What You Really Need to Know about Counselling and Psychotherapy Training

Becoming a counsellor or psychotherapist is a transformative and life-changing experience. Some trainees manage this process well, while others struggle to come to terms with the personal impact of their training.

In *What You Really Need to Know about Counselling and Psychotherapy Training,* Cathy McQuaid provides an in-depth but accessible guide to the processes of understanding individual motivations for wanting to undertake training and choosing the most appropriate course. Backed by extensive research, the book explains the training process from beginning to end, covering topics including:

- entry requirements, course curriculum and terms and conditions of training;
- the training relationship and group process;
- the challenges of training;
- the outcomes of counselling and psychotherapy training.

McQuaid leads the reader through the process of choosing a course, working with the course leader and with a group of peers and considering potential employment prospects upon completion.

Prompting the reader to consider their own personal, professional and educational needs within the framework of training, this is essential reading for anyone thinking of training as a counsellor or psychotherapist and for trainers and training course providers.

Cathy McQuaid is a UKCP registered transactional analysis psychotherapist and integrative psychotherapist in private practice. She is an EATA accredited trainer and supervisor and has a passion for training, training standards and research. She is also a freelance trainer and external examiner for a number of counselling and psychotherapy training organizations and higher education establishments.

What You Really Need to Know about Counselling and Psychotherapy Training

An essential guide

Cathy McQuaid

Routledge
Taylor & Francis Group
LONDON AND NEW YORK

First published 2014
by Routledge
27 Church Road, Hove, East Sussex, BN3 2FA

and by Routledge
711 Third Avenue, New York, NY 10017

Routledge is an imprint of the Taylor & Francis Group, an informa business

British Library Cataloguing in Publication Data
A catalogue record for this book is available from the British Library

Library of Congress Cataloging in Publication Data
McQuaid, Cathy.
What you really need to know about : counselling and psychotherapy training : an essential guide / Cathy McQuaid.—First Edition.
pages cm
Includes bibliographical references and index.
1. Counseling—Vocational guidance. 2. Psychotherapy—Vocational guidance. I. Title.
BF636.64.M37 2014
361′.060683—dc23
2013035361

ISBN: 978-0-415-81333-4 (hbk)
ISBN: 978-0-415-81334-1 (pbk)
ISBN: 978-1-315-81800-9 (ebk)

Typeset in Times
by Swales & Willis Ltd, Exeter, Devon, UK

Contents

Illustrations

Figures

Tables

Foreword

I am delighted to offer a foreword to this book.

Training in counselling or psychotherapy is a serious and, increasingly, expensive undertaking and should, therefore, not be entered into unadvisedly or lightly, but reverently and soberly. There are three principal aspects to this undertaking and education: first, the 'taught' component, i.e. the education and/or training course or programme itself, its theoretical perspective/s, its 'terms and conditions', the status or standing of the qualification it offers, and the implications of that training and qualification for the graduate's career and prospects for accreditation, registration, progression and advancement; second, the 'personal' component, i.e. the desirability and/or requirement for the healer to 'know thyself' through personal therapy, and personal development in both individual and group settings; and third, the 'experiential' component, i.e. the supervised practice of counselling and psychotherapy, which involves practice in the context of training, practice on placement/s and, possibly, private practice; and, of course, working with a supervisor.

Unfortunately, in my experience, too many potential trainees or students enter therapy training with very little or, in some cases, no knowledge of the field and these aspects or elements of the whole training experience. This book addresses this lack of knowledge and brings together in one volume a thorough consideration of all the components of such training, and does so in a logical sequence which takes the interested reader – and potential applicant/trainee/student – through the relevant issues, considerations and implications so that they can indeed undertake this particular 'marriage' advisedly.

Based on the author's own doctoral research, for which she interviewed a number of people at various stages of their training experience – good, bad and indifferent – this book stands as an honest, reflective, accessible and essential consumer's guide to therapy training, as a part of which each chapter concludes with a number of questions on which the reader is invited to reflect. A particular strength of the book is the author's mindfulness that trainees are people in context, i.e. that they – and indeed all of us – have life beyond therapy and training, and that committing to such training impacts on our lives, friends, families and relationships. Indeed, as it is a highly personal undertaking – and some of us would see therapy as a spiritual and/or political as well as a personal practice – for many, training in therapy challenges our most personal relationships and, thus, the book also contains questions for the potential trainee to ask themselves and others who are significant in their lives.

The author herself is a certified transactional analyst – and a teaching and supervising transactional analyst – and transactional analysis clearly and usefully informs her thinking about people, personality and processes; nevertheless, this book is generic in that the issues identified and raised apply to all forms of training in counselling and psychotherapy. As well as the information about all aspects of training, the book contains some useful reflections and ideas about personal stories, narratives or 'life scripts'; the difference between education and training, and between learning and being taught; different theoretical approaches or modalities of counselling and psychotherapy; learning and training contracts; the terms and conditions of training; attachment styles; the context of such training with regard to debates about the desirability (or otherwise) of the accreditation of training courses and the regulation of the professions of counselling and psychotherapy; and much more!

Although the book is aimed at trainees and potential trainees, it also offers both information and some useful challenges to trainers. By and large, the educators and/or trainers of therapists are not formally trained as *educators and/or trainers*, with the result that some trainers have not necessarily thought through issues and questions of their philosophy of education and/or training (and even whether these terms offer different paradigms about their respective activities); their working model of the student and whether it is based on one informed by theories of child development or of adult development; their curriculum and its development; their understanding of their responsibilties as trainers; and so on. Trainers will find information in these pages which is also useful to them in providing a training programme which is transparent about all its terms and conditions and, therefore, ethical.

I have had the privilege of seeing these pages fresh from the printer prior to going to press and, in reading them as well as earlier drafts, I have been struck by Cathy's passion for the subject of therapy training; her commitment to the project of bringing her research forward and making it accessible to the public; and her ambition to raise the standard of this particular – and, given its personal component and nature, arguably – unique training. I congratulate her on seeing this project to fruition and, you, the reader, for having bought the book; and, if you are or are considering training in counselling and/or psychotherapy, I wish you well in your journey, which I know will be the more advised and informed as a result of your reading of this book.

Keith Tudor PhD, CQSW, Dip. Psychotherapy, CTA (P), TSTA (P)
Keith is a transactional analyst and Associate Professor at AUT University, Auckland, where he is the Head of the Department of Psychotherapy and Counselling and the Programme Leader for the Master of Psychotherapy. He has a small private practice in West Auckland.

Acknowledgements

I would like to express my appreciation, and thanks, to my trainers, peers and trainees, without whom I would not have had the inspiration to undertake my research in the first place, and to all my research participants for their willingness to engage with me in relating the stories of their training experiences. I would also like to thank the following contributors and organizations that gave permission for selections of their material to be published:

Andres Fortino and the EvoLLLution; Angela Harrison, Chair of the British Association for Music Therapy (BAMT); Ann Salter, Chair, Gestalt Psychotherapy Training Institute (GPTI); British Association for Counselling and Psychotherapy (BACP); Dawn Bennett and Maddy Jevon from the Association for Cognitive Analytic Therapy (ACAT); British Association for Behavioural and Cognitive Psychotherapies (BABCP); British Association of Art Therapists (BAAT); Catherine Hayes of the British Association for the Person-Centred Approach Coordinating Group (BAPCA-CG); Centre for Counselling & Psychotherapy Education (CCPE); Centre for Transpersonal Psychology (CTP); College of Sexual and Relationship Therapists (COSRT); Counselling and Psychotherapy in Scotland (COSCA); European Association for Psychotherapy (EAP); Group Analytic Society (GAS); Independent Practitioners Network (IPN); Irish Association for Counselling and Psychotherapy (IACP); Institute of Group Analysis (IGA); International Transactional Analysis Association (ITAA); John Roberts; Leilani Mitchell, Chair, United Kingdom Association for Transactional Analysis (UKATA); Martina Vaughan, Chair, Irish Council for Psychotherapy (ICP); Quality Assurance Agency of Higher Education (QAA); Regent's School of Psychotherapy and Psychology; The Association for Family Therapy and Systemic Practice in the UK (AFT); The British Association of Dramatherapists, (BADTH); The Council for Psychoanalysis and Jungian Analysis (CPJA); The Institute of Psychoanalysis (IOPA); The National College of Hypnosis and Psychotherapy (NCHP); The Personal Construct Psychology Association (PCPA); The Psychosynthesis and Education Trust (PET); United Kingdom Association of Humanistic Psychology Practitioners (UKAHPP); United Kingdom Council for Psychotherapy (UKCP).

Excerpt from *A Way of Being* by Carl Rogers. Copyright © 1980 by Houghton Mifflin Company, renewed 2008 by David E. Rogers and Natalie Rogers. Reprinted by permission of Houghton Mifflin Harcourt Publishing Company. All rights reserved.

Thanks also go to Dr Keith Tudor for his encouragement in compiling this book, his editorial advice, and for writing the foreword.

Finally, I would like to express my deep gratitude to my husband and children for their continued love and encouragement and to my friend and colleague, Sue Parker Hall, for her unwavering support and editorial expertise.

Abbreviations

BABCP	British Association for Behavioural and Cognitive Psychotherapies
BACP	British Association for Counselling and Psychotherapy
BPC	British Psychoanalytic Council
CBT	Cognitive behavioural therapy
COSCA	Counselling and Psychotherapy in Scotland
CPD	Continuing professional development
EAP	European Association for Psychotherapy
HCPC	Health and Care Professions Council
HIPC	Humanistic and Integrative Psychotherapy College
IACP	Irish Association for Counselling and Psychotherapy
IAPT	Improving Access to Psychological Therapies
ICP	Irish Council for Psychotherapy
NICE	National Institute for Health and Care Excellence
PCA	Person-centred approach
PSA	Professional Standards Authority for Health and Social Care
PWP	Psychological Wellbeing Practitioner
TA	Transactional analysis
UKAHPP	United Kingdom Association for Humanistic Psychology Practitioners
UKCP	United Kingdom Council for Psychotherapy

Introduction

If you are thinking of undertaking training to be a counsellor or psychotherapist, or you are a trainer, or training provider, for counselling or psychotherapy courses in the UK or Republic of Ireland, then this book is a must for you.

Some people have experienced training as a counsellor or psychotherapist as the most rewarding and transformative experience they have ever encountered, and one that can be deeply reparative. However, others begin the training with no idea of what to expect, and can feel puzzled, confused, frustrated, and even betrayed, when they discover the reality of what they have taken on. There are many training courses that are run by ethical and professional trainers who provide clear and comprehensive information about all the requirements and implications of the training in this field or discipline, but, sadly, some establishments are not so transparent.

This book provides you with guidance on courses, professional and academic requirements, therapy modalities and post-training employment opportunities. As well as information and practical guidance, the book also conveys the subjective, phenomenological experience of counselling and psychotherapy training, so that you get a sense of the highs and lows of what, for most trainees, is an important and significant professional and personal journey. By presenting both – the practical and the phenomenological – I help you, the next generation of trainees, to make an informed decision about whether counselling or psychotherapy training really is right for you and, if it is, how to find the very best course for you that contains all the necessary and key elements essential for a comprehensive education and training.

Personal background

This book has been born out of my own experiences as a trainee counsellor, then as a psychotherapist, and now as a trainer of counsellors and psychotherapists, plus the experiences of my doctoral research participants.

My training experience was diverse; the quality varied, depending upon the trainer's skills and their capacity to be authentic, and how congruent their teaching style and material delivered was with the philosophy of the counselling or psychotherapy approach being taught. I went into training because of a curiosity about why people do what they do, as well as a personal inquisitiveness about my own thoughts, feelings and behaviours. Initially I enrolled on a counselling skills course, which I thoroughly enjoyed, and then I continued training until I gained my diploma in counselling. The courses were challenging and enlightening; I began to learn more about myself, and increased my interest in others. After completing my diploma, I had a break for a couple of years before embarking on psychotherapy training. One reason for going into the psychotherapy field was because I felt my knowledge was limited and I wanted a greater depth of understanding to be able to help clients get to the root cause of their difficulties.

My training as a psychotherapist was educational and demanding. I had not been fully aware at the start of what the training would entail, and yet I knew I had enthusiasm and motivation to continue. I think it was this passion that helped me when I felt down, or disillusioned. A key moment for me was when I attended a transactional analysis (TA) conference during my third year of training. I watched during the gala dinner as, one by one, successful exam candidates were called forward to be celebrated. Seeing the happiness, excitement and degree of rejoicing was pivotal for me, and I thought, 'That's what I want'. Three years later, I was one of those called up and celebrated.

Since passing my exam as a 'Certified Transactional Analyst Specializing in Psychotherapy Applications' (CTA (P)), I have been involved in training and examining others, as well as continuing my professional development. Partly because of my experience as a trainee, and the subsequent work I have undertaken in the area of examinations and training standards, I have become increasingly passionate about the education of therapists. In 2006, I decided to work towards a doctorate by researching the experiences of people who had trained either as counsellors or as psychotherapists. As a result, in 2010, I was awarded my 'Doctorate in Psychotherapy by Professional Studies', and I then passed my 'Teaching and Supervising Transactional Analyst Specializing in Psychotherapy Applications' (TSTA (P)) exams in the same year.

Research

I wanted to explore how trainees perceived their counselling or psychotherapy training, and to find out what, for them, helped make the training a positive experience.

I interviewed about 50 people, all of whom had undertaken some form of counselling or psychotherapy training, many of whom had gone on to gain their professional qualifications and accreditations or registrations, and a number who had become trainers themselves. Others had started the training, but, for one reason or another, decided against finishing it. All the participants were interviewed and the transcripts of those interviews were analysed using Interpretative Phenomenological Analysis (IPA) (Smith, 1995). The analysis created a number of themes and these were further analysed using transactional analysis.

Since completing my main piece of research, I have continued to speak with qualified counsellors and psychotherapists to ascertain the degrees to which the findings of the research matched their experiences, and to gather further information.

The main factors that impacted on the research participants' experiences were their personal belief system, their motivation for undertaking the training and their relationships with their trainers, their peers and the profession as a whole.

Five main themes emerged from the project:

1 The personal gains and losses from undertaking the training.
2 The nature of the relationship with the trainer and peers.
3 The challenges of undertaking the training.
4 The experience of examinations and accreditation/registration systems.
5 The reasons why people decided to stop their training.

What became clear from the research was that many of the participants had concerns in the following areas:

- a lack of information for trainees prior to the commencement of training;
- the lack of clear information from professional bodies concerning the quality of service trainees could expect from their training establishment, including procedures for dealing with grievances or concerns;
- the lack of consistency, and the idiosyncratic nature of the training offered by different training establishments;
- the reasons for trainees entering training in the first instance, accompanied by the trainers' reasons for accepting students onto their training programmes;
- the significant length of time and resources that the training entails for trainees, particularly with respect to psychotherapy trainees.

Purpose of the book

What became clear through the research is that counselling and psychotherapy training impacts on you personally, and on your relationships. The very nature of the training is unlike any other. You learn about theories of personality and how change happens within the counselling and psychotherapy relationship, but, more fundamentally, you learn about yourself and your relationships – past and present. Therefore, the purpose of this book is to help you decide whether such a potentially transformative process is really for you and, if you believe that it is, to give you a good idea of what you can expect and how to choose the most appropriate course for you.

In the UK, and the Republic of Ireland, there is a great diversity of training within the various mental health professions, such as counselling, nursing, psychiatry, psychology, psychotherapy and social work. Mental health nurses have a pre-registration nursing degree that leads to registration, in the UK, with the

Nursing and Midwifery Council, and, in the Republic of Ireland, with An Bord Altranais. Depending upon the route and method, training can take between three and five years.

Training to be a psychiatrist requires a medical degree, followed by foundation training, and then three years of speciality training. Psychiatrists in the UK are licensed by the General Medical Council (GMC), and, in Ireland, registered with the Medical Council.

Training as a psychologist in the UK usually requires a psychology degree, followed by postgraduate clinical training, which can lead to Chartered Membership of the British Psychological Society (BPS). Psychologists are statutorily registered with the Health and Care Professions Council (HCPC). In Ireland, psychologists have similar training to that in the UK, and become Graduate or Registered members of the Psychological Society of Ireland (PSI). Statutory regulation is not yet in place for psychologists in Ireland, but there are plans for this to be introduced.

Training as a social worker usually requires a social work degree specializing in either adults' or children's services. Courses which are at graduate or postgraduate level usually take three years. Social workers in the UK are also statutorily registered with the HCPC, or, in Ireland, with CORU.

The structure of the book

This book consists of eight chapters. Each chapter in this book has its own theme. You will find questions at certain points throughout, which are intended to be useful prompts for the relevant questions you may wish to ask yourself or your friends and family, as well as any potential trainer or training provider. I have shared my research participants' stories within the chapters to illustrate the processes involved.

Chapter 1 begins with a discussion about the definitions of counselling and psychotherapy that you may find useful when deciding on which course to take. The personal impact of the training is briefly introduced, alongside some theoretical ideas to help you to understand your motivation for undertaking the course and to identify the outcome that you hope to achieve. The chapter then explores a variety of theories of learning, and argues that counselling and psychotherapy training is more of an educative rather than a training process. The remainder of the chapter proposes that choosing the right academic level is very important. If you start too low, you may feel bored, or under-stimulated, and if you start too high, then you may become overwhelmed by the demands of the course. Beginning your training at a level that is akin to where you are currently, in terms of academic ability, is likely to provide the right amount of challenge for you. The various academic levels and benchmarks across the UK and Ireland are discussed, and links are made with educational levels elsewhere in Europe.

In Chapter 2, you are introduced to a variety of possible modalities in which you can train, including a selection of arts therapies, cognitive therapy, constructivist therapy, family, couple and systemic therapy, humanistic and integrative therapies, hypno-psychotherapy, psychoanalytic and Jungian analysis, and sexual and relationship psychotherapy. There are too many modalities – one study suggests there are over 400 (Karasu, 1986, cited in McLeod, 2013) – for them all to be included in this book, and so I have selected those that are most common. Choosing the most appropriate approach for you is important, because there needs to be a congruence, or 'fit', between the models that you learn and subsequently practise, and your own personal values, ethics, and views on human development and relationships; this will maximize your chances of assimilating and integrating all that you are learning.

Chapter 3 begins with the general entry requirements for a counselling certificate, a counselling diploma and a psychotherapy training course, and then outlines the application and selection processes involved. The chapter also considers the curriculum of training, which can be separated into three component parts:

> Taught Training – this covers areas such as ethics and ethical codes, practical work, working with difference and diversity, the theoretical orientation of the course, the taught elements of the mental health familiarization placement and training in research methods.
>
> Supervised Clinical Placement – this is the requirement for trainees to have a placement where they can practise under the supervision of a more qualified and experienced practitioner. For psychotherapy trainees, this would also include the clinical element of the mental health familiarization placement.
>
> Personal Development – this focuses on the personal ability of a trainee to be able to manage the training. Maslow's (1987) 'hierarchy of needs' is used to explain how differing requirements can be met both inside and outside of the training. The personal impact of the training is significant, and the trainee's ability to self-reflect will be enhanced through the training. Later in the chapter, the Quality Assurance Agency for Higher Education benchmark statement for counselling and psychotherapy (QAA, 2013) is introduced. This will give you a much clearer idea of the knowledge, skills and competencies that you may develop during your training. Finally, some of the usual terms and conditions of training are introduced, along with some other areas for you to consider, such as costs, time, outcome, or termination of training.

The personal impact of training is at the heart of Chapter 4. The challenges and changes involved in training, including personal relationships, self-discovery, and the significance of the underlying motivations for embarking on the training, are discussed. The chapter also considers the differing requirements for personal therapy, and, also, the ability to be self-reflective, a demonstrable skill necessary for certain accrediting or registering bodies, along with a discussion about whether therapy should be required, or 'imposed', on trainees. There is some information on how to find a therapist, and a number of suggested questions to ask of them; these are offered to assist you in finding the right therapist for you.

Chapter 4 is probably the most important chapter for you to read, in order for you to gain an understanding of the phenomenological experience of training; you may even choose to share this chapter with your partner and family, as they, too, are likely to be impacted upon by your undertaking.

Chapter 5 considers the nature of the relationships that may develop between the trainee, their peers and the trainer, and some ethical principles that underpin most training courses. The relationship with the trainer, and whether they 'walk the talk', is key to the outcome of the training. If a trainer demonstrates congruence between the modality and their behaviours, then the trainee is more likely to experience their relationship in positive terms. Later in the chapter, the advantage of encountering different trainers and approaches is discussed. Also, the relationships between peers are explored, with some trainees viewing them as synonymous with having a new family. The chapter continues with a discussion on the ten phases of transformational learning (Mezirow, 1991, 2000) and the various stages of learning that appear to be evident in many trainees' experiences of counselling and psychotherapy training, and how they impact on the self-esteem of the trainee. Additionally, the chapter considers the stages of group development, and how a trainee's attachment pattern can influence their experiences of being in a group, and their relationships with their peers and trainer; this is followed by a brief mention of the issue of power.

Chapter 6 focuses on the notion that often, during training, many trainees reach a point of disillusionment, or disappointment. This may be with the course itself, in terms of the trainee not being fully aware of what the course would entail, or a mismatch between the trainee's hopes and what the course can actually provide. A common complaint concerns the amount of work involved, either academically, in terms of how much written work is required, or personally, in terms of the amount of time training takes up, especially when adding in the extra features, such as personal therapy, supervision, placement and self-study; and then, professionally, a student may become discouraged in terms of the difficulty in finding placements or employment. The chapter explores other common areas for challenge, including incongruity between the course philosophy and what actually occurs, and the difficulty, for some, in going back into education after a long break, which may even lead to the discovery of additional learning needs, e.g. dyslexia, of which the trainee may have previously been unaware. Some hints and tips on planning a written assignment are offered, and this is followed by an exploration of how trainees perceive examinations, and the stories and myths that surround qualifying examinations and professional accreditation or registration systems. Finally, the significance of the costs of training, and the perceived viability of training and any subsequent paid employment, are discussed.

Chapter 7 begins with a consideration of post-training employment opportunities, includes suggestions about where to look for jobs, and also outlines some points to consider if you intend, at some stage, to set up a private practice. There is discussion about your possible options to work with children and young people, as well as with other client groups, and this is then followed by an examination of some of the political issues that impact on the counselling and psychotherapy profession, including NICE guidelines, which may influence which modality you choose, statutory regulation, and assured voluntary registration. The chapter then explores a variety of professional accreditation and registration schemes that are available through a number of professional bodies. One way you may like to think about your options could be to have an idea of where you'd like to end up. So, for example, would you like to work in the NHS, or in a specific agency, or prefer to have your own business? Do you feel drawn to joining a particular professional organization, and, if so, what are their accreditation or registration requirements? Once you have this information, you will be better equipped to select a course.

Chapter 8 brings all the themes together. A suggested plan of action is proposed that offers various steps to help you in deciding whether the training is for you, and, if so, what you may like to consider when choosing a course. The steps are by no means exhaustive, but they give you an idea of some of the most important considerations for you to think about.

A glossary is provided at the back of this book. It defines a number of concepts that have been used, and is intended to help you become familiar with some of the terminology used in counselling and psychotherapy.

A number of appendices support the material presented in the book. Appendix 1 comprises a list of accrediting or registering organizations, along with their contact details and website addresses. These will be useful if you are researching whether a course you are contemplating meets any necessary training requirements should you plan to join that organization.

Appendix 2 provides the contact details for a range of organizations that offer training and/or information on specific modalities.

Appendix 3 offers you a suggested template for collating your training, supervision and personal therapy hours. You may find it useful to begin recording these hours from the very start of your training.

Appendix 4 provides a template for a learning contact, often used in student-centred learning.

Chapter 1

Definitions, learning theories and levels of education and training

This chapter introduces you to some of the diverse definitions of counselling and psychotherapy that exist because the various professional bodies have different views on the nature of, and, more specifically, the requirements for, training. You may find it helpful to understand these differences when choosing your course as it will influence the type of training you receive, and the options you will then have later in your career.

After presenting you with the assorted definitions of counselling and psychotherapy, I introduce you to one of the most important aspects of the training that you need to be aware of, but which is not often commented upon, and that is the personal impact it will have on you.

Then I present some theories on how adults learn, and put this in a wider educational context which may be helpful to you when considering undertaking a training course.

Finally, I explain the academic levels of training. It is important that you are aware of these because choosing the right level of entry for you will ensure you are a competent and confident learner; it will also influence the other course options available to you later in your training, and determine the professional accreditation or registration scheme that you can apply for once you have completed training.

What is counselling and psychotherapy?

This may seem like a straightforward question, but there can be as many answers as persons asked. This is not helped by the fact that, in the UK, the terms 'counselling' and 'psychotherapy' tend to be used interchangeably. Some people disagree about whether there are any differences. For example, Sue Aldridge of the British Association for Counselling and Psychotherapy (BACP), in a response to the Health and Care Professions Council (HCPC) concerning the then proposed statutory regulation, wrote:

> The Association does not support the specific proposals to differentiate between counselling and psychotherapy and the consequent differentiation

> within the Standards of Proficiency and threshold entry levels to the register . . .
>
> The proposal to differentiate between counselling and psychotherapy is out of step with research and other developments in the field of the psychological therapies for example New Ways of Working and IAPT [Improving Access to Psychological Therapies]. The work undertaken by Skills for Health to develop National Occupational Standards for the Psychological Therapies does not differentiate between counselling and psychotherapy. There are an increasing number of training courses that title themselves 'counselling and psychotherapy'.
>
> (BACP, 2009a)

The BACP defines counselling and psychotherapy as:

> umbrella terms that cover a range of talking therapies . . . delivered by trained practitioners who work with people over a short or long term to help them bring about effective change or enhance their wellbeing.
>
> (BACP, 2010a)

The United Kingdom Council for Psychotherapy (UKCP), on the other hand, states that their organization:

> strongly supports the Strasbourg Declaration – particularly in identifying psychotherapy as a profession independent of, and distinct from counselling, psychology and psychiatry, and in upholding the multiplicity of psychotherapy modalities.
>
> (UKCP, 2008a: 7)

With regard to any differences between counselling and psychotherapy:

> Different people use the words counselling and psychotherapy in different ways, so there is no commonly agreed definition. There is a general understanding that a psychotherapist can work with a wider range of clients or patients and can offer more in-depth work where appropriate.
>
> UKCP believes the difference lies in the length and depth of training involved and in the quality of the relationship between the client and their therapist. UKCP-registered psychotherapists are trained to Master's level.
>
> UKCP registers psychotherapists and psychotherapeutic counsellors. Psychotherapeutic counsellors are counsellors who have received more in-depth training than that undertaken by most counsellors. UKCP's training standards for both qualifications seek to ensure that UKCP registrants are competent to practice to the highest standards.
>
> (UKCP, 2013)

The Irish Association for Counselling and Psychotherapy (IACP), while embracing both, states that:

> Counselling tends to deal more with immediate issues that may have arisen more recently e.g. bereavement or relationship breakdown. Psychotherapy tends to deal with deeper, more long-term issues that may be rooted in the past e.g. a trauma, or, serious mistreatment, where the affects of such are ongoing.
>
> (IACP, 2010: 2)

In a document written for Counselling and Psychotherapy in Scotland (COSCA), Bondi (2004) states that:

> Counselling and psychotherapy are ways of responding to a wide range of human needs. Counselling and psychotherapy provide opportunities for those seeking help to work towards ways of living in more satisfying and resourceful ways.
>
> In their current form, counselling and psychotherapy are less than 100 years old, but they have roots in much older ways of providing help and care. Counselling and psychotherapy have developed in order to respond to modern circumstances. They are living practices which are open to change and which evolve in response to changing needs. Consequently, it is impossible to define counselling and psychotherapy once and for all.
>
> (Bondi, 2004: 1)

She does, however, make some interesting points regarding the differences between counselling and psychotherapy when compared with other allied activities such as befriending, mentoring and coaching, advocacy and mediation. Bondi further considers that the main differences between counselling and psychotherapy lie in their origins:

> [Psychotherapy] began with the arrival and development of psychoanalytic and psychodynamic ideas in the 1920s, joined later by a variety of other approaches. These various approaches to psychotherapy developed in the private sector, and initially psychodynamic ideas also secured a place in the medical speciality of psychiatry, although when the National Health Service was established, practitioners without medical qualifications were forced out. Psychotherapeutic ideas also influenced other professions and professional training, including teaching and social work. Through the middle of the twentieth century, psychotherapy flourished in the public sector and in the private sector, with training offered primarily in the independent sector. Recently there has been a partial shift in the location of training into universities. Training fees are paid either by trainees' employers (e.g. public sector bodies such as the NHS) or by trainees themselves.
>
> (ibid.: 4)

She continues:

> Counselling services and counselling training began to develop in the 1950s, with both originating in the voluntary sector. In contrast to this, with rare exceptions, psychotherapy services and training have not developed in the voluntary sector. The first counselling services to be developed were offered by voluntary sector organisations, with the counselling delivered free of charge by trained volunteers.
>
> (ibid.: 5)

Finally, the United Kingdom Association of Humanistic Psychology Practitioners (UKAHPP), an organizational member of the UKCP, defines a counsellor as:

> Someone trained to deal with immediate problems and crises which arise, such as bereavement, a broken relationship, a difficult marriage, a specific illness like cancer or AIDS, problems with children, alcohol/drug problems etc. Many counsellors also deal with long-term problems. Counselling can also be done on a couple, family or group basis. Some counsellors also use active techniques and give specific advice.
>
> (UKAHPP, 2012)

They define a psychotherapist as:

> Someone with a specialised, professional and broad-based training and the ability to work in depth with clients, sometimes for two or three sessions a week and often over an extended period of time. Psychotherapists may use a wide range of approaches or may concentrate on one in particular. Short-term psychotherapists usually specialise in more intense work with clients but of limited duration.
>
> (ibid.)

From reading these extracts, it is clear that there is a lack of consistency in defining counselling and psychotherapy within the professional organizations. This lack of clarity could cause some confusion for potential trainees in determining what a course is actually offering.

What's in a name?

The *Longman Dictionary of Contemporary English* (2009) defines 'counselling' as 'advice and support given by a counsellor to someone with problems, usually after talking to them' (p. 383), and 'psychotherapy' as 'the treatment of mental illness . . . by talking to someone and discussing their problems rather than giving them drugs' (ibid.: 1401).

If we take on board these two definitions, it is clear that counselling and psychotherapy will require different skills, and, depending upon their training, that some psychotherapists may be able to offer counselling, and that a number of counsellors may be able to provide psychotherapy.

Unfortunately, because the terms are often used interchangeably, it may not be clear from the outset which discipline a training course is offering, and what employment you can undertake as a result of that training.

Being conversant with the differences, or implied differences, between counselling and psychotherapy can be helpful for a number of reasons. First, knowing if you want to be a 'counsellor' or a 'psychotherapist', about the types of clients or issues you want to work with, or which professional body you wish to belong to, will help you determine the most appropriate course for you. Second, that decision will help you to get the type of employment you would like once you are qualified. For example, some jobs are advertised specifically for a 'counsellor', or a 'psychotherapist', or both, so your choice of course may broaden or limit your employment opportunities. Third, having an appreciation of all the elements of training, whether as a counsellor or a psychotherapist, means that you will have a greater understanding of the likely impact the course will have on you. Most psychotherapy training programmes tend to be more personally and academically challenging than counselling training courses in terms of personal therapy requirements, the depth of the knowledge-base needed, and the increased number of clinical hours with a higher supervision ratio, and they will probably have more of an impact on you and your relationships with friends and family. Finally, you will be clearer about the costs you will need to pay, as, overall, a psychotherapy training programme with all its extra requirements will cost more than counselling training.

In order to decide which route to take, initially you may find it helpful to have an idea of the outcome you want at the end of your training. If you want to be able to work with people who have issues such as anxiety, stress, relationship problems, low self-esteem or confidence, then counselling training would probably be advantageous. If you wish to work with clients suffering from a more complex range of mental health problems, such as unresolved childhood issues, or abuse and trauma, then psychotherapy training would be beneficial.

It's a personal process

Counselling and psychotherapy training is a very personal process. In order to demonstrate the significance of the personal processes involved, I offer some theoretical concepts throughout this book and invite you to apply them to your own life. Another reason for doing this is to help you become familiar with some of the terminology you may come across during your search for a training course. (There is a glossary at the end of the book to help you get acquainted with specific terms that may not yet be familiar to you.)

To begin, I want to introduce you to the idea of a 'life story', or 'script'. Eric Berne (1910–70), the founder of transactional analysis (TA), coined the term and described a life script as, 'An ongoing program, developed in early childhood under parental influence, which directs the individual's behavior in the most important aspects of his life' (Berne, 1975: 418). In essence, this means that each of us has a life-plan, although it may not be in our conscious awareness, and that we make decisions, think, feel and behave in particular ways that are in keeping with that plan. For example, we will make relationships, or not make relationships, or take on jobs or careers, or not work at all, in order to maintain our script.

What's in your script?

A fun way of finding out what is in your script is to think about your favourite story from childhood, and which character you most identified with. It may have been a fairy story, a comic-book story, or a TV programme, film or book. Take your time, and, if you can, do this with someone else so you can ask each other questions to prompt memories.

What is important is the story as you remember it, which may be quite different from how it was actually written. This does not matter. It is your version that is significant.

What are the qualities of the character with whom you can identify? What are their strengths? What are their weaknesses? What happens in the story? Is it an adventure story, a tragedy, a love story, a triumph of good over evil? Who are the other main characters in the story? How do they interact with your character?

Once you have all these answers written down, consider them in relation to your own life. Are there any similarities or discrepancies? If you can recognize some aspects of this story in your own life story, where do you think you are in terms of the beginning, middle or end? Are you waiting for someone to come along and rescue you? Or, perhaps, you are the rescuer making things right for others, but not quite getting the rewards you feel you deserve? Finding out this type of information can be very helpful in finding out aspects of your life script.

Say, for example, your favourite story was *Cinderella*, and you identify with her. Do you have a relationship with someone who is like the 'wicked stepmother'? What about the 'ugly sisters'? Do you find yourself looking after other people? Are you hoping for a fairy godmother to come along? Are you hoping that one day a handsome prince will find you? Do you already have your prince? Whatever stage you think you may be in, ask yourself the following question: what am I waiting for so the story can continue? If the answer involves someone else – forget it. Sadly, fairy godmothers, magic wands and magical thinking can't help. Only *you* can sort your life out; a therapist can be very helpful but, ultimately, the final decisions are up to you.

Now consider your life story in terms of the relationships you get into with other people, and the processes you become involved in with them. How do they work? How does it all end? What do you end up believing about yourself, other people and life in general? How do those beliefs fit in with your life story? What you are looking at here is just the tip of what may be a very large iceberg, but, if you can get an idea of how this process works, then you will begin to understand yourself better, and, maybe, your reasons for doing what you do.

What's this got to do with being a counsellor or psychotherapist?

The answer is 'quite a lot, really'. Why do you want to be a counsellor or psychotherapist? What is your underlying motive? What is your secret reason, the one you don't tell anyone else? Could it be one of the following?

1 I want to sort out my mum, dad, brother, sister or partner.
2 I want to make people happy.
3 I want to make loads of money.
4 I want to sort myself out.
5 I want to cure the world.
6 There's nothing else to do.

If you have given any of the answers shown above, then, for you, training as a counsellor or a psychotherapist probably won't work.

If you have the following motivations, then you are more likely to succeed as a counsellor or a psychotherapist:

1 I want to develop some new skills to add to my existing skills.
2 I want to have a career whereby I can help other people to help themselves.
3 I've already done some basic counselling skills training and really enjoyed it, so now I'd like to do more.
4 Having had my own therapy, I can really see the benefits; I'd like to be able to do this work with others.
5 I'm fascinated by people, by how, and why, they do things. I'd like to understand others better, and find a way I can relate to others that is more rewarding.

You may have other reasons for undertaking the training, but what is important is that you are honest with yourself with regard to your motivations. Some counselling training, and, certainly, psychotherapy training courses, will be inviting you to answer some tough questions. Are you up for the challenge? How will doing this training impact on your life script and those of your partner, friends or family? Indeed, are you destined to fail, as being with someone who does not succeed is part of their script as well as yours, and so, unconsciously, they may sabotage you? Alternatively, are you both ready for change?

Another way to look at this is to consider how you make decisions in your life? Do you decide for yourself? Do you rely on your own judgements and opinions? If so, you would be said to have an internal locus of evaluation (see Glossary). Or do you rely on others to advise you what to do? Do you doubt yourself and constantly seek reassurance from others? If this is what you do, then you would be said to have an external locus of evaluation. Where is your locus of evaluation? Is it internal or external? If external, to whom do you look to seek that evaluation?

Having answered all these questions you are likely to have a greater understanding of yourself and your reasons for becoming a counsellor or psychotherapist.

Once you have a clearer idea of your motives for undertaking training, the next step is to consider how you learn.

Learning, education and training

The reason for beginning with learning, education and training is to provide you with information about the process of learning, to invite you to consider how you learn, to help you understand the differences between education and training, and finally, to consider how this may influence your choice of course.

What is learning?

Napper and Newton offer their definition of learning as 'the bringing together of information, abilities and experiences – both internal and external – to create a new insight or competence which becomes freshly integrated into an individual's understanding of the world' (2000: 1.3)

There are numerous papers and authors that have considered the different means by which people learn. Significant to this book is how adults learn, so that will be the area that is more fully explored and discussed.

For Knowles (1984), andragogy, or the techniques and methods used to teach adults, is based on at least five central assumptions about the characteristics of adult learners (they differ from the assumptions about child learners upon which traditional pedagogy is based), and they are:

1 Self-concept: As a person matures, his self-concept moves from one of being a dependent personality towards one of being a self-directed human being.
2 Experience: As a person matures, he accumulates a growing reservoir of experience that becomes an increasing resource for learning.
3 Readiness to learn: As a person matures, his readiness to learn becomes oriented increasingly to the developmental tasks of his social roles.
4 Orientation to learning: As a person matures, his time perspective changes from one of postponed application of knowledge to immediacy of application, and, accordingly, his orientation towards learning shifts from one of 'subject-centeredness' to one of 'problem-centeredness'.
5 Motivation to learn: As a person matures, the motivation to learn is internal.

(Knowles, 1984: 12)

Here, it is possible to see that the significance of the goals, motivations and maturity of the learner – in this case, a counselling or psychotherapy trainee – will be central to the learning process, and that each needs to be considered. This is essential in graduate and postgraduate levels of training where, presumably, most students are there because they want to be, and they have an interest in the subject matter. This means that training programmes tend to focus more on the process and less on the content; therefore, experiential methods such as case studies, role-play exercises, simulations and self-evaluation are more appropriate with the trainers adopting the role of facilitator, or resource, rather than lecturer. Clearly, the motivation of the learner (assumption 5) will be significant in any outcome of this style of learning. (Read more about personal motivation and determination in Chapter 5.)

How do people learn?

Laird (1985) considers that people learn via sensory stimulation, and that, in order to learn, the facilitator needs to use teaching methods that will stimulate as many senses as possible. According to Laird, the vast majority of knowledge held by adults (75 per cent) is learned through seeing. Hearing is the next most effective (about 13 per cent) and the other senses – touch, smell and taste – account for 12 per cent of what we know.

Behavioural approaches

This is markedly different from the behavioural methods proposed by Skinner (1965), who suggests that people learn by continual positive or negative reinforcement. In other words, people keep repeating certain behaviours in order to obtain the same experiences. This can be seen in education on a very basic level – from praise for work that is well done, to punishment for unsatisfactory behaviours. A set of conditions is therefore created which is designed to eliminate undesirable behaviour and encourage desired behaviour (Burns, 1995: 108). The advantage of this type of learning is that procedures or methods can become automatic responses on the part of the learner, but the disadvantage is that it does not allow for individual idiosyncrasies, or the higher level of learning required in postgraduate programmes in terms of the ability to synthesize and critique theory and practice, and to develop a personal style.

Cognitive-gestalt approaches

Cognitive-gestalt approaches place significance on the importance of experience and 'meaning making' accompanied by problem-solving techniques. Burns (1995: 112) suggests that this theory develops the awareness of the differing needs and attitudes of people at different times and in different situations. For example, how a person responds to a particular situation in one context may differ with respect to that same situation in a dissimilar context. Cognitive-gestalt methods make use of Constructivism (Dewey, 1938; Piaget and Inhelder, 1969) and Personal Construct Theory (Kelly, 1955), and help the learner to problem-solve the current situation in a way that accounts for past experience within the learner's own framework. This links into the area described by Bandura (1977) as 'Social Learning Theory', which explains human behaviour in terms of continuous reciprocal interaction between cognitive, behavioural and environmental influences. He goes on to say that:

> Learning would be exceedingly laborious, not to mention hazardous, if people had to rely solely on the effects of their own actions to inform them what to do. Fortunately, most human behaviour is learned observationally through modelling: from observing others one forms an idea of how new behaviours are performed, and on later occasions this coded information serves as a guide for action.
>
> (Bandura, 1977: 22)

This is developed further by Vygotsky's theories that stress the fundamental role of social interaction in the development of cognition (Vygotsky, 1978; Wertsch, 1985). He believed strongly that community plays a central role in the process of 'making meaning', and this way of thinking about learning links together the behavioural and cognitive-gestalt theories mentioned above.

The humanistic approach

Leading on from cognitive-gestalt approaches, Kolb (1984; Kolb and Kolb, 2006), Honey and Mumford (1986, 1992), Rogers (1969), Rogers and Freiberg (1994), Maslow (1987), and Knowles (1950, 1975, 1978, 1984, 1990) are the main contributors to this approach.

Kolb (1984) views learning theory in a different way. He considers that people have different styles and cycles of learning. His learning theory sets out four distinct learning styles, or preferences, which are based on a four-stage learning cycle (see Figure 1.1).

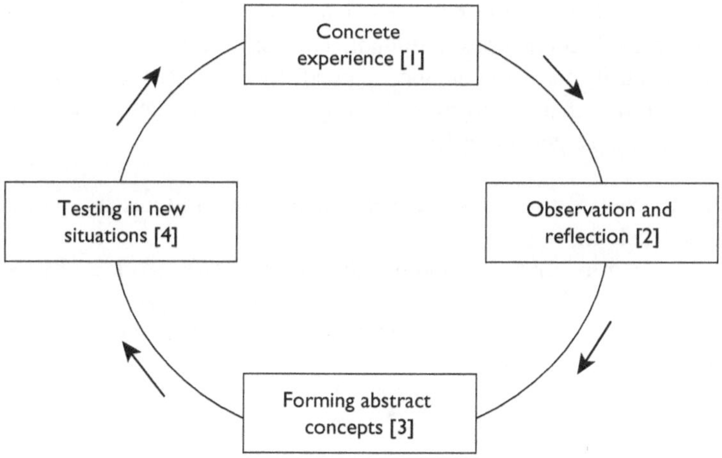

Figure 1.1 Kolb's learning cycle (1984)

The process can begin at any of the stages and is continuous; there is no limit to the number of cycles you can make in a learning situation. Indeed, during the learning process, a learner may go around the cycle numerous times. This theory asserts that without reflection we would simply continue to repeat our mistakes.

The strengths of Kolb's model are that the learning styles are not fixed personality traits, but relatively stable patterns of behaviour that are also flexible. Over the years, the model has been critiqued; for example, Rogers states that 'learning includes goals, purposes, intentions, choice and decision-making, and it is not at all clear where these elements fit into the learning cycle' (Rogers, 1996: 108). Nevertheless, it can be used as an introduction to how people learn. The model is based on the theory of experiential learning, which incorporates growth and development, and tends to be more for the benefit of teachers in terms of teaching styles and methods than for individual learners.

Honey and Mumford (1986, 1992) took Kolb's model and used it as a basis from which they developed their own 'Learning Styles Questionnaire' (LSQ), an 80-item, self-report questionnaire designed to identify an individual's relative strengths in each of four learning styles: 'Activist' (stage one), 'Reflector' (stage two), 'Theorist' (stage three) and 'Pragmatist' (stage four). Honey and Mumford seem to agree with Kolb that people learn most usefully from reflecting on experience. Similarly, they suggest that simply having experiences does not guarantee effective learning. The experience needs to be reviewed and conclusions made; and then it requires action to be taken on the strength of the conclusions drawn.

Honey and Mumford's contribution has been to provide a way for trainers and learners to identify specific learning styles in order that the trainer can facilitate different learning styles within the learning situation. They define a learning style as being 'a description of the attitudes and behaviour which determine an individual's preferred way of learning' (Honey and Mumford, 1992: 1).

Kolb and Kolb (2006) suggest that each person naturally prefers a certain learning style which then becomes dominant. They say various factors influence this, and our propensity to reconcile and successfully integrate the dominant and the remaining non-dominant learning styles improves as we mature through particular developmental stages, identified as:

1 acquisition: from birth to adolescence where basic abilities and cognitive structures develop;
2 specialization: from formal schooling through the early work and personal experiences of adulthood where social, educational, and organizational socialization forces shape the development of a particular, specialized learning style; and
3 integration: in mid-career and later life where non-dominant modes of learning are expressed in work and personal life.

(Kolb and Kolb, 2006: 8)

Clearly, when considering adult education, trainers need to take into consideration the fact that learners have already developed a style and method which, on returning to academic study after a prolonged period away, may not be compatible with current thinking concerning student-led education.

Rogers (1969) and Rogers and Freiberg (1994) suggest that there are two types of learning – 'cognitive', or the acquisition of academic knowledge, and 'experiential', or applied knowledge. Rogers also identified the following principles of learning:

1 Human beings have a natural potential for learning.
2 Significant learning takes place when the subject matter is perceived by the student as having relevance for his/her own purposes, when the individual has a goal he/she wishes to achieve and sees the material presented to him/her as relevant to the goal, learning takes place with great rapidity.
3 Learning which involves a change in self-organization in the perception of oneself is threatening and tends to be resisted.
4 Those learnings which are threatening to the self are more easily perceived and assimilated when external threats are at a minimum.
5 When the threat to the self is low, experience can be perceived in differentiated fashion and learning can proceed.
6 Much significant learning is acquired through doing.
7 Learning is facilitated when the student participates responsibly in the learning process.
8 Self-initiated learning which involves the whole person of the learner – feeling as well as intellect – is the most lasting and pervasive.
9 Independence, creativity and self-reliance are all facilitated when self-criticism and self-evaluation are basic and evaluation by others is of secondary importance.
10 The most socially useful learning in the modern world is the learning of the process of learning, a continuing openness to experience and to incorporate into oneself the process of change.

(Rogers, 1969: 114)

These principles suggest that given the optimal learning environment, a student who is actively involved and at the centre of their learning is more likely to learn and change as a result of that experience.

Student-centred learning

A number of my research participants mentioned that 'how' they were taught was often of more significance than 'what' they were taught. Here, I discuss some different methods used in student-centred learning that you may experience during your training. Some aspects may already be familiar to you.

Rogers (1969) suggests that experiential and student-centred learning requires the trainee to be at the heart of their educational experience, to take charge of their learning process, and to initiate and evaluate their experience. The implication of this is that the student has an equal share of power in the learning process; they are in control of their learning and development, and, as a result, are more likely to 'own' their goals, and to reach them.

This is in contrast to more behavioural methods of learning that may be viewed as the teacher holding the power and the knowledge, and, also, deciding the goals. You may be more familiar with this way of learning if you have been away from education for quite some time.

Knowles (1975) refers to self-directed learning, which he describes as:

> a process in which individuals take the initiative, with or without the help of others, in diagnosing their learning needs, formulating learning goals, identifying human and material resources for learning, choosing and implementing appropriate learning strategies, and evaluating learning outcomes.
>
> (Knowles, 1975: 18)

Learning contracts, participation in curriculum development, and personal goal-setting, are three methods that can facilitate the process of self-directed learning on a counselling and psychotherapy course.

Learning contracts

Learning contracts are often used as they allow the student to become an active participant in their educational experience.

According to Knowles (1986), a learning contract is:

> an alternative way of structuring a learning experience: It replaces a content plan with a process plan. Instead of specifying how a body of content will be transmitted (content plan), it specifies how a body of content will be acquired by the learner (process plan).
>
> (ibid.: 39–40)

He goes on to say that a learning contract typically specifies:

1. The knowledge, skills, attitudes, and values to be acquired by the learner (learning objectives);
2. How these objectives are to be accomplished (learning resources and strategies);
3. The target date for their accomplishment;
4. What evidence will be presented to demonstrate that the objectives have been accomplished; and
5. How this evidence will be judged or validated. In academic settings the contract also specifies how much credit is to be awarded, and what grade is to be given.

(ibid.: 38)

Learning contracts can be developed for different aspects, or modules, of the training, as well as having a general overall agreement. As the contracts are unique to the individual student, the process is often experienced as 'empowering'. The trainee, in agreement with their trainer, or supervisor, can also develop the plan to suit their learning style, e.g. 'Activist', 'Reflector', 'Theorist' or 'Pragmatist' (Honey and Mumford, 1986, 1992). (For an example of a contract, see Appendix 4.)

Curriculum development

Student participation in curriculum development, on the other hand, builds on the work initiated by Dewey (1916), which was further developed by Rogers (1969), and others (Aronowitz, 1981, 1994; Pinar, 1981; Rogers and Freiberg, 1994; Shor, 1992). In essence, students share the responsibility for the curriculum (hooks, 1994; Rogers and Freiberg, 1994) with the trainer, who then becomes a co-learner. The process of focusing on the trainee's own experience as the basis for the curriculum design enhances and supports learning for the student as their knowledge becomes more relevant and meaningful. The power differential, common in many training situations, is broken down, and this enables the student to experience the freedom to develop their critical thinking and analysing skills (Barnett and Coate, 2005; Freire 2003; Rice, 2004; Rogers, 1969; Rogers and Freiberg, 1994). Rogers and Freiberg (1994) also consider that one indicator of effective learning taking place is that an element of personal change is involved, and that this can be a transformational experience (Mezirow, 2000). (See Chapter 5 for more information on transformational learning.)

Student participation in curriculum development can be used for many areas, including the determination of the course learning outcomes, the methods of learning, which include classroom activities, and the defining of assessment methods.

Personal goal-setting

Goal-setting, although behavioural, is widely used in many training settings, and is similar to using learning contracts. The main difference between goal-setting and using contracts is that the former is often completed by the trainee on their own, whereas a learning contract is an agreement between the student and the trainer, or supervisor. When setting goals, the learner is invited to answer a number of questions to help them identify what successful completion of the course, or module, will entail for them. If you want to use goal-setting for the first year of your course, some questions you may ask yourself could be:

1 What do I want to get from this year of training?
2 What three goals would I like to achieve this year?
3 What help do I need to achieve those goals?
4 How will I get that help?
5 How might I sabotage myself?

Ensure your goals are: 'Specific, Measurable, Achievable, Relevant and Time-specific' (SMART):

> 'Specific' – This is being clear about what you would like to achieve, and it involves using positive language to state what you want, rather than what you don't want. One way to start this process is by saying to yourself, 'By the end of this course, or year, I will be able to . . .'. An example would be, 'By the end of this year, I will be able to understand, and apply, at least five key elements of the Person-Centred approach to counselling'. By being specific, it is much easier for you, and others, to verify whether you have achieved your goals.
>
> 'Measurable' – Is your goal measurable in some way? The example above is measurable, as it states 'five key elements'. Having a goal that is measurable will make it easier for you to plot your progress.
>
> 'Achievable' – Is your goal achievable? The above goal is achievable because its focus was on one approach; also, it is reasonable to expect that a trainee may learn at least five different concepts and apply them to their practice within a year. It may not be achievable if the goal were to be focused on five different *approaches*, such as 'cognitive analytic', 'integrative', 'personal construct', 'psychoanalytic' and 'relational psychotherapy'. Identifying a number of achievable goals that you can attend to during the year, and then acknowledging completion each time you achieve one of them, can help to increase your confidence, in both yourself and your training.
>
> 'Relevant' – Is your goal relevant to the course you are undertaking? It may not be helpful to identify five key requirements of 'constructivist psychotherapy' when you are on the first year of a 'group analysis' course, as, although you may appreciate being able to compare and contrast the two approaches, the time you take to do this may distract you from understanding aspects of your core model. Making your goal relevant will keep you focused.
>
> 'Time-specific' – Having a clear time-frame keeps you aware of your goals, and gives you a set point at which you can identify whether or not you have achieved them.

Once you have your list of goals, you may like to review them throughout the year and confirm whether, or by how much, you have achieved each target. Goal-setting can be flexible. These are *your* goals, for *you*; if, part way through the year, you decide that some fresh targets are also appropriate, then you can make modifications to include them, too.

Identifying what help you may need, such as academic support, child care, encouragement, financial assistance, or time off from work, and verifying the sources for that support, for example your bank, college or training provider, friends and family, or employer, may also help you to stay on target.

The last question in the list, 'How might I sabotage myself?' is just as important as the others. You could even widen this to, 'and how might others sabotage my progress?'

Imagine, for a moment, that you left school at 16 years of age with a few O levels, or GCSEs, or no qualifications at all. Since you did not go on to further or higher education, you may have a few concerns about school, education and your own intelligence or cleverness; these may be conscious or unconscious. Such worries or fears can permeate all aspects of our lives, so I now invite you to be curious about how they may get in your way. Using the above example, if you have a belief that you are unintelligent and worthless, then one way you might sabotage yourself would be to not ask for help should you begin to struggle. Without the necessary help, you may not pass the assignments; and thereby prove yourself to have been 'correct'. If you do ask for help, but don't get what you need, this, too, may prove your underlying belief. For example, you ask someone who you know is unreliable to babysit, you get ready to attend your study group session, the babysitter, unsurprisingly, doesn't turn up, and so you cannot attend the meeting.

Using learning contracts, student involvement in curriculum development and goal-setting enables a trainee to have a deeper sense of engagement in their learning. Most counselling and psychotherapy courses will use at least one of these methods, depending upon their approach to training. For example, a gestalt course may be more inclined to use student participation in curriculum design, or the development of learning contracts, while a 'cognitive behavioural therapy' (CBT) course may prefer to use goal-setting.

Training or education?

The *Longman Dictionary of Contemporary English* (2009: 1875) defines 'training' as 'the process of teaching or being taught the skills for a particular job or activity' and 'education' as 'the process of teaching and learning, usually at school, college, or university' (ibid.: 540). In Table 1.1, Fortino (2012) summarizes the attributes of education and training, and suggests a critical question for the learner to consider when choosing between these processes.

Using the definitions and the information contained in Table 1.1 suggests that most counselling and psychotherapy programmes would come under the heading of education, rather than training, although there will be elements of training within the learning process. Convention in the 'counselling and psychotherapy' world tends to use the term 'training' when referring to courses, and, in order to keep with custom, 'training' is used throughout this book to refer to the whole learning experience of becoming a counsellor or psychotherapist. This is even though the processes for this type of training are actually educational, transformational, lifelong and, as you will read in this book, life-changing.

Consider, briefly, the last time you were in any kind of formal educational or training situation. How do the earlier principles and learning theories apply to your experience? Similarly, think of a time when you learned something new that you identify as being valuable. How do these theories apply to that situation? Were there any similarities or differences? If so, what were they, and how do you think the above concepts could be used to illustrate the parallels and distinctions? As

Table 1.1 The difference between education and training

Attribute	*Education*	*Training*	*Determining factor*
Purpose of the Learning experience	Acquire or deepen mindset or profession	Acquire new skills and knowledge	Do I want to be transformed into a different person or just be more skilful?
Evidence of Learning success	Course grades, GPA [credits]	Testing, certification, job performance	How will others and I know I was successful with my learning experience?
Credentials	Degrees, graduate certificates	Certificates and licences	Do I want to get a degree or certificate?
Difficulty to learn	Harder	Easier	I am ready to undertake a lengthy and hard learning process or can I just do something quickly?
Length of the learning process	One to three years	Typically from one to five days or several weeks	How long do I expect the learning process to take?
Persistence of the learning outcome	Lasts a lifetime	Short half-life, five years on average	How long should I expect the results of this learning to last or remain current?
Style of learning	Draw out, mentoring by instructor	Drill in, developing skills, habits, practice	What can I expect my educational experience to be like?
Behaviour after learning took place	Acting after deep thought and analysis; broad	Acting out of new habits and skills; narrow	How will I behave after this learning experience?
Change	Skilful at thinking, transformational, deeper more radical	Skilful at doing; shallower, more superficial	What kind of change am I looking for?

(continued)

Table 1.1 (continued)

End result	Makes you different from others, thoughtful and mindful, educated	Make you the same as others with the same training, measure up	What am I looking for as an end result of my learning experience
Institutions providing learning experience	Colleges and universities	In-house seminars, training companies, self-taught	Where can I obtain this learning experience?
Examples	College courses and degree programmes	Training seminars, job training	What are some examples of education and training?

Source: Fortino, 2012.

you reflect on these ideas, what do you believe are the most important aspects of learning for you? What do you think is your preferred learning style? Are you an 'Activist' – do you favour concrete experiences, exercises, role-plays, problem-solving, simulations; or are you more of a 'Reflector' – would you rather observe and reflect, compare and contrast, or evaluate; or perhaps you tend to be more of a 'Theorist' – do you like to form concepts, generalize, theorize and hypothesize; or would you identify with being a 'Pragmatist' – do you like testing out new things, experimenting and action-planning? Once you have an idea of your own preferences for learning, you will be able to see where you would 'sit' on Kolb's learning cycle (Figure 1.1) and usefully consider ways of developing the other areas in the sequence.

In Table 1.2, a number of educational models are shown with their uses and methods. Most counselling and psychotherapy training courses are likely to come under the 'humanistic' and 'radical' education headings, with some of the more cognitive and behavioural approaches coming under the 'liberal' and 'technological' education headings, depending upon the skills and knowledge needed. (You can read more about the different modalities in Chapter 2.) When looking at Table 1.2, and your answers to the questions posed above, do you have a sense of which style of education would suit you best? When considering the learning experiences you identified earlier, can you recognize which style was being used then? Did this work for you? If not, are you able to identify which style would have worked better for you in that situation?

Once you have a clearer idea of your own preferences, you may find it helpful to attend a 'taster-day' with your proposed new trainer to see if their style of facilitation, and the methods used in that approach, would suit you and your way of learning. Other aspects to consider, in terms of education, are the appropriateness

Table 1.2 Educational models adapted from comparison of educational models

	Liberal (traditional)	*Progressive*	*Humanistic*	*Technological*	*Radical*	*Dogmatic (guru)*
Emphasis	Thinking, knowledge, and pluralism	Emerging skills, individual commitment, vision, aspiration and caring	Personal value and worth, growth and development	Increasing competence, efficiency, clarity, and standards of excellence	Genuine change, autonomy and empowerment	Need for structure and certainty and received tradition
Discount	Learners' experience	Personal needs	Social relationships, others' perceptions	Creativity, flexibility, reflection	Need for structure and safety	Personal as individual, new ideas
Metaphor	The learner as: . . . a container to be filled	. . . committed and obligated	. . . a growing plant	. . . inert material to be shaped	. . . imprisoned by their context	. . . burdened by mistakes and ignorance
Contract	I tell you, I give you information, you learn from school	I may guide you, we problem-solve together	I support you in your search for wholeness	I assess and accredit you when competent	We learn and change together	I reward you for orthodoxy
Uses	Teach theory, academic and research skills	Address problems and needs for change	Personal development in group and creativity	Practise skills	Increasing awareness, developing praxis	Giving basic tools and setting boundaries
Methods	Lecturing, films, discussion and book reading	Active problem-solving, increase skills through role-play, group work, fact sheets, account of personal experience	Group discussions, self-study, practice exercises that focus on personal growth, development and wholeness, e.g. triads, using personal experiences	Learning on the job under the guidance of another. The basis of S/NVQs	Experience/reflection/action and community development. This is a social action problem-solving approach	Iteration and reiteration, learning by heart, committing to memory
Roots	Socrates, Plato, mediaeval church and the enlightenment	Social action and political movements, and democracy	Person-centred ideas of Rogers, Maslow and existential philosophy	Behavioural psychology and systems theory	Liberation theology, ideas of Freire and Illich	Cultural and religious models of law and authority

Source: Adapted from Newton, 2003.

of the course to the practice of being a counsellor, or psychotherapist, and the academic level of the course you would like to complete.

How to choose a course

Before you opt for the course that is the most convenient or the cheapest, you may wish to spend some time researching your options; it might be convenient, or more affordable, but it may not be right for you.

Counselling and psychotherapy are professions whereby, with a few exceptions, e.g. some short-term, problem-solving or computerized cognitive behavioural therapy (CBT), the therapeutic relationship is central to the work. Therefore, while online or distance-learning courses may prove helpful in learning theory, you will miss out on the essential ingredients of building rapport, and the development of trust and skills practice. Although these courses are often very cheap, it is one of those cases where the saying 'you get what you pay for' is highly pertinent. Consider, for a moment, whether you yourself would go to see a counsellor or psychotherapist who had completed only an online, or distance-learning, training course? I expect you probably would not. So, although these courses may sound appealing – cheap and short – they are usually not accepted in the wider counselling, psychotherapy or mental health fields as part of your core training.

You may wish to think about looking for a course that offers you practical training in building and developing a therapeutic relationship. Many courses which have 'studies' in the title (as in 'Psychotherapy Studies') are not clinical in nature, meaning that no client-work is involved. These courses will not qualify you to undertake counselling or psychotherapy work with clients, although they may well offer you some theoretical understanding of the processes, so this type of course could be used as an introduction to a clinically based course. The next thing to consider is the academic level of the course.

Levels of training

During my research, I found that a number of the participants had no idea of the type or level of training they were to undertake. This did not cause a problem for some, but for others it led to a degree of confusion regarding what clinical work they would be able to undertake post-qualification, and several struggled with the written coursework. Whilst being interviewed, a number of the trainees said that they wished they had known and understood more about the academic side of the training. As Ben said:

> I had no idea that there were different levels of training. Part way through, I began to really struggle with the academic side of the course. I left school with a handful of O levels and two A levels about 20 years ago, and hadn't studied since. This part of the course was an almost vertical learning curve. I needed lots of help. In hindsight, I think I would have been better starting with a lower level course, first, to get me back into learning again.

Most counselling courses are 'entry-level'. This means that they usually start with an introductory course before progressing on to certificate and then diploma courses. In England, Wales and Northern Ireland, counselling is generally taught at levels one to six (see Table 1.3). This means that they start at a higher-grade GSCE, or A level, and then go up to graduate diploma level. This can be confusing, as courses run at different levels are called 'certificate' and 'diploma' courses. Most people would, understandably, assume that one certificate or diploma course would be at the same level as any other certificate or diploma course, but sadly this is not true. This variation has sometimes led to confusion, frustration and upset when a trainee has completed a certificate course and then decided to change training establishment to continue their diploma training elsewhere, only to then discover that they are expected to complete another certificate course as their previous training course does not give them eligibility for the diploma course they had hoped to attend.

In the Republic of Ireland, counselling certificate courses usually start at level 6, and, in Scotland, at level 7.

In England, Wales and Northern Ireland, the academic levels have been simplified by the combination of the National Qualifications Framework (NQF), the Qualifications and Credit Framework (QCF) and the Framework for Higher Education Qualifications (FHEQ) levels, so the levels are sequential. This does not necessarily impact on the actual name given to the qualification, so bear in mind the academic level any course claims to be set at and, if it is not clear, ask the course provider.

In the UK, the Quality Assurance Agency for Higher Education (QAA) published a subject benchmark statement for counselling and psychotherapy (QAA, 2013). This statement refers to bachelor degrees with honours (level 6 in England, Wales and Northern Ireland, and level 10 in Scotland) and master's degrees in counselling and psychotherapy (level 7 in England, Wales and Northern Ireland, and level 11 in Scotland). This document states that: 'The curriculum that evolves from the benchmarks described here will in most cases be the minimum required by professional bodies before registration or accreditation is granted' (QAA, 2013: 1). This suggests that, in time, accreditation and professional registration systems may be amended to incorporate higher education levels of achievement, and, although some already do this, it is not consistent between organizations. You may wish to bear this in mind when choosing a course because these higher academic levels may be required by the awarding bodies by the time you come to apply for your accreditation or registration.

Most counselling courses range from one to three years' duration. Predominantly, a one-year certificate or foundation course is followed by a two-year diploma course. Some training establishments offer a shorter, say, six to twelve weeks introductory course to help potential students decide if counselling is the path they wish to take. These can be helpful in allowing you to experience a short course to see if the skills taught and the manner of teaching suits you and your style of learning. If, for whatever reason, you do not feel comfortable in the

Table 1.3 Academic levels across the UK and Ireland

Main stages of education/ employment	*Level*	*FHEQ in England, Wales and Northern Ireland www.qaa.ac.uk*	*Level*	*QCF/NQF for England, Wales and Northern Ireland* www.ofqual.gov.uk*	*Level*	*Credit and Qualification Framework For Wales www.cqfw.net*	*Level*	*National Framework of Qualifications for Ireland www.nfq.ie*	*Level*	*The Scottish Credit and Qualifications Framework www.scqf.org.uk*
Professional or postgraduate education, research or employment	8	Doctoral Degrees	8	Vocational Qualifications Level 8	8	Doctoral Degrees	10	Doctoral Degrees Higher Doctorate	12	Professional Development Awards, Doctoral Degrees
	7	Master's Degrees, Integrated Master's Degrees, Postgraduate Diplomas, Postgraduate Certificate in Education (PGCE), Postgraduate Certificates	7	Fellowships, NVQ Level 5, Vocational Qualifications Level 7	7	Master's Degrees, Integrated Master's Degrees, Postgraduate Diplomas, Postgraduate Certificate in Education (PGCE), Postgraduate Certificates	9	Master's Degree, Post-graduate Diploma	11	SVQ Level 5, Professional Development Awards, Postgraduate Diplomas, Master's Degrees, Integrated Master's Degrees, Postgraduate Certificates
Higher education Advanced skills training	6	Bachelor's Degrees with Honours, Bachelor's Degrees, Professional Graduate Certificate in Education (PGCE), Graduate Diplomas, Graduate Certificates	6	Vocational Qualifications Level 6	6	Bachelor's Degrees with Honours, Bachelor's Degrees, Professional Graduate Certificate in Education (PGCE),	8	Honours Bachelor Degree, Higher Diploma	10	Bachelor's Degrees with Honours, Professional Development Awards, Graduate Diplomas, Graduate Certificates
							7		9	

(continued)

Table 1.3 (continued)

Main stages of education/ employment	*Level*	*FHEQ in England, Wales and Northern Ireland www.qaa.ac.uk*	*Level*	*QCF/NQF for England, Wales and Northern Ireland* www.ofqual.gov.uk*	*Level*	*Credit and Qualification Framework For Wales www.cqfw.net*	*Level*	*National Framework of Qualifications for Ireland www.nfq.ie*	*Level*	*The Scottish Credit and Qualifications Framework www.scqf.org.uk*
						Graduate Diplomas, Graduate Certificates		Ordinary Bachelor Degree	8	Bachelor's/Ordinary Degrees, Professional Development Awards, SVQ Level 4, Graduate Diplomas, Graduate Certificates
Entry to professional graduate employment	5	Foundation Degrees, Diplomas of Higher Education (DipHE), Higher National Diplomas (HND)	5	NVQ Level 4, Higher National Diplomas (HND), Vocational Qualifications Level 5	5	Foundation Degrees, Diplomas of Higher Education (DipHE), Higher National Diplomas (HND)	6	Advanced Certificate, Higher Certificate	7	Higher National Diplomas, SVQ Level 4, Professional Development Awards, Diplomas of Higher Education (DipHE) Access 2, National Progression Awards, National Certificates Professional Development Awards, Higher National Certificates,
Specialised education and training	4	Higher National Certificates (HNC), Certificates of Higher Education (CertHE)	4	Vocational Qualifications Level 4, Higher National Certificates (HNC)	4	Higher National Certificates (HNC), Certificates of Higher Education (CertHE), NVQ level 4, Essential Skills				

				Wales (ESW), Wider Key Skills (WKS), Higher Apprenticeship Framework				Certificates of Higher Education (CertHE), SVQ Level 3, Scottish Baccalaureate, Advanced Highers
Qualified/Skilled worker Entry to higher education Completion of secondary education	3	NVQ Level 3, Vocational Qualifications Level 3, GCE AS and A Level, Advanced Diplomas (England)	3	NVQ Level 3, ESW, WKS, Vocational Qualifications Level 3, GCE AS and A Level, Welsh Baccalaureate Qualification Advanced, Apprenticeships Framework	5	Level 5 Certificate, Leaving Certificate	6	Highers, SVQ Level 3, Professional Development Awards, National Progression Awards, National Certificates
Progression to skilled employment. Continuation of secondary education	2	NVQ Level 2, Vocational Qualifications Level 2, GCSEs at grade A*–C, ESOL skills for life, Higher Diplomas (England), functional skills Level 2 (England) (English, mathematics & ICT), Essential Skills Qualifications (NI)	2	NVQ Level 2, Vocational Qualifications Level 2, Welsh Baccalaureate Qualification Intermediate, GCSEs grade A*–C, ESW, WKS, Foundation Apprenticeship Framework	4	Level 4 Certificate, Leaving Certificate	5	Intermediate 2, Credit Standard Grade, SVQ Level 2, National Progression Awards, National Certificates

(continued)

Table 1.3 (continued)

Main stages of education/ employment	*Level*	*FHEQ in England, Wales and Northern Ireland www.qaa.ac.uk*	*Level*	*QCF/NQF for England, Wales and Northern Ireland* www.ofqual.gov.uk*	*Level*	*Credit and Qualification Framework For Wales www.cqfw.net*	*Level*	*National Framework of Qualifications for Ireland www.nfq.ie*	*Level*	*The Scottish Credit and Qualifications Framework www.scqf.org.uk*
Secondary education. Initial entry into employment or further education			1	NVQ Level 1, Vocational Qualifications Level 1, GCSEs at grade D–G, ESOL skills for life, Foundation Diplomas (England), functional skills Level 1 (England) (English, mathematics & ICT), Essential Skills Qualifications (NI)	1	NVQ Level 1, ESW, WKS, Vocational Qualifications Level 1, GCSEs at grade D–G, Welsh Baccalaureate Qualification Foundation	3	Level 3 Certificate, Junior Certificate	4	Intermediate 1, General Standard Grade, SVQ Level 1, National Progression Awards, National Certificates
			Entry Level	Entry Level Certificates (sub levels 1–3), ESOL skills for life, functional skills Entry Level (England) (English, mathematics & ICT), Essential Skills Qualifications (NI)	Entry Level	Entry Level Qualifications, ESW	2	Level 2 Certificate	3	Access 3, Foundation Standard Grades, National Progression Awards, National Certificates
							1	Level 1 Certificate	2	Access 2, National Progression Awards, National Certificates
									1	Access 1

Source: © The Quality Assurance Agency for Higher Education, 2011.

training course, then it may be an indication that this is not an appropriate one for you.

Psychotherapy training is usually at postgraduate level (level 7 in England, Wales and Northern Ireland, level 9 in the Republic of Ireland, and level 11 in Scotland), meaning that it is often a second qualification. Some courses may have a preliminary course to bridge the gap between previous training courses and the postgraduate course. Many people who start psychotherapy training may have already completed a counselling course, or have a psychology degree or some significant experience working within the helping professions, e.g. social work, teaching or nursing.

Postgraduate study requires far more from the student in terms of their ability to analyse, evaluate, critique and synthesize information; in contrast, further education will usually require a more basic level of knowledge, understanding and application of theory to practice.

Read through the training prospectus, brochure or online information for the courses you are interested in exploring, see the levels at which they are running, and then decide if that is the right level for you and your academic abilities. It may also be an idea to ask the training providers to give details of the help they can offer you in terms of academic support, access to a library and skills development; for example, how to make notes, or how to write an essay, should this be what you need. This will be especially helpful if you are returning to education after a long break. As one of the research participants, Claire, said:

> I really wanted to do the psychotherapy training as it looked so interesting but I looked at the levels of the course and realized that I needed to start at the beginning. I am so glad I did because I feel as though I started slowly and then built up my training and experience. I sought help from the trainers as I had no idea how to structure an essay; their help was invaluable and made the whole learning experience much easier. It has taken a lot longer than I originally thought but I have found it a very rewarding process.

Before deciding whether a course is right for you, you may want to consider exploring another course, or courses, for comparison purposes. If, having done this, your first course 'feels right', then take notice of your intuition. Similarly, if you have an intuitive response that says 'No!' – even if you don't really know why not – then it may be worth considering that this is unlikely to be the right course for you. Charlotte had this experience, and she said:

> I applied to and was accepted onto an advanced diploma course. I'd already completed a counselling diploma and this was to be the next stage. I was keen to resume my training as I'd had a break for a couple of years, but I had a niggling doubt about the course. I couldn't put my finger on why I didn't feel OK about it. All I knew was I found myself thinking of excuses why I would find it difficult to get there. So I decided to withdraw my application. I'm glad I did as I found a postgraduate course later that better suited me and my level of training.

Table 1.3 accounts for qualifications across England, Wales, Northern Ireland, the Republic of Ireland and Scotland. As some people are moving more widely across Europe, it may also be worth bearing in mind how these qualifications compare elsewhere.

The QAA states that:

> Within Europe, two overarching qualifications frameworks exist to which the national qualifications frameworks of the UK and Ireland relate: the European Qualifications Framework (EQF) and the Framework for Qualifications of the European Higher Education Area (FQ-EHEA) also known as the Bologna Framework.
>
> (QAA, 2011: 1)

Table 1.4 shows the association of levels established between national qualifications frameworks and the EQF.

The Bologna Framework was created in 1999, and it aims to create a European Higher Education Area (EHEA) to promote the European system of higher education worldwide, to increase mobility and employability for people, to enhance competitiveness, and to positively influence the social dimensions of education by creating 'participative equality', so that there is a consistent and level playing field for all.

What this means, in principle, is that the EHEA will have three cycles – 'Bachelor', 'Master' and 'PhD'. Within the first and second cycles, there will

Table 1.4 Association of levels between national qualifications and EQF

European Qualifications Framework (EQF)	*Qualifications and Credit Framework England/Northern Ireland (QCF)*	*Credit and Qualifications Framework for Wales (CQFW)*	*Scottish Credit and Qualifications Framework (SCQF)*	*The National Framework of Qualifications for Ireland (NFQ IE)*
8	8	8	12	10
7	7	7	11	9
6	6	6	10/9	8/7
5	5/4	5/4	8/7	6
4	3	3	6	5
3	2	2	5	4
2	1	1	4	3
1	E3	E3	3	2/1
	E2	E2	2	
	E1	E1	1	

Source: © The Quality Assurance Agency for Higher Education, 2011.

Table 1.5 Comparisons between national qualifications and EHEA cycle

Typical higher education qualifications within each level	*FHEQ level*	*FQHEIS /SCQF level*	*NFQ IE level*	*FQ-EHEA cycle*
Doctoral Degrees	8	12	10	Third cycle (end of cycle) qualifications
Master's Degrees including Integrated Master's				Second cycle (end of cycle) qualifications
Postgraduate Diplomas	7	11	9	Intermediate qualifications within the second cycle
Postgraduate Certificates				
Bachelor's Degrees with Honours/ Honours Bachelor Degrees		10	8	First cycle (end of cycle) qualifications
Irish Higher Diploma				
Bachelor's Degrees/ Ordinary Bachelor Degree	6		7	
Graduate Diplomas		9		Intermediate qualifications within the first cycle
Graduate Certificates				
Foundation Degrees (e.g. FdA, FdSc)				Short cycle (within or linked to the first cycle) qualifications
Diplomas of Higher Education (DipHE)	5	8		
Higher National Diplomas (HND)			6	
Irish Higher Certificate				
Higher National Certificates (HNC)	4	7		Intermediate qualifications within the short cycle

Source: © The Quality Assurance Agency for Higher Education, 2011.

be descriptors which will identify different learning outcomes, competencies and credits for qualifications. There will be a shift away from a degree structure, based on years of study, to a credit system. Each course will attract a number of credits based on the student's workload, which can then be added together to achieve a qualification. Credits can be transferred from one programme to another. The focus will be on a student-centred approach based on meeting learning outcomes.

Table 1.5 compares national qualifications with the EHEA cycle and will probably only be of interest to you if you are thinking of moving to another country and would like to work there with your existing qualifications.

Once you have decided on the level of study that would be the most appropriate for you, the next thing you may want to consider is what modality you should choose; this is the focus of the next chapter.

Conclusion

This chapter has defined counselling and psychotherapy, and briefly introduced the personal processes that you may wish to reflect on, especially with regard to your motivation for doing the training. A number of learning theories were introduced, and the levels of training that are available have been explained.

In relation to the content covered in this chapter, some questions for you to consider include:

1. What do you think is your preferred learning style?
2. What academic level do you feel would be most appropriate for you at this time?
3. When looking at a specific course, or courses, at what academic levels are the courses set? If it is not clear in the literature, then you may want to ask.
4. What types of issues and levels of work will the course train you to work with? Does it mainly equip you to work in the 'here and now' with clients, or will you be trained to work with clients whose more complex difficulties originate at a much earlier time in life?
5. Does the course only qualify you to work in specific settings, or with a specific client group?

Chapter 2

Counselling and psychotherapy modalities

> A major challenge for everyone who enters training as a counsellor or psychotherapist is the number of different therapy theories that are in circulation. One widely publicized survey, by Karasu (1986), found more than 400 different named approaches to therapy. It is clear that, in reality, there are not 400 unique ways to practice therapy.
>
> (McLeod, 2013: 121)

This is very true. There is not enough space within this book to explore each modality, so I have decided to limit the scope, here, to include some of the main approaches accredited by the BACP, COSCA, HCPC, IACP, ICP and the UKCP, as they are the main professional accrediting bodies in the UK and the Republic of Ireland.

The BACP, COSCA and IACP accredit specific courses that meet certain criteria, and no differentiation or distinction is made between approaches in the accreditation process. In contrast, the HCPC, ICP and UKCP recognize training and/or accrediting organizations that meet general criteria across all disciplines, and then further specify criteria related to a particular modality or field as laid down by that organization. Hence, the HCPC, ICP and UKCP are more modality-focused than the BACP, COSCA and IACP, although they all require members to be trained in a core theoretical approach.

Which modality or approach?

I think of the counselling and psychotherapy modalities as being in the form of a tree. Freud forms the roots, and then psychoanalysis, which was the only therapy option available for quite some time, forms the main trunk. Then, as time has progressed, various different branches have developed, each with its own specific way of operating. Today, we have so many ways of working that, at times, it is hard to know where one model ends and another one starts. New approaches emerge that combine elements from other models, or take concepts and rework them into a new way of working. Increasingly, modalities are discovering gaps in their approach, and they then borrow ideas from one another to fill those missing areas.

So, where does this leave you as a potential trainee? Quite possibly, a little confused and unsure about which route to take. In this chapter I offer you insights into a number of the various approaches; how they view themselves, the nature of their training and the options that will be available to you on completion. Table 2.1 shows the different colleges that make up the UKCP and the range of modalities available within each college. Table 2.2 presents the approaches recognized by the ICP, Table 2.3 displays those available on BACP and IACP accredited courses, and Table 2.4 those available on COSCA validated or approved courses.

I asked the following questions of the main professional body for each of the below approaches:

1 How would you describe your approach of counselling or psychotherapy to a layperson?
2 What prerequisites are there for someone who wishes to train in that model, e.g. previous qualifications/experience, etc.?
3 What are the training requirements, e.g. the number of hours of training, weekday/weekend/time commitments, and are there additional requirements, e.g. personal therapy, supervision, client work, written coursework or oral exams, etc.?
4 What form does the training take? How would you describe that to a layperson?
5 What are the professional accreditation/registration requirements (if any) for this specific model, or, if there are no specific requirements, what form of accreditation/registration is open to trainees who have completed their training?

The following information has been taken either from their responses, or from the relevant website. If you want more information on any specific approach, the website addresses for the main professional bodies are provided.

I have selected a number of modalities that appear on more than one table, and have then grouped them together to reflect the various branches of the counselling and psychotherapy tree. The branches are: Arts therapies, Cognitive therapy, Constructivist therapy, Family, Couple and Systemic therapy, Humanistic and Integrative therapies, Hypno-psychotherapy, Psychoanalysis, and Sexual and Relationship Psychotherapy. These names are in line with those used by the UKCP colleges. I have ensured that at least one modality (shown in bold in Table 2.1) is given for each college, so you have the fullest possible information.

Arts therapies branch

The Arts therapies are shown under the Humanistic and Integrative College of the UKCP, but I have put them under their own heading as they are the only psychotherapy approach to be regulated in the UK by the Health and Care Professions Council (HCPC). They consist of the three separate disciplines of art, drama, and music therapies.

Table 2.1 UKCP colleges and modalities of training

UKCP college	*Modalities*
Cognitive Psychotherapies College (CPC)	**Cognitive Analytic Therapy**
College for Sexual and Relationship Psychotherapy (CSRP)	**Sexual and Relationship Psychotherapy**
College of Constructivist Psychotherapies (CCP)	Autogenics **Existential Analysis** Neuro-Linguistic Psychotherapy **Personal Construct Psychotherapy**
College of Family, Couple and Systemic Therapy (CFCST)	**Family and Systemic Therapy**
College of Hypno-psychotherapies (CH-P)	Contemporary Psychotherapy **Hypno-psychotherapy** Neuro-Linguistic Psychotherapy
Council of Psychoanalysis and Jungian Analysis College (CPJA)	Analytical Psychology Attachment-based Psychoanalytic Psychotherapy Educational Psychotherapy **Group Analysis** Group Psychoanalytic Psychotherapy Intersubjective Systems Theory **Jungian Analysis** **Psychoanalytic Psychotherapy** Psychodynamic Psychotherapy
Humanistic and Integrative Psychotherapy College (HIPC)	**Arts Psychotherapy** Biodynamic Psychotherapy Body Psychotherapy Core Process Existential Psychotherapy **Gestalt** Humanistic Psychotherapy **Humanistic and Integrative Psychotherapy** Integrative Child Psychotherapy and Counselling Integrative Psychotherapy **Person-Centred** Process Oriented Psychology (Process Work) Psychodrama **Psychosynthesis** Psychotherapy with Children and Young People **Transactional Analysis** **Transpersonal**
Psychotherapeutic Counselling and Intersubjective Psychotherapy College (PCIPC)	Dynamic Interpersonal Therapy **Humanistic Counselling** Integrative Counselling Relational Centred Counselling
Universities Training College (UTC)	**Existential** Group Analytic Integrative Psychodynamic

Table 2.2 Modalities recognized by ICP

Cognitive Behavioural Therapy	CBT
Constructivist Therapy	Personal Construct Psychology
Couple and Family Therapy	Systemic Therapy
Humanistic and Integrative	Humanistic and Integrative
Psychoanalytic	Analytical Psychology Child and Adolescent Psychoanalytic Psychotherapy Group Analytic Human Relations Psychoanalysis

Table 2.3 Modalities available on BACP and IACP accredited courses

Anthroposophy	CBT	Cognitive
Existential	Gestalt	Humanistic
Integrative	Object Relations	Person-Centred
Psychodynamic	Psychosynthesis	Relational
Relationship Therapy	Systemic	Transpersonal

Table 2.4 Modalities available on COCSA validated or approved courses

CBT	Christian Counselling	Integrative
Interpersonal Dialogue	Person-Centred	Psychodynamic
Transactional Analysis		

Art therapy

According to the British Association of Art Therapists (BAAT):

> Art therapy is a form of psychotherapy that uses art media as its primary mode of communication.
>
> Clients who are referred to an art therapist need not have previous experience or skill in art, and the art therapist is not primarily concerned with making an aesthetic or diagnostic assessment of the client's image. The overall aim of its practitioners is to enable a client to effect change and growth on a personal level through the use of art materials in a safe and facilitating environment.
>
> The relationship between the therapist and the client is of central importance, but art therapy differs from other psychological therapies in that it is a three-way process between the client, the therapist and the image or artefact. Thus, it offers the opportunity for expression and communication and can be

> particularly helpful to people who find it hard to express their thoughts and feelings verbally.
>
> Art therapists have a considerable understanding of art processes underpinned by a sound knowledge of therapeutic practice, and work with both individuals and groups in a variety of residential and community-based settings, for example: adult mental health, learning disabilities, child and family centres, palliative care and the prison service. The diversity of these areas of work is reflected in the number of special interest groups that have developed in affiliation with the British Association of Art Therapists.
>
> The art therapist's work is sometimes challenging and calls for skill and sensitivity; it follows that those who wish to pursue a career in art therapy should be mature, flexible people. The training course, which combines theoretical and experiential work, is a Masters Degree to be completed over two years full-time or three years part-time. Applicants must have a first degree in art, although other graduates are sometimes considered, and some proper experience of working in an area of health, education or social care.
>
> (BAAT, 2011)

The following websites display more information about art therapy:

The British Association of Art Therapists – www.baat.org
Irish Association of Creative Arts Therapists – www.iacat.ie
Northern Ireland Group for Art as Therapy – www.nigat.org

Drama therapy

The British Association of Dramatherapists (BADTH) is the professional body recognized by the HCPC, and, according to them:

> Dramatherapy is a form of psychological therapy in which all of the performance arts are utilised within the therapeutic relationship. Dramatherapists are both artists and clinicians and draw on their trainings in theatre/drama and therapy to create methods to engage clients in effecting psychological, emotional and social changes. The therapy gives equal validity to body and mind within the dramatic context; stories, myths, play-texts, puppetry, masks and improvisation are examples of the range of artistic interventions a Dramatherapist may employ. These will enable the client to explore difficult and painful life experiences through an indirect approach.
>
> Dramatherapists work in a wide variety of settings:
>
> - in schools
> - in mental health
> - in general health social care settings
> - in prisons
> - in the voluntary sector.

> Thus the clients they work with will have differing needs; from children on the autistic spectrum to older people with dementia; adolescents who self-harm, people with histories of sexual and/or physical abuse, those suffering from a mental illness and women with post-natal depression.
>
> (BADTH, 2011)

The following websites display more information about drama therapy:

The British Association of Dramatherapists – www.badth.org.uk
Irish Association of Creative Arts Therapists – www.iacat.ie
Northern Ireland Group for Art as Therapy – www.nigat.org

Music therapy

Angela Harrison, Chair of the British Association for Music Therapy (BAMT), and Lead Music Therapist for the North Yorkshire Music Therapy Centre, a registered charity providing a rural, community-based service, supplied the following information:

> Music therapy is an established, psychological intervention which uses the beneficial effects of shared music-making to help those whose ability to communicate and express themselves has been compromised by illness or disability. Group and individual sessions are provided in a range of settings and are tailored to meet the needs of those involved. Music therapists work in multi-disciplinary teams with children and adults with autism, learning disabilities or emotional and behavioural problems, with acquired brain injury or neurological conditions, life-threatening illness, psychosis, dementia and those in end of life care.
>
> Music therapists are trained musicians as well as therapists and use their skills to support and enrich the music of those with whom they work. Acoustic instruments and voices may be used in sessions alongside the rapidly developing world of music technology, which offers opportunities for expressive music-making and provides analytic tools for evaluation/research.
>
> Music therapy training is at postgraduate master's level and most candidates have a degree/degree equivalent in music, occasionally in related topics such as psychology. All the UK trainings require previous experience with one or more of the client groups with whom music therapists work. Recommended age for entry is 23+ for maturity of approach. There is also the requirement for a level of self-understanding and an ability to communicate effectively through a musical instrument and/or voice.
>
> The seven training courses have a common core curriculum delivered from the perspective of different models and are approved by the Health and Care Professions Council (HCPC). Each requires personal therapy to be undertaken throughout the training and includes supervised clinical placements, case work presentations, vivas and dissertation.

Training is an intensive experience which breaks down the familiar elements of music into a communicative process. Students gain knowledge and experience of medical and psychological conditions and therapeutic techniques and become more musically expressive, intuitive, analytical and flexible, and from their personal self-experience (e.g. psychotherapy) they work through a parallel process of change from musician to therapist. They also learn about audit and research, now an essential part of the job. Music therapy training supports the student to develop a reflective stance, the personal resilience required to support families in troubled circumstances and a belief that people are capable of positive change. Models of training present different emphases on the role of music within the therapy, ranging from music being the primary catalyst for change, to music being a medium for the 'playing out' and understanding of unconscious processes.

There is currently no registration requirement for trainees. Once qualified, registration with the HCPC allows practitioners to use the title 'Music Therapist'. The HCPC regulates fitness to practise, based on adherence to a code of ethics and profession-specific standards. Biennially, they audit the continuing professional development records of a percentage of registrants to ensure safe, up-to-date practice.

The British Association for Music Therapy (BAMT) represents the profession in the UK and, amongst its many services, provides cross-curricular events for trainees to help prepare for the business world ahead. Membership of BAMT is an expectation for many posts, as it demonstrates an additional level of support and guidance, thus raising standards.

(Harrison, A., Personal Communication, 16 August 2012)

The following websites display more information about music therapy:

The British Association for Music Therapy – www.bamt.org
Irish Association of Creative Arts Therapists – www.iacat.ie
Northern Ireland Group for Art as Therapy – www.nigat.org

Cognitive branch

Traditional psychoanalysis was often undertaken over many years; the founders of the cognitive therapies that are now available wanted to be able to offer shorter-term work. In the UK, Dr Anthony Ryle (born 1927), a GP, developed cognitive analytic therapy (CAT) in the 1980s in response to the need in the NHS for short-term focused therapy that could be tailored for each client. It would take into account their personal history, earliest life experiences and coping strategies, and then support them in developing new ways to cope with life-challenges. CAT training is available in the UK and, with limited availability, in Ireland.

Aaron Beck (born 1921), who developed cognitive behavioural therapy (CBT), focused on the client's thoughts, which, if changed, will directly change the emotion that the client feels in response to a specific set of circumstances. The focus of CBT tends to be on 'here and now' problem-solving, challenging outdated, or distorted, thinking. Although CBT is not available via any UKCP college, it is one of the most popular modalities available in the NHS, and, as such, is included in this section. Training in CBT is widely available across Britain and Northern Ireland.

Cognitive analytic therapy

Maddy Jevon, Liaison Officer, and Dr Dawn Bennett, trainer for the Association for Cognitive Analytic Therapy, provided the following information:

> Cognitive Analytic Therapy (CAT) is a collaborative process that looks at the way a person thinks, feels and acts, and the events and relationships that underlie their experiences. As its name suggests, it brings together ideas and understanding from different therapies into one integrated, user-friendly and effective therapy.
>
> CAT respects a person's individual needs and his or her own manageable goals for change. It is time-limited – typically 16 to 24 weeks. Briefer CAT interventions can be used in primary care and with clients who self-harm (Cowmeadow, 1994). CAT focuses on what a person brings to the therapy ('target problems') and explores the deeper patterns of relating that underlie them.
>
> CAT has been widely used with people who have experienced childhood physical, emotional or sexual abuse, neglect and trauma. Therapists may work with adults, adolescents, older people, those with learning difficulties and in forensic settings.
>
> **Training requirements**
>
> A two-year training, usually with ten training days per year, typically weekdays but occasional weekends. The training comprises a combination of workshops, training days, seminars, peer group work, personal learning, supervision, clinical practice and personal CAT therapy. Experiential work focuses on personal exploration and the development of CAT skills and their clinical application.
>
> Trainees must complete a minimum of eight supervised cases and pass all written work required by the course – one case study and one theoretical essay each year before accreditation. Trainees are required to have weekly supervision; this is usually group supervision (three trainees) for one and a half hours a week.
>
> CAT Psychotherapists are qualified as CAT Practitioners and have undertaken an additional in-depth two-year training with more practice hours, equivalent to UKCP requirements, and further personal therapy. This allows UKCP and CAT accreditation as psychotherapists.
>
> (Jevon, M., Personal Communication, 19 June 2012)

Professional accreditation

There are twelve course centres in the UK delivering CAT Practitioner training and leading to the ACAT CAT Practitioner Diploma. ACAT is currently exploring collaboration with a new higher education provider for courses to replace the collaboration with Sheffield Hallam University which ended in 2013. It intends to continue to offer the dual award at Postgraduate Diploma and ACAT CAT Practitioner Level. The award can be followed by:

(i) CAT psychotherapy training: psychotherapy training enables CAT practitioners to become cognitive analytic psychotherapists via an additional two-year assessed course, which leads to eligibility for registration with the United Kingdom Council for Psychotherapy.
(ii) MSc: ACAT has offered an MSc in CAT in collaboration with Sheffield Hallam University (2008–13). This award constituted the completion of a research stage of the CAT Practitioner training (PG Diploma). From 2013 the MSc programme at Sheffield Hallam University continues to be open to prospective MSc students who can apply via the Advancing Professional Practice programme. There may be additional opportunities in the future with a new higher education partner.

(Bennett, D., Personal Communication, 28 April 2013)

Cognitive behavioural therapy

John Roberts, lecturer in psychological therapies at the University of Plymouth, and a BABCP Cognitive and Behavioural Psychotherapist, states:

> Cognitive Behavioural Therapy (CBT) is a collaborative and structured activity. It features active engagement of the client and therapist; it is a time-limited, empirical and problem-oriented form of talking treatment. It takes a 'here and now' approach to problems – though taking account of historical developmental influences will be important for the most severe of difficulties.
>
> Experimentation between sessions is important within CBT. These are mutually designed by the client and therapist and can take a number of forms, for example collecting further data regarding a problem such as monitoring a mood or a problematic activity. Later, it may focus on change – for instance, interrupting or changing an activity or a thought that may have been hypothesised to be unhelpful. The client then reports back to the therapist so that further experiments can be designed.
>
> There are no prerequisites for a professional membership of the BABCP should someone wish to become accredited. However, typically accredited therapists will be psychiatric nurses, counsellors, clinical psychologists, occupational therapists or social workers. Although there is not a pre-requirement for any educational qualifications, graduates in the humanities or helping professions feature strongly.

Typically, a training programme in CBT is now a postgraduate diploma consisting of approximately 400 hours of taught study (a balancing of theory and practice) and 200 hours of supervised clinical practice – this leads to provisional accreditation as a Cognitive Behavioural Psychotherapist.

Roughly speaking, this will involve studying six postgraduate modules: assessment and formulation, key techniques in CBT, research methodologies, CBT for depression, CBT for anxiety, and CBT for complex presentations. The submission of a portfolio of experiential learning and supervision is required for module seven. Students on CBT programmes will typically submit six 5,000-word client-based assignments and multiple taped sessions for evaluation by supervisors and tutors. A final module will include a reflective-experiential journal and a final taped session that meets the threshold of competence in the Cognitive Therapy Training Rating Scale (CTS-r).

There is no requirement to have personal therapy in CBT but increasingly courses are grounding themselves in modern, scientific experiential teaching and clinician growth methods. 'Self-Practice–Self-Reflection' (SP-SR) (Bennett-Levy, 2006; Bennett-Levy *et al.*, 2001) are now seen as vital components of clinician development.

Typically, a high-intensity CBT student will be employed within IAPT in a primary care setting; they will work with a caseload and attend university two days a week. Their course will involve a range of teaching strategies and methods, a strong experiential component, role-plays and problem-based learning.

Most recently, there is a new group of professionals known as Psychological Well-Being Practitioners (PWPs) who are trained to postgraduate diploma level in CBT skills and techniques for the low-intensity patients within the stepped care model of mental health difficulties.

For accreditation with the BABCP you have to have 450 hours' training and 200 hours' supervised clinical practice, the supervision must be provided by a BABCP accredited therapist, and you have to pass the CTS-r. This forms the basis of a provisional accreditation. The demand for full and further accreditation is dependent on receiving further supervision and undertaking a further 30 hours of CPD.

(Roberts, J., Personal Communication, 27 April 2013)

It is possible to undertake counselling training with a CBT focus with the academic levels ranging from two to five. The frequency of training varies from half a day, or one full day, per week, to one weekend per month.

The following websites display more information about cognitive therapies:

The Association for Cognitive Analytic Therapy – www.acat.me.uk
The British Association for Behavioural and Cognitive Psychotherapies – www.babcp.com

Constructivist branch

According to Brion Sweeney (2010), Chair of the UKCP College of Constructivist Psychotherapies:

> Constructivism as a philosophical stance sees the world's 'reality' as mediated through the experience of each individual. This is not to deny the reality of lived experience, rather that a person can change their lived experience by making sense of the world in different ways. Constructivist positions see existence as contextual and relational. The act of the construal – i.e. making both sense and meaning of being human – can only be understood in terms of living in a shared world which is socially negotiated through shared perspectives with others.
>
> (Sweeney, 2010)

One approach that comes under this umbrella is existential psychotherapy.

Existential psychotherapy

According to Regent's School of Psychotherapy and Psychology, Regent's University, London (2012):

> Existential psychotherapy is a professional, down-to-earth form of therapy which responds to an inner curiosity to find out who we really are and how we really want to live. The emphasis is on a person's existence rather than just his or her mind, their experience rather than psychological theories. The course provides a safe and contained setting for a deep and philosophical exploration and discovery of those elements which have a bearing on being and ways of working therapeutically with clients.
>
> The practice of existential psychotherapy is informed by existential philosophy. The focus of this course is the practice of actively doing as opposed to talking about philosophy. Although there is an intellectual demand in engaging with existential philosophy this is only a means for the possibility of breaking through into radical new understandings about the very way we make sense of phenomena.
>
> (Regent's School of Psychotherapy and Psychology, 2012a)

The academic seminars introduce the central concerns of the existential-phenomenological way of viewing the world, the antecedents and foundations of this world view in existential philosophy and, critically, applications of this world view to the practice of psychotherapy. Detailed examination of the work of major philosophers of existence is encouraged to promote an existential approach to psychotherapy as a means of understanding concepts such as 'truth' and 'meaning' in the context of clinical practice. The training seminars look critically at the concept of techniques and skills, examining

> their relevance to the practice of existential psychotherapy, and also provide a practice forum.
>
> (Regent's School of Psychotherapy and Psychology, 2012b)

Another approach under this umbrella is Personal Construct Psychology.

Personal construct psychology

Personal Construct Psychology (PCP) was developed by George Kelly (1905–67), in 1955. In essence, PCP considers how the client makes sense of their world, and is about finding out how the client construes the meaning of their life within their social and cultural contexts. It is frequently used in organizations, coaching and in businesses, and can also be used in psychology, counselling and psychotherapy.

Primarily, two methods of assessment are used: Self-Characterization and Repertory Grids. The training for PCP appears to be available via an initial five-day course. This is followed by a tutorial-based programme mainly using internet groups.

The following websites display more information about Constructivist Psychotherapy:

Irish Constructivist Psychotherapy Association – www.irishconstructivists.org
Regent's School of Psychotherapy and Psychology – www.regents.ac.uk/about/schools/regents-school-of-psychotherapy-psychology
The Centre for Personal Construct Psychology – www.centrepcp.co.uk
The Personal Construct Psychology Association – www.pcpassociation.net

Family, couples and systemic branch

Family, couple and systemic therapy is a distinct form of therapy that focuses on the family, couple, or system, as a whole, rather than on specific individuals. A problem in the family is framed as a systemic issue, rather than an individual's problem and, as such, the family members work together to find the solution. Family in this context can mean anything from a couple, whether married or not, to a multi-generational family, including grandparents, parents, children and step- and half-siblings. The Association for Family Therapy and Systemic Practice (AFT, 2013) states that:

> [Family and systemic psychotherapy] helps people in a close relationship help each other.
>
> It enables family members, couples and others who care about each other to express and explore difficult thoughts and emotions safely, to understand each other's experiences and views, appreciate each other's needs, build on strengths and make useful changes in their relationships and their lives. Individuals can find Family Therapy helpful, as an opportunity to reflect on important relationships and find ways forward.
>
> Research shows Family Therapy is useful for children, young people and adults experiencing a very wide range of difficulties and experiences.

The training to become a Family and Systemic Psychotherapist requires that students have already trained in, and had experience in, another relevant profession. To qualify as a Family and Systemic Psychotherapist it is necessary to undertake a four-year part-time training at Foundation, Intermediate and Qualifying levels.

[The foundation level] is usually a part-time course, lasting for one academic year, consisting of theoretical input and teaching in small and larger groups. There is a strong emphasis on active learning and there will usually be opportunities to work in pairs and small groups and to be involved in role-play and other experiential exercises.

[The intermediate level] is also usually part-time and lasts for one academic year. There is a continuation of theoretical input and opportunities to process ideas in small groups. This year also places a firm emphasis on the application of theoretical ideas to practice and clinical work. Students are required to undertake a minimum of 50 hours of systemic practice during the year.

[The qualifying level] is usually completed part-time over two academic years and must be at postgraduate level. Students at this level will be required to do at least 200 hours' work-based systemic practice over the period of the course.

Courses have the following components:

- Theoretical teaching. Personal and professional development – at present there is no requirement for students to undertake personal therapy although many do so.
- Live supervised clinical practice within a small supervision group, led by an appropriately qualified supervisor. Generally, this uses a video link and often a one-way screen to allow the supervisor and other team members to observe sessions.
- Research teaching. Discussion of work-based clinical practice (200 hours).

Courses are very demanding because of the active clinical component and heavy assessment schedule. In order to successfully complete the course, students will have to demonstrate both academic and practice competence and a level of competence appropriate to independent practice. The latter is often assessed through reports from clinical supervisors and other teachers, and a clinical portfolio together with a formal presentation to a panel.

(AFT, 2013)

The following websites display more information about Family and Systems Therapy:

The Association for Family Therapy and Systemic Practice – www.aft.org.uk
Family Therapy Association of Ireland – www.familytherapyireland.com
European Family Therapy Association – www.europeanfamilytherapy.eu

Humanistic and integrative branch

This is probably the largest grouping of therapies that are available today. Many BACP accredited courses refer to themselves as 'humanistic' or 'integrative', sometimes with a further clarification, e.g. 'humanistic (person-centred)'. Some of the humanistic therapies developed as a departure from psychoanalysis, which some saw as being too elitist or restrictive, or engendering a dynamic whereby the therapist has more power than the client. In the 1940s and 1950s, Carl Rogers (1902–87) developed client-centred therapy (CCT), which later became known as the person-centred approach (PCA), in which he advocated a non-directive approach:

> The central hypothesis of this approach can be briefly stated. Individuals have within themselves vast resources for self-understanding and for altering their self-concepts, basic attitudes, and self-directed behaviour; these resources can be tapped if a definable climate of facilitative psychological attitudes can be provided.
>
> (Rogers, 1980: 115)

Around the same time that Rogers was developing client-centred therapy, Eric Berne became disillusioned with psychoanalysis. He felt that it was too rigid and slow, and that the knowledge and power lay in the therapist rather than the client. Berne wanted to share theory and power with his clients, and so he developed transactional analysis (TA), where concepts could be easily understood and used by both clients and therapists alike. Similarly, Fritz Perls (1893–1970) and Laura Perls (1905–90) were moving away from traditional psychoanalysis, with its emphasis on introjections and interpretation, towards assimilation and encouraging discovery, and where the phenomenological experience of the client is central. This was the beginning for gestalt therapy. All these approaches have been developed over the years and are increasingly popular today.

Other theories that are now included under the humanistic umbrella have earlier roots. For example, in the late 1920s and early 1930s, Wilhelm Reich (1897–1957) developed Freud's ideas about the body and became the pioneer of what is now called Body Psychotherapy. Earlier still, William James (1842–1910) began to recognize the existence of the spiritual self, and a higher self, and was one of the founders, along with Otto Rank (1884–1939), Gustav Jung (1875–1961), Abraham Maslow (1908–70) and Roberto Assagioli (1888–1974), of what is today called Transpersonal Psychology, which also includes Buddhist and other Eastern philosophies and practices. Assagioli then went on to develop Psychosynthesis. In the 1950s and 1960s all these approaches became widely recognized in their own right.

More detailed information is included here about some of the different modalities available under the humanistic and integrative umbrella. They are presented in alphabetical order.

Gestalt therapy

Ann Salter, chair of the Gestalt Psychotherapy and Training Institute (GPTI), states:

Gestalt practitioners work on a short or long-term basis, with individuals, couples, groups, families and organizations. Gestalt therapy is an existential approach which emphasizes personal responsibility and choice, whilst equally recognizing the importance of interconnection and interdependence. There is an understanding that we are all influenced by our surroundings, and by each other; none of us can be understood in isolation. The practice of awareness (sometimes called mindfulness in other approaches) is central to the methodology of gestalt. Our belief is that increased awareness leads to greater choice, the possibility for change and more fulfilling ways of being in the world. At the heart of gestalt is a recognition of every individual's dignity and worth.

The Diploma in Gestalt Psychotherapy (GPTI) is at postgraduate level. Applicants for training will normally be qualified in one of the helping professions (e.g. counsellor, social worker or General Practitioner) or will be able to show that they have achieved graduate-level competence and have experience of working with people in a helping capacity.

The core training takes place over a period of four years; traditionally this has been one weekend a month or a long weekend (three days) every two months. Trainees are required to undertake a minimum of 500 GPTI accredited training hours for the diploma.

Trainees will normally be in regular weekly personal psychotherapy during the course of their training. They are required to be in personal psychotherapy during the formal training period and the year preceding their final examination.

The minimum number of supervision hours to be undertaken by the trainee before the oral exam is 150 hours. Six hundred hours of experience in seeing a range of clients is required, of which at least 300 should be using the gestalt approach. A psychiatric placement or an equivalent is required for those without relevant experience.

A case study of between thirteen and fifteen thousand words is required to demonstrate theoretical and clinical competence. Once all the requirements have been met, a candidate needs to pass an oral examination (or viva) to gain the diploma.

The core training takes place over a period of four years, in a group setting. The training format includes theoretical input from the trainer, experiential exercises, skills practice and seminar discussion groups. The training group is recognized as an important resource for trainees, in which they can learn from their own ways of relating to others and their environment. A carefully calibrated mixture of support and challenge enables trainees to work towards becoming practising psychotherapists.

On qualification, trainees are awarded the Diploma in Gestalt Psychotherapy and become accredited members of GPTI. They are also usually eligible for UKCP registration.

(Salter, A., Personal Communication, 7 May 2013)

It is also possible to undertake gestalt counselling training at undergraduate level at other centres, which can then be used as entry to postgraduate training, if necessary.

The following websites display more information about gestalt psychotherapy:

The Gestalt Centre – www.gestaltcentre.co.uk
The Gestalt Psychotherapy and Training Institute – www.gpti.org.uk
The Irish Gestalt Centre – www.irishgestaltcentre.com
European Association for Gestalt Therapy – www.eagt.org

Person-centred approach

Catherine Hayes, a member of the British Association for the Person-Centred Approach Coordinating Group (BAPCA CG), and a trainer in 'Counselling for Depression' at the University of Nottingham, provided the following information:

> Underpinning all person-centred psychotherapy and counselling is a fundamental respect and regard for the client and their unique experience of life and a belief that being fully heard and understood has a powerfully beneficial effect. Practitioners do not analyse or pathologise. The therapeutic encounter ensures the client is able to determine and identify aspects of their experience they wish to explore.
>
> Rogers (1951, 1957, 1961, 1974, 1979, 1980) referred to 'the necessary and sufficient conditions of therapeutic personality change and for constructive personality change to occur, it is necessary that these conditions exist and continue over a period of time'. The conditions are:
>
> - Two persons are in psychological contact.
> - The first, whom we shall term the client, is in a state of incongruence, being vulnerable or anxious.
> - The second person, whom we shall term the therapist, is congruent or integrated in the relationship.
> - The therapist experiences unconditional positive regard for the client.
> - The therapist experiences an empathic understanding of the client's internal frame of reference and endeavours to communicate this experience to the client.
> - The communication to the client of the therapist's empathic understanding and unconditional positive regard is to a minimal degree achieved.
>
> (Rogers, 1957: 96)
>
> The therapist offering and communicating these conditions may enable the client to find or rekindle emotional and cognitive resources that generate growth and enhance their ability to accept themselves, thereby diminishing the adverse effects of distress in all its manifestations. Carl Rogers is renowned for developing the person-centred or client-centred approach to psychotherapy. Its impact was of such great significance that the person-centred approach is fundamental to positive psychology, education, mediation and peace and reconciliation movements.

Training establishments will have various routes via introductory/certificate courses in order to qualify to study at diploma, postgraduate or master's level. The personal and academic standard is very high once entry to a qualification level training is achieved.

[Some] diploma-level training courses match the requirements set out by BACP in order for trainees to achieve accreditation. Trainees are required to attend with an increasing time commitment which peaks at year two and then reduces by year three. Apart from group work, skills development and lectures, trainees will need to attend one-to-one supervision, group supervision (some placements providers will have additional requirements) and personal development groups. Trainees need to attain a particular level of academic achievement in order to progress to the subsequent years and can defer if necessary. Diploma level qualifies the trainee to be a practitioner and, if desired or necessary for employment, to apply for accreditation from the BACP [provided they have met all the requirements]. Any further development (BA, MA, MSc or PhD) follows the requirements of examining bodies.

Other than outcomes of requirements set out by the university or further education exam board and, if relevant, any accrediting body, there is no standard formula. Students are encouraged to maintain confidentiality to their fellow trainees. The whole group meets on a regular basis (usually called community time), for skills and academic lectures/presentations over one or two days. Students also have smaller groups and will usually remain in those groups for their entire training. Triads may also form. Video and audio recording is used throughout the training process. Trainees need to be fully aware of their own processes and prejudices, limitations and attributes and, as a result of that, many people leave courses with a thirst to learn and progress more.

The person-centred approach has a national membership body called the British Association for the Person-Centred Approach (BAPCA). Membership is open to anyone who is interested in the approach in all its applications.

(Hayes, C., Personal Communication, 7 May 2013)

The following websites display more information about the person-centred approach:

The Association for Person Centred Therapy Scotland – www.pctscotland.co.uk
The British Association for the Person-Centred Approach – www.bapca.org.uk
The Irish Association for the Person Centred Approach – www.iapca.ie
The Network of the European Associations for Person-Centred and Experiential Psychotherapy and Counselling – www.pce-europe.org

The person-centred approach is probably one of the most popular modalities in counselling courses. Training levels range from a basic 'Introduction to Counselling Skills' course up to postgraduate level for an 'MSc in Person-Centred Psychotherapy and Counselling'.

Many counselling courses have some element of the person-centred approach contained within them even if they are not specifically named as such.

Psychosynthesis

The Psychosynthesis and Education Trust (PET) (2012a) states:

> Psychosynthesis is concerned with the realisation of individual and collective potential and the harmonisation of all elements of the personality.
>
> The first step is the attainment of a certain level of self-knowledge, and the techniques used help to understand the different parts of our psyche and how to integrate them.
>
> Among the therapeutic methods used are creative visualisation, free drawing, the training of the will, physical expression, writing, meditation, and interpersonal and group work.
>
> (PET, 2012a)

> The introductory course that gives an intensive experience of what psychosynthesis can offer is the Essentials course, run more than six times a year (both in London and outside) as either a five-day intensive or over two long weekends.
>
> For those wishing to develop their understanding of both themselves and psychosynthesis further, there is our Foundation Year consisting of ten weekends, validated by the University of East London (UEL). This (or an approved equivalent) is a prerequisite for entry into our Postgraduate Diploma/MA Programme.
>
> The entry point to our professional training programme is the Postgraduate Certificate in Psychosynthesis Foundations. Successful completion of this course (or a similar level psychosynthesis course) is the prerequisite for the next step, the Postgraduate Diploma in Psychosynthesis Counselling, which lasts two years and is accredited by the British Association for Counselling and Psychotherapy, as well as being validated by UEL.
>
> This may be followed by the two-year psychotherapy training leading to the Master of Arts in Psychosynthesis Psychotherapy, also validated by UEL and accredited by the United Kingdom Council for Psychotherapy.
>
> (PET, 2012b)

The following websites display more information about psychosynthesis:

The Institute of Psychosynthesis – www.psychosynthesis.org
The Psychosynthesis and Education Trust – www.psychosynthesis.edu
The European Federation for Psychosynthesis Psychotherapy – www.psychosynthesis.net

Transactional analysis

Leilani Mitchell, Chair of the United Kingdom Association for Transactional Analysis (UKATA), formerly the Institute of Transactional Analysis

(ITA), and Co-Director of the Link Centre, Sussex, provided the following information:

> Transactional Analysis (TA) offers a variety of theories that seek to understand how our past influences our thoughts, feelings and behaviour today. Its founder, Eric Berne, was keen to make TA accessible to all. One of its strengths today is the range of useful concepts, such as the Drama Triangle (Karpman, 1976) and the Ego State models that offer clients and practitioners alike a simple tool to understand complex personal and relationship dynamics. TA offers a humanistic (focused on the individual) approach to counselling and psychotherapy, within which there is a spectrum of working styles from the more cognitive and behavioural through to the more relational. With such a broad range of tools and concepts to draw on, TA can be used for both short-term and in-depth, long-term work.
>
> There are a variety of ways to train in TA, including a short two-day course (TA 101), a one-year foundation theory training, or a longer four-year psychotherapy training. There are no prerequisites for someone looking to undertake a 101 course. A degree, or equivalent life/work experience, is required to undertake TA Psychotherapy training. TA training centres aim to be as inclusive as possible so it is worthwhile talking to your local training centre if you are interested in undertaking TA training.
>
> Psychotherapy training is usually offered as ten two-day weekend courses per year over a period of four years. It usually consists of both experiential and theoretical learning together with the opportunity to practise skills at weekends. Personal development comes about through insights and during group time at weekends, which is then enhanced by personal therapy and self-reflection during the weeks in between training weekends. Strong bonds often develop between trainees during training with some friendships continuing long after training has been completed.
>
> Trainees are required to have weekly personal therapy for a minimum of four years, complete written coursework and undertake supervised client work, usually achieved through placement with counselling agencies.
>
> TA offers a wide range of theories and concepts that make it useful across a diverse range of clinical settings. These may include working with children and teenagers, or adults with mild to complex physical, emotional and behavioural problems such as illness, drug or alcohol misuse and bereavement.
>
> At the end of training there are a variety of qualification options. These range from a TA Counselling Diploma from the relevant TA training centre, to accreditation as a TA Practitioner, through to becoming a Certified Transactional Analyst (CTA). This final qualification requires both a written and oral exam to be taken to qualify as a UKCP registered psychotherapist.
>
> TA has a large membership within the UK and offers regular regional and national conferences, together with European and international conferences from its linked memberships.
>
> (Mitchell, L., Personal Communication, 27 April 2013)

The following websites display more information about transactional analysis:

The Institute of Developmental Transactional Analysis – www.instdta.org
The Scottish TA Association – www.scottishta.org.uk
The United Kingdom Association for Transactional Analysis – www.uktransactionalanalysis.co.uk
The European Association for Transactional Analysis – www.eatanews.org
The International Transactional Analysis Association – www.itaaworld.org
International Association of Relational Transactional Analysis – www.relationalta.com

Transpersonal psychotherapy

The Centre for Transpersonal Psychology (CTP) (2011) states:

> Transpersonal Psychology embraces and draws upon the wisdom of the world's spiritual traditions and developments in modern psychology. It includes theories and approaches pertaining to the development and health of the personal ego. It seeks to understand our human ambitions, our worries and loves, as we make our passage through this worldly life with its inevitable ups and downs. Importantly, it places these within a larger perspective. It draws upon spiritual traditions which point us towards intimations of an enduring reality beyond the world of impermanence and changing forms; a reality which beckons us to uncover a deeper meaning and purpose to our lives along with the discovery of our deepest Self.
>
> All transpersonal perspectives affirm the spiritual potential of human beings to move beyond the ego to both heights and depths of the human psyche. Such perspectives acknowledge the importance of both transcendent and unitive states of consciousness, cultivated and nurtured over thousands of years by traditions which, until relatively recently, were ignored by traditional psychology and psychotherapy.
>
> Transpersonal Psychology is concerned, therefore, not only with understanding 'breakdown and repair' or with restoring healthy functioning to the personal ego. Its primary concern is exploring those aspects of consciousness and being that are to do with realising humanity's highest potential – a potential which is released as we discover and reveal the source and depth of our own Being. It provides an opportunity for us to recognise and value our true worth and that of all individuals, indeed of all forms of life.
>
> (Centre for Transpersonal Psychology, 2011)

The website for the Centre for Counselling and Psychotherapy Education (CCPE) (2012) provides the following information regarding training:

> A one-year course in the *Foundations of Counselling and Psychotherapy* from a spiritual perspective that embraces the psychodynamic, humanistic

> and transpersonal approaches. It offers a thorough grounding in basic counselling skills.
>
> The course focuses on personal growth encompassing body, mind and spirit. It is aimed at students wishing to go on and pursue a career in counselling or psychotherapy, holistic health practitioners wanting to improve client contact skills and for those with a general interest in counselling.
>
> (CCPE, 2012)

This can be followed by a diploma:

> The emphasis on this course is on developing a spiritual perspective on human interaction, on learning practical techniques to help people with psychological problems as well as those who are seeking to unfold their own potential.
>
> The four-year part-time Diploma course involves 900 contact hours, including one six-day intensive, one residential weekend, 24 weekend seminars and 120 evening meetings spread over four years. The evening meetings include a period for lectures and group supervision. In addition, students undertake a minimum of 160 hours of individual therapy and at least 550 hours of supervised counselling/psychotherapy practice and 100 hours at an approved psychiatric observational placement.
>
> Students will draw on their supervised counselling/psychotherapy practice hours to submit case histories for assessment. Finally, they are required to develop an individual counselling practical project, which reflects their beliefs, personality and therapeutic style of working.
>
> (ibid.)

The following websites display more information about Transpersonal Psychotherapy:

> The Centre for Transpersonal Psychology – www.transpersonalcentre.co.uk
> The Centre for Counselling and Psychotherapy Education – www.ccpe.org.uk
> The European Transpersonal Association – www.eurotas.org

Hypno-psychotherapy branch

This branch of psychotherapy uses hypnosis and neuro-linguistic psychotherapy as well as an integration of a number of other modalities. According to Fiona Biddle, Chair of the UKCP College of Hypno-psychotherapists:

> Hypnotherapy, or 'neuro-hypnotism' – meaning sleep of the nervous system – uses hypnosis to induce a deep state of heightened relaxation and altered awareness, during which the unconscious mind is highly receptive to new or alternative perspectives and ideas.
>
> In the field of hypno-psychotherapy the unconscious mind is looked upon as a resource for wellness and creativity; accessing this part of the mind,

> through hypnosis, opens up possibilities for the maintenance of the body towards health via the autonomic processes.
>
> Hypno-psychotherapy can be applied to modify a client's behaviour, attitudes and emotions, as well as manage pain, anxiety, stress-related illnesses, and dysfunctional habits, promoting personal development.
>
> (Biddle, 2013)

According to the National College of Hypnosis and Psychotherapy:

> Training . . . may be undertaken on a part-time basis by combining weekend attendance for practical tuition and lectures at one of the tuition venues, together with a programme of home study, the ideal method for students with domestic and/or work commitments. Each weekend consists of some fourteen hours of practical instruction in the application of therapeutic techniques, combined with lectures on the various theories involved. Starting at 9.30am each day and finishing at 5.15pm, allowing for breaks, gives approximately 258 hours of class contact for the first three stages of the training up to Diploma level.
>
> The total number of study hours required to complete the course varies depending on what prior knowledge a student brings to the course. However, monitoring of past students' study patterns suggests that for a student with little prior knowledge of hypnosis, psychotherapy or psychology, total study hours up to UKCP registration level may amount to 1,800 hours over a four-year period.
>
> The National College courses are structured in accordance with the needs of two groups of people. These are:
>
> - People who wish to embark on a new career in hypno-psychotherapy, and require a recognized training to assist them to achieve their goal.
> - People who, although not wishing to enter practice, may wish to pursue their serious interest in the subject within the context of a recognized training programme.
>
> Two further considerations have influenced the structure of the training.
>
> - The Academic Board is aware that many applicants, although having an interest in hypno-psychotherapy, have little experience in its use.
> - Many applicants, although being able to meet the educational standards required to gain enrolment, may not have had the opportunity for many years to engage in serious study, and they will require a gradual reintroduction to a learning environment.
>
> With these points in mind, the National College courses commence with practical instruction, the academic content of the course being introduced gradually. Therefore, once having gained enrolment, if a student is prepared to follow the training and instruction provided, then he or she will experience little or no difficulty.
>
> In addition, students and/or prospective students may be referred to an appropriate course in psychology to preface, supplement or complement their regular National College training.

> Personal development is not central to National College training, though it forms an important corollary, with self-therapy being a compulsory component for UKCP Registration.
>
> (NCHP, 2013)

The following websites display more information about hypno-psychotherapy:

> The National College of Hypnosis and Psychotherapy – www.hypnotherapyuk.net
> The Beeleaf Institute for Contemporary Psychotherapy – www.beeleaf.com
> The Institute of Clinical Hypnotherapy and Psychotherapy – http://hypnosiseire.com
> The European Association for Hypno-Psychotherapy – www.hypno-psychotherapy.com

Psychoanalysis branch

Psychoanalysis is as popular today as many other modalities. Sigmund Freud (1856–1939) developed psychoanalysis in the 1890s, and, since then, a variety of different branches of psychoanalysis have emerged. Traditionally, Freud's patients would lie on a couch and he would sit behind them so that the patient could not see him. He would invite the client to talk freely (sometimes called 'free association') about their dreams, thoughts and fantasies. He believed in three aspects of personality: the id, the ego and the super-ego (Freud, 1923), and in two basic instincts, which later became known as love (Eros) and death (Thanatos) (Freud, 1920). He made links between sexual developmental stages, e.g. oral, anal, phallic and genital, and later problems in life, and he developed the idea of different levels of consciousness, e.g. conscious, preconscious and unconscious. Freud believed that neurosis was the result of these various stages and processes being in conflict with one another, and that the aim of therapy was to remove the neurosis so that the patient could be cured.

Two areas of this branch will now be discussed: 'Group Analysis' and then 'Psychoanalysis and Jungian Analysis'.

Group analysis

According to the website of the Group Analytic Society:

> Group Analysis explores the theory, practice and experience of analytical group psychotherapy, embracing concepts derived from psychoanalytic psychology, social psychology, group dynamics, sociology and anthropology.
>
> At the heart of Group Analysis is the idea that human beings are fundamentally social beings, whose lives are inextricably linked with other people in manifold ways. The source of personal puzzles that are difficult or impossible to resolve, or behaviours or motives that are difficult to understand, which individuals may encounter in their personal lives and at work, are to be found not only in the dynamics of the groupings that they inhabit in the present, but also in the groups in which all of us are rooted, across time and throughout our development. These groupings include the family, friendship groups, schools and so on.

> On the basis of this S.H. Foulkes [1898–1976], the founder of Group Analysis, reasoned that as one's difficulties arise in groups, then these difficulties are best explored, understood and changed specifically in a group context. Foulkes, in the 1950s, proposed that there is no such thing as an individual that exists apart from and outside the social (Foulkes, 1948; Foulkes and Anthony, 1957).
>
> (Group Analytic Society, 2013)

According to the Institute of Group Analysis (2013), the training starts with a foundation year which aims:

> to familiarise students with the principles of Group Analysis through a range of lectures/seminars and experiential group work. Theoretical and experiential learning encourages participants to gain a more informed general understanding of how groups operate. The course provides the opportunity for personal and professional development.
>
> (Institute of Group Analysis, 2013: 4)

This is followed by a diploma course in Group Work Practice:

> The course offers an advanced introduction to the Group Analytic approach to general group work as it is currently practised in social, health care and educational settings. It is aimed towards the development of the theoretical knowledge, skills and techniques necessary to successfully facilitate a wide range of group work approaches.
>
> **Intensive Learning Experience (ILE)**
>
> The Intensive Learning Experience is an annual national event led by eminent group analysts, which includes a series of lectures and discussion seminars as well as opportunities for experiential learning. This event provides the opportunity for students from across the IGA trainings to develop their membership of the wider national IGA community. The ILE is an integral part of the Diploma in GWP course.
>
> **Group Work Practitioner**
>
> Successful completion of this course, together with appropriate clinical experience can lead to the status of Group Work Practitioner and Associate Membership of the IGA. By conferring the status of Group Work Practitioner, the IGA recognises that graduates have demonstrated a high degree of competence in group work skills. This provides a beneficial addition to any existing clinical competences graduates may already possess. Group Work Practitioners have a good understanding of the theory and practice of group work at a level that is appropriate to conductors of a range of creative or educative groups, and to auxiliary workers for therapy groups.
>
> (ibid.: 6–7)

After successful completion of the diploma course, trainees may be eligible to undertake the Qualifying Course in Group Analysis:

> This . . . course aims to provide students with a fundamental understanding of Group Analytic theory and practice that will enable them to become practising Group Analysts. The course aims to help students develop a critical and enquiring mind towards psychoanalytic and social theory.
>
> These aims are achieved through the tripartite structure of clinical and theoretical learning; supervised clinical practice and twice weekly or block Group Analysis.
>
> Successful graduates are eligible to become full members of the IGA and to gain professional registration with the UKCP.
>
> (ibid.: 9)

Psychoanalysis and Jungian analysis

The Council for Psychoanalysis and Jungian Analysis (CPJA, 2012) states:

> Psychoanalytic relationships are generated by the desire to find meaning as well as relief from psychological suffering. Different schools of psychotherapy have emerged and continue to develop from Freud's original work. In psychoanalytic psychotherapy, particular attention is paid to analysing transference and resistance issues, so that the patient is helped to find a more creative relationship between conscious and unconscious processes and to discover their own personal truths.
>
> Psychoanalytic theory explores the connection between events in early life (which may be unconscious) and current disturbance and distress. The therapy offers a reliable setting for free association to past and present fantasies, feelings, dreams and memories.
>
> Particular attention is given to the developing relationship with the therapist; through this, the patient re-experiences relationships from their early life and explore new ways of relating, released from the characteristics that previously caused distress. Through this transference relationship, the patient may achieve a new and better resolution of long-standing conflicts and overcome resistances to change and growth.
>
> (CPJA, 2012)

There are a number of different schools of psychoanalysis, and they include Freudian, Jungian, Kleinian and Lacanian. According to Nick Hall, formerly of the Institute of Psychoanalysis, the method and purpose of the training is threefold:

> **Personal Training Analysis**
>
> All students have a personal psychoanalysis with an approved training analyst of the British Psychoanalytical Society. This analysis consists of daily fifty-minute sessions, five days a week (Monday to Friday), which continues throughout the

training. Students choose their training analyst, with whom they then agree a schedule and fee. A list of training analysts is available from the Institute training administrator. The therapeutic goals of the personal training analysis are the same as those of a therapeutic psychoanalysis, to enable the analyst and to gain as full an understanding as possible of their unconscious mental functioning and its relationship with their conscious experience. The additional educational goals include freeing the student from those unconscious factors that would interfere with his or her ability to feel, think, and work as a psychoanalyst.

Theoretical and Clinical Seminars

The curriculum provides an intensive study of the theory and clinical practice of psychoanalysis. The seminars aim to teach and facilitate the development of therapeutic skills and crucially to enable the student to adopt a critical engagement with the underlying theory of clinical practice.

After a *minimum* of one year of a personal training analysis the student is eligible to start the theoretical training. Theoretical and clinical seminars take place up to three times a week during term time and are usually spread over a period of not less than three years. The first year of theoretical seminars consists of the study of Freud's writings and psychoanalytic theories of human development. An equally important component of the first year are seminars of Infant Observation: each student makes weekly home visits to observe a mother and baby; their observations are then discussed in a weekly seminar. From the second year onwards, seminar series are offered on a wide range of theoretical and technical issues including for example: *approaches to depression, clinical studies of perversion, narcissistic and borderline states, dreams, theory and practice, character and personality disorders, psychosomatic medicine and psychoanalysis, understanding trauma, assessment for analysability, ethical issues in psychoanalytic practice and technique.* Further, there are seminars on the three main schools of the British Psychoanalytical Society – Contemporary Freudian, Independent and Kleinian.

From the second year until qualification, every student attends weekly clinical seminars in which they present clinical material from their training cases and discuss their psychoanalytic work with fellow students and a senior clinician.

The faculty of the Institute of Psychoanalysis is a diverse and experienced body drawn from a spectrum of theoretical views in the British Psychoanalytical Society. Just as important as the quality of teaching is the unique experience of studying with accomplished and motivated students from around the world.

Supervised Psychoanalysis of Two Patients

Supervised work with a first training patient is usually begun during the second year. The second case may be started a year later depending on satisfactory reports of progress from their supervisor. Training patients are seen for a fifty-minute session each day, five days a week, Monday to Friday.

> The first case must be continued for a minimum of two years and the second case for a minimum of one year before a student is eligible to qualify as a psychoanalyst. Students are expected to continue treating both their training cases until completion of the analysis.
>
> (Hall, N., Personal Communication, 29 April 2013)

The core of a psychoanalytic approach is that the analyst will work with, and explore, the unconscious conflicts of feeling, emotion and fantasy that are at the root of their patient's symptoms, and the problems that are troubling them. To do this effectively, the analyst needs to be able to become aware of their own unconscious processes so as not to contaminate their work with their clients'. Hence, a significant element of the training is personal analysis.

The following websites display more information about psychoanalysis:

The Council for Psychoanalysis and Jungian Analysis – www.cpja.org.uk
The Institute of Psychoanalysis – www.psychoanalysis.org.uk
The College of Psychoanalysts in Ireland – www.psychoanalysis.ie
Human Development Scotland – www.hdscotland.org.uk
European Confederation of Psychoanalytic Psychotherapies – www.ecpp.org

Sexual and relationship branch

Most of the therapists who offer sexual and relationship therapy have undertaken core training in one or more of the modalities mentioned above, or have been working with psychosexual and relationship issues within their practice or workplace, e.g. medicine, psychology, social work or graduate nursing. They have gone on to complete specific training in this area of work. According to the website of the College of Sexual and Relationship Therapists (COSRT):

> COSRT members offer a range of treatments encompassing sex therapy, psychosexual therapy and relationship therapy. These are all talking therapies where an individual or couple work with an experienced therapist to assess and treat their sexual and/or relationship problems. Together they will identify factors that trigger the problems and design a specific treatment programme to resolve or reduce their impact.
>
> (COSRT, 2013)

Although not offering training itself, COSRT provides a framework for the approval of courses in sexual and relationship psychotherapy. They currently approve four training courses ranging from two to four years' duration (COSRT, 2012: 17–18).

The following websites display more information about sexual and relationship therapy:

The College of Sexual and Relationship Therapists – www.cosrt.org.uk
Relate – www.relate.org.uk

Relationships Ireland – www.relationshipsireland.com
Relationships Scotland – www.relationships-scotland.org.uk

What next?

Some of the websites listed above have details of recognized or accredited training courses and training providers. There are also some generic websites that list a whole range of both counselling and psychotherapy training courses across the different modalities. The most popular ones are shown in Appendix 1.

Consider researching as many courses as you can find, taking your time, so that you discover the one that is right for you. It will be worth it in the long run.

Umbrella terms

Some training courses may not specify in their title the models or theories that are taught on that course. Phrases such as 'integrative' and 'humanistic' are common, but can mean different things. Check with the course provider for what model(s) are taught, and how you will be trained in each approach.

Above all, when deciding which model or approach to choose, consider how well it will work for you personally, as well as how you think it may work for you professionally.

Conclusion

In this chapter we have looked at various counselling and psychotherapy modalities that are available. In the next chapter, we consider the entry requirements and methods of training used on counselling and psychotherapy courses.

Questions to ask yourself

1. Which modality, or modalities, appealed to me?
2. Does this course/model/approach suit me at this time?

   Check your intuitive response.

Questions to ask the training provider

1. What models are taught on the programme? Is there an opportunity to compare and contrast the model(s) taught with other models or approaches?
2. If the course is called 'humanistic', or 'integrative', how do you utilize this way of working during the course? Do you see 'humanistic', or 'integrative', as a specific model or way of working, or as an amalgamation of different approaches? If so, which model, or models, are taught on the programme?
3. What additional course requirements are there, e.g. personal therapy, placements, observations, supervision, etc?
4. Is the course externally validated, approved, accredited or registered by a professional body? If so, which body?

Chapter 3

Entry requirements, course curriculum and terms and conditions of training

During my research, I noticed that four specific areas were unclear for a number of the participants:

1 Entry routes and ongoing course requirements, including direct admission or non-standard pathways.
2 The content and purpose of the course. Is it to train counsellors, or psychotherapists, or both? The elements of the core curriculum, the methods used to facilitate learning, and how the trainee will be assessed;
3 The nature of additional course requirements.
4 The terms and conditions of training.

The ambiguities that a number of the participants experienced in these areas left some of them uncertain about what was required to pass the course, or disappointed that the course was not going to provide them with what they had anticipated. (For more information about some of the challenges experienced by the research participants see Chapter 6.)

Conversely, there were a number of research participants for whom these were not issues as they had been given clear information from the start, which they had been able to take on board; these participants generally had a more positive experience of their training.

This chapter addresses some of the above concerns and provides you with clear information regarding what you may expect, whether you embark on a counselling or a psychotherapy course.

To begin the chapter, I offer some information on the entry requirements and selection procedures that you may encounter during your application process, and then I present some of the key elements necessary for a training course, which can be summarized under the headings of 'taught training', 'supervised clinical practice', and 'personal development'. Finally, I provide some information regarding costs and general course terms and conditions.

Entry requirements

There was a general consensus among the research participants that clear and unambiguous entry and selection criteria for their courses would have been appreciated.

Certificate in Counselling courses

Usually one year in duration, there are no formal qualification requirements for entry on to a counselling certificate course, although the following personal skills are often sought (ABC Awards, 2013; CPCAB, 2012; COSCA, 2011):

- to be able to manage the course content and requirements;
- to be emotionally stable, and capable of taking advantage of personal development;
- to have an awareness of difference and diversity.

Some courses may ask you to complete a short introductory course before the certificate course.

Diploma in Counselling courses

These are usually two-year programmes, and the entry requirements often consist of successful completion of a counselling certificate, or other preparatory course at the academic level immediately preceding that of the diploma. In addition, the following personal skills are often sought (ABC Awards, 2013a; BACP, 2009b; COSCA, 2013; CPCAB, 2012; IACP, 2013b):

- to be able to cope with the academic and emotional demands of the course;
- to be able to work with difference and diversity;
- to be able to identify their motivation for undertaking the training;
- to be able to take advantage of personal development;
- to be able to form a therapeutic relationship that demonstrates sensitivity and empathy towards others;
- to demonstrate the basic ethical principles of respect, honesty and integrity;
- to be sufficiently robust to manage challenge;
- to have arranged a supervised clinical placement.

Psychotherapy courses

These are usually four-year postgraduate-level programmes. Generally, you will be expected to have already completed an undergraduate degree, or have relevant professional training in an allied field, such as counselling, psychology, psychiatry, social work or teaching. Some courses may also expect you to have completed a specified number of personal therapy hours. In addition to these entry requirements, the following personal qualities are sought:

- a lively and enquiring mind;
- a capacity for critical reflection and self-directed learning;
- an ability to listen and respond with compassion and respect;

- awareness of prejudice, and the ability to respond openly to issues of race, gender, age, sexual preference, class, disability, ethnic, spiritual/religious and cultural differences, and diversity;
- awareness and sensitivity in relation to the political, socio-cultural and religious/ spiritual contexts of people's lives [including] in-depth self-reflection;
- self-awareness and commitment to self-development. Applicants should have sufficient emotional competence and the internal resources necessary to engage with the demands of the training and the work of psychotherapy.

(UKCP, 2011: 2)

If you meet the entry requirements, then your application process will be straightforward. If you don't, but you still want to undertake the course, you may like to ask about 'non-standard entry'. This is a way that potential trainees may still be able to apply, provided that they can demonstrate the key skills, or attitudes, necessary for the course.

Accreditation of Prior Learning (APL)

Many courses offer a system that acknowledges and gives you credit for previous training and experience through a mechanism known as 'Accreditation of Prior Learning' (APL). APL may give you credit for formal certificated study, called 'Accreditation of Prior Certificated Learning' (APCL), or for learning arising from professional experience and related study or training, which may not be certificated, called 'Accreditation of Prior Experiential Learning' (APEL).

This credit means that you may be able to enter your course at a higher level; for example, if you have completed a counselling studies training course, you may have already met the learning outcomes of year one (level four) and so be admitted onto year two (level five). If you have a formal certificate for this course, you would use the APCL option, or, if not, then you would use APEL.

If you think that either of the APL processes applies to you, it would be useful to ask what you need to submit to provide evidence of this; and, as there is usually a charge for this application, to ask about the associated costs, which can be significant, while the process can be time-consuming. Sometimes, students decide not to apply for APL, even if they have previously met the relevant learning outcomes, because they would rather enter at the beginning, and then use the training as a refresher.

Application and selection process

In order to apply for a place on a counselling or psychotherapy training course, you will be asked to complete an application form, which often includes the request for a personal statement outlining why you want to do the course. This will be expanded upon later in the selection process, which usually includes an interview with one or two members of the teaching staff (ABC Awards, 2013a; BACP, 2009b; COSCA, 2013; CPCAB, 2012; IACP, 2013b; UKCP, 2011).

During your interview you are likely to be asked some of the following questions:

1. In your personal statement, you have said that you want to do this training because . . . so, would you now say more about what underpins your motivations for embarking on the training?
2. What are your hopes and concerns for the course?
3. What has been your experience of training and education in the past?
4. What were the high points, and what were the challenges?
5. What are the positive qualities that you will bring to the training, and your work as a counsellor or psychotherapist?
6. What aspects of your personality do you struggle with? How will you manage those characteristics? What additional help will you need?
7. What life experience will you bring to the training group?
8. Why this training course as opposed to any other?
9. How will you manage all the course requirements, which are . . . ? What support do you have to help you?
10. What are your final plans, if any?

Another aspect of the selection process may be a group exercise facilitated by the course trainers. This offers you an opportunity to experience how your trainers work, and get a flavour of how the course will be run. The selection process is not only for the trainers to assess your suitability, but also for you to assess the appropriateness of the course for you.

Curriculum

During my research, I noticed that the participants had varied training experiences – some courses were more academically focused than others, some were residential training marathons (a mixture of teaching, therapy and supervision) that lasted anything from a week to a couple of months, some were evening classes, and others were weekend courses. Some trained the student to work with specific clients, or in a certain setting, and others were more generic in their approach.

Each of the three main components of training – taught training, supervised clinical practice and personal development – will be now be discussed in turn.

Taught training

There are some similarities and differences in the curriculum when training either as a counsellor or as a psychotherapist. The similarities concern training in areas such as ethics and professional practice, practical skills training, and working with difference and diversity. The main differences concern the theoretical, mental-health familiarization placement, and research components. Each element will now be discussed with distinctions made between counselling certificate, counselling diploma and psychotherapy training courses, as necessary.

Ethics and professional practice

Ethical practice underpins the counselling and psychotherapy professions.

Certificate-level courses will include a basic knowledge and understanding of ethics, and the ability to work within appropriate boundaries.

Counselling diploma and psychotherapy courses will usually spend a significant amount of time discussing and exploring ethics and ethical dilemmas. You may find it helpful to become familiar with at least one code of ethics, ethical framework or set of professional practice requirements, as they are there to protect your clients, you and the profession.

Ethical principles

The core ethical attitudes used in counselling and psychotherapy are usually grounded in the following principles, synthesized from various codes and frameworks (BACP, 2013a: COSCA, 2007; GPTI, 2010; IACP, 2013a; UKATA, 2008; UKCP, 2009):

> *Above all, do no harm* – this is the primary underlying principle, and is a commitment to not do anything that would intentionally, or accidentally, harm another.
>
> *Trustworthiness, honesty and integrity* – acting in a way that shows an ability to be reliable, trustworthy and honest, and to act with congruence in terms of one's own personal values, beliefs and principles. Does the person 'walk the talk'? Do they behave in a way that invites trust? Do they keep promises? Will they admit it if they make a mistake, or get something wrong?
>
> *Justice and being fair minded* – demonstrating the ability to do what is right when taking into account all the factors involved, without prejudice or bias, and while attending to inequality and prejudice.
>
> *Compassion and respect* – demonstrating the ability to show care and concern for another while respecting their autonomy and life decisions.
>
> *Courage and humility* – demonstrating the ability to do what you believe to be right, even though you feel you may be criticized for doing so, and the ability to appreciate you may have your own vulnerabilities and weaknesses. Being willing to look at your own behaviours, and receive constructive feedback.
>
> *Competence* – indicating your ability to regularly monitor and develop your professional skills, knowledge, ethical awareness, expertise and capacity for work, seeking support from colleagues and supervisors, as necessary.

An ethical counselling or psychotherapy course will probably have such principles, or something similar, as the foundation of the training programme, and they will be evident throughout your training experience, no matter which approach you are studying. On such a course, your trainer will adhere to and, hopefully, embody these principles.

Second, you and your peers will also be encouraged to engage with such principles, and you may well be invited to explore your own values and morals to see whether you feel able to embrace, embody and work within the ethical code, or framework, of the course.

Each training programme will have its own set of ethical guidelines that are usually consistent with the philosophy of the approach that is being taught. For example, a person-centred course will have principles concerning the ability to offer the necessary and sufficient conditions of therapeutic personality change, and to act at all times in the client's best interest. A transactional analysis course will have principles concerning clear and open communication, contracting and the belief that everyone is 'OK'; that everyone has the capacity to think and influence their life by the decisions they make, and that any decision can be changed. You will be introduced to any codes of ethics applicable to the modality in which you are training during your course.

An interesting point about ethics is that, usually, there is no single right answer; resolving an ethical dilemma will depend upon a number of factors, such as your own personal and moral qualities and expectations, and those of your client, the circumstances of the clinical placement, or practice, any ethical and professional practice guidelines held by the placement, and any relevant professional bodies, the situation that was in place when the dilemma arose, and the context of that situation. Ethical discussions can be incredibly challenging, and also rewarding, as you may be continually questioning your 'frame of reference' (Mezirow, 2000), which can then lead on to transformational learning (Mezirow, 1991). (For more information on frame of reference and transformational learning see Chapter 5.)

Practical work

The use of active listening skills is invaluable in developing the therapeutic relationship. The ability to understand body language, and to learn such skills as paraphrasing, reflecting and summarizing, can help to develop an accepting and empathic attunement with a client. These skills are generally taught on certificate-level courses, in dyads (working in pairs), or triads (working in threes), during classroom-practice sessions. There may also be small-group exercises and tutor demonstrations, and the use of video, to illustrate the skills and the approach being taught.

One of the main purposes of training is to help you to develop the skills and techniques of the specific modality you are learning. The most effective way of doing this is with your peers in a supportive learning environment, where repetition of skills strengthens your practice, and the making of mistakes is a key opportunity for learning. Half the time on your course is likely to be taken up with this type of experiential learning. The participants in my research commented that they found the practical work to be the most rewarding and enlightening because they were able to use these live experiences to make personal meaning of the theory being taught.

How you develop these skills, this knowledge and these abilities will depend upon your learning style, the teaching methods used, and what you have agreed in your learning contract, if you have one. Practical skills assessments may include tutor observation and feedback, the use of audio or video work, self- and peer-assessment, and written assignments.

Difference and diversity

All counselling and psychotherapy courses will include some aspects of working with difference and diversity. The IACP refers to the trainee needing to develop an ability to work within a social system (IACP, 2013b: 10), COSCA requires training courses to 'help participants understand the variety of social, cultural and religious backgrounds in which they will be expected to work as counsellors/psychotherapists' (COSCA, 2013: 8), and the BACP course accreditation criteria has the stipulation that trainees should 'demonstrate awareness of diversity and the rights and responsibilities of all clients, regardless of their gender, age, ethnicity, culture, class, ability, sexuality, religion and belief' (BACP, 2013c: 18). The UKCP requires that:

> All trainings should operate within an equality and diversity framework. Trainings should include:
>
> a a broad understanding of some of the key systemic hurdles affecting those, but not exclusively those, covered by the Equality Act 2010.
> b the contemporary and significant discriminatory discourses throughout trainings.
> c raising awareness of conscious and unconscious bias.
> d equipping students and trainees to work with clients across the diversity spectrum.
> e equipping students and trainees to engage with their own fears and prejudices, and those of their clients, re difference.
> f arrangements to ensure that the students and trainees can identify and manage appropriately their personal involvement in and contribution to the processes of the psychotherapies that they practise.
>
> (UKCP, 2012: 6)

According to my research participants, this element of training can be personally testing and transformational, as previously held beliefs, fears, values and prejudices, some of which you may not be aware that you possess, can arise. (For the phases of transformational learning, see Chapter 5.)

Theory

Both counselling and psychotherapy courses require a thorough grounding in at least one central theoretical approach.

COUNSELLING COURSES

Having a core model helps to provide a framework for the training. On skills courses, students are usually introduced to an approach, and are then invited to apply the theory to themselves, their relationships and their developing skills practice.

My research participants suggested that students in counselling training would be better off with a course that offers a single core theoretical approach that is studied in depth for at least the first couple of years. The introduction to another model, or models, can then be used so that the counsellor has an opportunity to compare and contrast the two approaches. The advantage of doing this is that once you have integrated a core model, you can then more easily complement your existing practice with another approach. Beginning with an introduction to a range of models may prove confusing to a counselling beginner. (For more information about some of the different modalities, see Chapter 2.)

Generally, counselling courses cover the origins, philosophy and recent developments of the core model being taught. Students will learn the necessary skills that will enable them to evaluate the key concepts and then critique the approach, outlining its strengths and limitations, and research findings may be used to enhance practice. The academic requirements vary depending upon the level of the course. Each model will have a view on the nature, significance and use of the therapeutic relationship, and students will learn how to develop such relationships during the practical sessions, as well as how the approach considers that the therapeutic change occurs.

There is much variation in the nature and quantity of theoretical knowledge needed by accrediting bodies. For example, the BACP requires that applicants can 'describe a rationale for your client work with reference to the theory/theories that inform all your practice' (BACP, 2013a: 3); COSCA requires students to be able to have an understanding of human growth and development, theory and other therapeutic traditions, the therapeutic relationship and psychopathology (COSCA, 2012: 10); and the IACP states that their accredited courses 'must provide a detailed study of at least one major school of counselling/psychotherapy with an introduction to other schools/models of counselling/psychotherapy for comparison, contrast and critical analysis' (IACP, 2013b: 6).

PSYCHOTHERAPY TRAINING

Psychotherapists are typically expected to have a broad theoretical base, with at least one core theoretical model studied in depth. They are typically expected to be able to not only compare and contrast modalities, but also to critique and combine elements of those theories which the practitioner finds most helpful, in order to develop their unique approach, and to locate it within the wider field of psychotherapy.

According to the UKCP (2012), the core curriculum for psychotherapy training needs to include, as a minimum:

1 A model of the person and mind.
2 A model of gendered and culturally influenced human development.
3 A model of human change and ways in which change can be facilitated.
4 A set of clinical concepts to relate theory to practice.
5 An extensive literature which includes a critique of the model.
6 Awareness of safeguarding issues in relation to clients and those likely to be impacted by their actions.

(UKCP, 2012: 5)

The European Association for Psychotherapy (EAP) requires the following theoretical elements:

- theories of human development throughout the life-cycle;
- an understanding of other psychotherapeutic approaches;
- a theory of change;
- an understanding of social and cultural issues in relation to psychotherapy;
- theories of psychopathology;
- theories of assessment and intervention.

(European Association for Psychotherapy, 2012)

The methods used for learning theory include personal reading, group discussions, presentations from tutors or peers, and explanations by the trainers when applying concepts to live material in the group.

The theoretical curriculum may be developed with the trainees, particularly on person-centred programmes, and some other humanistic courses. Often, there will be a balance between any course accreditation requirements, which may focus on the content of the course, and the wishes of the trainees, which may concern the process of learning. The use of learning contracts can be invaluable in making these needs explicit.

Assessment methods generally include written assignments, peer presentations and case studies.

Mental Health Familiarization Placements (MHFP)

These are not required on counselling courses, but some counselling accreditation systems do refer to the therapist having an understanding of psychopathology (COSCA, 2012). Typically, psychotherapists are trained to work with clients who have complex issues and presentations.

The MHFP is usually separated into taught elements and a clinical placement. The taught elements may be included on your course, and will help you with areas such as how to use the 'DSM V' or 'ICD-10' (books which list symptoms of, and codify, recognized psychiatric disorders), or learning to understand how psychopharmacology (the study of drug-induced changes in mood, thinking and behaviour) may impact on clinical work, or understanding the Mental Health Acts of 1983 and 2007.

Having a placement in your local community-health team, where you can work alongside psychiatrists, community psychiatric nurses (CPN), social workers and care workers, will give you some experience of the psychiatric system. This can be beneficial in broadening your knowledge of how people with mental health issues may present themselves, in learning how to differentiate between someone with traits of the various mental health problems and someone with a diagnosable disorder, and in gaining relationships with, and knowledge about, a range of professional colleagues from whom you may be able to seek additional help and support in your practice, should you need it.

The Humanistic and Integrative Psychotherapy College (HIPC) of the UKCP states that during the Mental Health Familiarization Placement (MHFP) trainees are to be able to:

1 develop a basic understanding of psychiatry and the mental health system, the rights of patients and the psycho-social issues involved;
2 understand the main principles of the Mental Health Act and the procedures for the compulsory admission and detention of patients;
3 enhance their ability to liaise with other mental health practitioners;
4 become familiar with psychiatric assessment, planning a range of forms of intervention and evaluation procedures;
5 understand the range of 'mental illness' that can lead to involvement in the mental health system;
6 familiarize themselves with the different types of intervention used, including medication and electro-convulsive therapy, etc., and their main side effects.
7 spend time with people who have been diagnosed with severe depression and psychosis so that they are able to recognize these in the future.
8 be able to empathize with clients who have been patients in the system.

(UKCP, 2011: 14)

How these learning outcomes will be assessed can vary, so there may be some flexibility for you. Some trainees may write a report outlining how they consider they have met them, and others may prefer to make a presentation to their peers and tutor. It may be an idea to discuss this with your trainer when developing your learning contract. In addition, if your course enables student participation in curriculum development, there could be a group consensus in terms of what is to be taught in the classroom, and what will be achieved on placement.

Research

Research is an essential component for monitoring the effectiveness of counselling and psychotherapy.

COUNSELLING COURSES

Some counselling courses introduce students to research findings to enhance their understanding of clinical work; this is usually during the diploma stage (CPCAB, 2012). The BACP requires students on their accredited courses to have some training in research findings and methods. There are no requirements for training in research in the counsellor accreditation systems used by the BACP, COSCA or IACP.

PSYCHOTHERAPY TRAINING

Research is one of the key elements for psychotherapy training in the UK. The UKCP (2012) standards include the following:

> 2.2.1 Research acquisition includes a critical understanding of the relevance of studies and research findings in human development, psychopathology, sexuality, ethics and social science.
>
> 2.2.2 Understanding of basic research techniques and their application to the investigation and evaluation of psychotherapeutic interventions from assessment to ending of treatment . . .
>
> 2.2.3 Specifically addressing research into practice and requiring that Trainings provide sufficient opportunities for their students and trainees to develop the following capacities so that at the point of registration the potential registrant has:
>
> 1 A basic understanding of different approaches to research to psychotherapy practice;
> 2 A capacity to critically understand a research report in relevant clinical and professional journals;
> 3 A capacity to evaluate the significance of research findings with respect to practice, and their practice;
> 4 A working knowledge of research findings in relation to assessment for therapeutic intervention, and a capacity to critique these;
> 5 A working knowledge of research findings regarding psychotherapy process and their implications for practice.
>
> (ibid.: 5–6)

Politically, in an environment where the purchasing of therapy services relies on a proven evidence base, research is certainly vital for the survival of both counselling and psychotherapy. Some recent and relatively interesting research projects have explored the efficacy of counselling and psychotherapy, generally (Baardseth *et al.*, 2013; Butler *et al.*, 2006; Cooper, 2008; Cooper *et al.*, 2010a; Duncan *et al.*, 2009; Fellows *et al.*, 2012; Hofmann *et al.*, 2012; Lindgren *et al.*, 2012; Markowitz and Weissman, 2012; McLeod, 2008; O'Hara and Schofield, 2008; Tolin, 2010), in a specific setting (Stiles *et al.*, 2006, 2008), or with a client-group suffering from specific issues, e.g. addictions (Evans and Ryan, 2012), depression (Moritz *et al.*, 2013; Peeters *et al.*, 2013; Wampold *et al.*, 2002; Widdowson, 2011, 2012) and post-traumatic stress disorder (Galovski *et al.*, 2013).

There is a wide range of outcome-measure research tools that can be used to collect data, such as the 'Beck Depression Inventory, BDI-II' (Beck *et al.*, 1996); 'Clinical Outcomes in Routine Evaluation (CORE) System' (Mellor-Clark *et al.*, 1999); 'CORE Outcome Measure' (CORE-OM) (Barkham *et al.*, 2006); 'Generalised Anxiety Disorder Assessment – GAD-7' (Spitzer *et al.*, 2006); 'Health of the Nation Outcome Scales' (HoNOS) (Wing *et al.*, 1998); 'Psychological Outcome Profiles Questionnaire (Psychlops)' (Ashworth *et al.*, 2004, 2012); 'Helpful Aspects of Therapy' (HAT) (Llewelyn, 1988); 'Personal Questionnaire' (PQ) (Elliott *et al.*, 1999), and the 'Patient Health Questionnaire – PHQ-9' (Kroenke *et al.*, 2001; Kroenke and Spitzer, 2002). Hopefully, your training course will provide you with a good grounding in a range of research tools and current research findings.

I run training courses on research methods in counselling and psychotherapy, and, at the start of the training, I ask the participants for their perceptions of 'research'. Many of them express concern, believing that research can only be completed by 'clever, academic people' or that it is 'boring' and 'number-crunching', but, by the end of a workshop, the participants usually agree, some with no little surprise, that this is not the case, and that research can be undertaken by anyone who has an interest in a particular field or topic, it does not have to include lots of statistics, and it can be positive and enlightening, and even fun.

How this aspect of training will be assessed may include the development of a research proposal, or you may be asked to submit a written assignment critiquing a specific piece of research, or explaining how you evaluate your work, drawing on current research to illustrate your findings.

The opportunity to become involved in research can feel daunting for some trainees, especially for those who may not believe they have the necessary skills or intelligence. If you use a learning contract for this aspect of the training, you may like to consider breaking the research element into small, manageable chunks, and ask your trainer to include in the taught elements of the course a basic introduction to research methods that covers the use of some of the aforementioned tools.

Supervised clinical practice

Once they have successfully completed an initial period of training, usually the certificate or foundation year of the course, trainees are generally expected to undertake some form of clinical practice. Therefore, at some stage during your course, you will be assessed by the trainer(s) to ascertain your suitability and readiness to begin to see clients.

The trainers will be looking for you to be able to demonstrate the key skills necessary for the model in which you are training, and that you work ethically and within professional boundaries. On some courses, this assessment is undertaken live during the course contact-time, and others make use of video presentations, which are then critiqued by the trainee.

You have some say in whether you feel ready to start seeing clients. Some trainees feel pretty confident fairly early on, especially, perhaps, if they already have experience of dealing with clients in an allied field. Another trainee, for whom this may be a change in career, may wish to take more time to feel confident in their abilities. If you feel unsure, ask your trainer to observe you on the course and then offer you feedback to support your development.

At some stage, hopefully, you will feel confident enough to be ready to see clients. Some trainees are ready to see clients after the first year of training, and others prefer to wait until they have completed year two, or even later. If, at the end of year two, you do not feel ready to see clients then consider talking with both your trainer and your therapist to discover what could be holding you back.

Your clinical work will need to be supervised by a more experienced practitioner who has also completed supervision training. Supervision does not mean that your supervisor is in the room with you and your client; it means that you and your supervisor discuss your client-work, together, in a separate meeting. On your course, you will also receive feedback on your experiential work, which is usually given by your trainer and your peers, from work undertaken with them during the practice dyad or triad sessions.

Some programmes offer group supervision during the course time, which may be facilitated by your trainer, or by an external supervisor. Supervision is seen as essential for ethical practice, the protection of the client and the professional development of the therapist (Bambling *et al.*, 2006; Bernard and Goodyear, 2009: Hess *et al.*, 2008; Holloway and Neufeldt, 1995; Lambert and Ogles, 1997; Vallance, 2004; Wheeler and Richards, 2007).

In supervision, you can discuss how confident you feel in your work, and talk about your mistakes, worries and concerns, as well as your excitement, triumphs and attainments. Your supervisor for your clinical work is usually external to your training course, unless this is specifically accounted for in the modality in which you are training.

Your training establishment is unlikely to secure a placement for you, so you will probably have to do this for yourself. The trainers may be willing to support you in this by giving you details of local organizations that have offered placements in the past, and providing information for the placement provider in terms of the trainee's stage of development, and any requests such as annual reports and supervision requirements. Some training providers monitor placements to make sure that the trainee is getting what they need in terms of access to appropriate clients, the receipt of sufficient and appropriate supervision, and, where necessary, access to any additional training.

Your participation on your supervised clinical placement is likely to be assessed by reports from the placement provider, your supervisor, and by your own reflections on your experience.

Personal development

Certain factors may influence your ability to undertake and experience training. Maslow (1987) considers that human beings have a propensity for self-actualization (see Glossary). By having their needs met sufficiently at different levels – physiological, safety, social, love and belongingness, and self-esteem – a person can develop in such a way as to reach their potential.

Maslow's 'hierarchy of needs' (Figure 3.1) suggests that in order to reach self-actualization at the top of the pyramid, it is necessary for the needs in the lower, supporting segments to have been sufficiently fulfilled. It is not suggesting that they have to be met fully, or for all of the time, but sufficiently for that time. For

Figure 3.1 Maslow's hierarchy of needs (original five-stage model) (Maslow, 1987)

example, if a trainee had a young baby, and, as a result, was suffering sleep deprivation, their physiological need for sleep may not be getting fully met, but arranging for their partner to look after the baby the night before the training course means they probably will have that need met sufficiently for that session. This will enable them to attend the course, join in with the group activities and thereby meet their belongingness needs and, possibly, their self-esteem needs.

In order for you to be in a position to fully engage with the learning, you may like to consider how your basic fundamental needs are being met, and whether they are being sufficiently met in order for you to be able to move further up the pyramid. The training provider will usually take responsibility for meeting basic needs at the training establishment, for example the provision of a comfortable training room with heating, ventilation, refreshments and toilets (physiological level). They will hopefully choose a venue that is sufficiently safe, and has a suitable environment, such as minimal noise and appropriate privacy (safety level), and the trainer will probably help to create a sense of belonging, thereby encouraging trainees to build relationships (social level).

Furthermore, by using Rogers' student-centred learning approach, and being active in your learning process, you may meet some of your needs at the 'social' and 'self-esteem' levels.

Maslow's hierarchy of needs, Rogers' student-centred learning and Mezirow's transformational learning are all models which suggest that if you are motivated, have a desire for self-discovery, and take ownership of your learning, you are much more likely to have a rewarding experience of training and a positive outcome.

Self-reflection

This was the area of training that all my research participants explicitly appreciated during their experiences on the course, and also found the most challenging. Many counselling and psychotherapy modalities value the therapeutic relationship as the vehicle for change (Asay and Lambert, 1999; Horvath and Luborsky, 1993; Lambert, 1986; Rogers, 1957; Strupp, 1977). One key aspect of such a relationship is the therapist's ability to reflect on their own experience with, and also as, a client.

During training you may be asked to keep a personal journal throughout the programme to enable you to develop this skill. This can be kept in any format that works for you. Some trainees like to use it in the same way as keeping a diary, writing in entries every week, or daily, and others write about particular experiences on their training course. Some things that trainees may include are how a training session went, what went well for them and what they struggled with, how their clinical practice is going, reflections on their relationships with others, and their experiences within the group.

Your ability to self-reflect will be enhanced through your own assessments of your practical work, your involvement in the training group activities, ethical debates, peer and tutor feedback, and via your own personal therapy. (For more information on personal therapy requirements and reflective practice, see Chapter 4.)

It can be quite difficult for someone else to assess a trainee's personal development, but methods such as the student's participation on the course as a whole, the self-reflective element of their written assignments, tutor, peer and self-assessments, and confirmation of their attendance at personal therapy sessions, may be used. Criteria used in accreditation systems usually invite the applicant to write about how they have developed their self-awareness, and how this has impacted on their clinical work (BACP, 2013b: 3), to write about their ability to be a reflective practitioner (COSCA, 2012: 16), or to be able to critically reflect on their own abilities, to engage with personal therapy and self-actualization, and to recognize, and appropriately respond to, unconscious material that may arise in the therapeutic work (UKCP, 2011: 19–20).

The training standards and learning outcomes for your course will be approved by its awarding body. Until 2013, the only agreed nationwide competencies in the UK were those established by the national occupational standards for psychological therapies (Fonagy, 2010) developed by Skills for Health. (For more information on these competencies, see Chapter 7.) In 2013 the Quality Assurance Agency for Higher Education (QAA) published a subject benchmark statement for counselling and psychotherapy courses, which is the first time that there have been national training requirements across modalities.

QAA subject benchmark statement for counselling and psychotherapy

According to the QAA benchmark, students are to have a broad knowledge in 'philosophy, human growth and development, psychological theories, ethics and the law, psychopathology and the functioning of groups and organisations' (QAA, 2013: 4). Students are expected to develop a range of skills and competencies, including 'relationship building, communication, assessment, formulation, psychotherapeutic strategies and interventions, reflective practice and monitoring, evaluation and research' (ibid.: 4–5). The statement also asserts that, typically, graduate trainees will develop the following skills:

- the capacity to work on their own initiative and in cooperation with others;
- the ability to make decisions in complex situations, and sometimes with incomplete information;
- the capacity to understand and critically evaluate research;
- the ability to communicate effectively both orally and in writing – to include skills such as the ability to articulate principal concepts and arguments, to give and receive feedback, and to include self-reflection in written communications where appropriate;
- the ability to work in small groups, with some understanding of the dynamics of such groups;

- the ability to form good, supportive, challenging and trusting relationships with others in which sensitive personal material can be considered;
- the capacity to tolerate the process of challenge, self-reflection and change;
- the use of IT skills, a capacity to use word processing facilities and a capacity to access library information;
- the ability to use virtual learning environments;
- the ability to identify appropriate sources of information and to extract relevant information to suit specific contexts;
- the capacity to acquire new knowledge and skills.

(ibid.: 6–7)

Those students who are undertaking a postgraduate level of training will also develop the following:

- research skills;
- a comprehensive understanding of analytical techniques applicable to their own research;
- the ability to evaluate and critique research methodologies.

(ibid.: 7)

Full details of all the standards, which represent the minimum requirements for training in higher education as a counsellor or psychotherapist, can be found on the QAA website: www.qaa.ac.uk.

Terms and conditions of training

Before joining the course, or on enrolment, you will want to know what you need to do in order to successfully pass the course. This may be in terms of written assignments, presentations, video or audio recordings of client-work, or the number of required training, clinical, supervision and personal therapy hours. This information is sometimes included in the training prospectus but more often is presented in the course handbook. These resources vary in quality: the most informative include all the course requirements, as well as additional material, such as accreditation, or registration requirements, appeals processes, codes of ethics, complaints and grievances procedures, fitness-to-practise criteria, placement opportunities and professional practice requirements.

Course considerations

Costs

Training costs vary, and your course provider will be able to supply you with information about necessary expenditure, including:

1 The course fees – there may be a discount if you pay in full, and in advance of the training, or there may be an opportunity to pay in instalments. Additional charges may be incurred if you pay your course fees in instalments, or by credit card.
2 An estimate of the costs for personal therapy – some therapists offer discounts to trainees, and fees range from £25 to £50 (€30 to €60) per session (2014 prices). You may also want to find out if you have to see a therapist from an approved list, or if you can choose your own whether they have to meet any specific requirements.
3 The cost of supervision – some placements provide free training and supervision in recognition of your voluntary work, but others ask you to pay for this. The training establishment is likely to know the average cost in your area.
4 The cost of books – courses often provide substantial booklists, but it could be expensive to buy them all. Books are usually identified as either 'required' or 'recommended', and your training establishment may have a library from which you can borrow books. Some training groups have a book-swap system, so you can borrow books from, and lend books to, your peers. Failing that, second-hand books may be available from ex-students, or on the internet through online booksellers. You may choose to buy the 'required' books for yourself, and then consider whether to borrow, or buy, second-hand copies of the 'recommended' books. If you have a local library, you may like to ask them for help.
5 Professional membership fees – it may be a requirement of your course that you join a professional body. The training provider will be able to give you an idea of the likely cost.
6 Professional indemnity insurance – this protects the counsellor, or psychotherapist, from bearing the full cost of defending against a complaint made by, or on behalf of, a client, or damages awarded in a civil lawsuit. Some placements may provide this for you, but you may wish to take out your own insurance. Costs vary according to whether you are joining as a member of a professional body, the amount of cover you need, and whether you are a counsellor or psychotherapist.
7 Membership fees – some training establishments ask trainees to pay a membership fee, or may have other additional fees.

Additional information

Other considerations that may be of interest to you include:

1 Time – you may find it helpful to ask how much time you are likely to need to devote to your training. Most training courses provide the number of face-to-face training hours, as well as a guide as to how many hours of home-study may be necessary. How much time the independent study takes will vary between trainees.

2 Grievance and complaints processes – training course providers, and, sometimes, a professional body, such as the BACP, COSCA, IACP, ICP or UKCP, publish clear guidelines for students on what they can expect from their training establishment, and on what to do if they have concerns about the quality of their training.
3 Termination of training policy – sometimes, trainees decide to leave a course part way through. This can be for various reasons, such as the course being unsuitable, or life events, such as changes in work patterns, bereavement, or a family issue. It is rare, but occasionally a student may be asked to leave a course. Course providers will have a policy in place should any of these circumstances arise. This will include an outline of the procedure to be followed, and whether a refund may be available. Some training establishments have an exit interview when a trainee leaves the programme, and this provides an opportunity to resolve any difficulties, for either the trainee or trainer; and, if necessary, an independent facilitator could manage this process.
4 Personal impact – trainers usually inform potential students that these kinds of courses involve significant personal change that may have an influence on existing relationships. Any personal therapy requirements are usually made clear at the outset. (For more information on the personal impact of the training, see Chapter 4.)
5 Qualifications awarded – course providers usually publish full details of the range of available qualifications in their training brochures, or on their website.
6 Examination, accreditation and registration procedures – information about the process of any final examination, or professional accreditation or registration system, is best introduced to trainees early on in the training programme, and regularly returned to thereafter. (For more information on accreditation and registration systems, see Chapter 7.)
7 The outcome of training – a number of my research participants commented that they considered it important to know what employment opportunities would be available on completion of the training. For example, some courses prepare you to work within an agency setting, and some teach you to work in a specific field, such as drugs and alcohol, sexual abuse or bereavement. Others will help you to work with clients who have mild to moderate problems, or with those who have a psychiatric diagnosis and need to be seen in a hospital setting. Counselling courses tend to focus more on the mild-to-moderate client-group, whereas psychotherapy training usually equips you to work with clients who have more severe mental health problems.

Consider asking your training establishment to indicate the nature of the clinical work that will be appropriate for your level of competence at the conclusion of your core training. Counsellors and psychotherapists are obliged to attend continuing professional development (CPD) training throughout their career so, even if your course doesn't cover a specific area that is of interest to you, it may be possible to consider additional training at a later date.

Conclusion

This chapter has explored the entry requirements and application processes relating to counselling and psychotherapy training courses. The core curriculum has been discussed, and general terms and conditions of training have been provided. In the following chapter we will consider the personal impact of training.

Chapter 4

'This time, it's personal!'

Counselling and psychotherapy training reaches the parts other trainings cannot reach, and this chapter considers two specific areas. The first is the indirect personal impact of training, and the second is the desire, or requirement, for personal therapy.

Personal changes

According to the participants in my research project, you are unlikely to be so personally and professionally involved and challenged in other types of training as you will be on a counselling or psychotherapy training course. I invite you to consider the fact that the training may have a significant impact on you and your relationships, and this may be experienced positively, or negatively, by others around you. You may also want to take this into account when considering whether this is the right type of training for you at this stage in your life.

Make no mistake, if you embark on counselling or psychotherapy training you will never be the same person again. You will begin to see yourself, your life, and your relationships, in a different light. In this chapter, I explain how this process happens and give some examples of the typical types of change. Later, I will discuss the role of personal therapy as an essential element of training.

First, here are some questions for you. Take your time, spend a while considering each one, and write down your answers:

1. How would you describe your marriage/partnership (if you have one)?
2. How would you describe your relationships with other family members, e.g. parents, grandparents, aunts, uncles, siblings and children?
3. How would you describe your friendships?
4. What changes have you experienced in your life?
5. Do you like change, or do you tend to avoid it?
6. What, if anything, would you like to change about yourself?
7. What would you like to change about your relationships?
8. What is your personal underlying motive for undertaking counselling or psychotherapy training?

The answer you have given to question one is very important. What would your spouse/partner say in answer to the same question? Would you both say that your relationship is robust enough to sustain you during your training? The aim here is to help you both to realize that you will be a different person at the end of the training. For some this is an exciting time, but for others it can be the end of a marriage. As Emma put it:

> The more I became me the less he liked me and the less I liked the way he responded to me. Potentially, I wouldn't have ended my first marriage, but, actually, the benefits have been huge.

No one can know at the start of training how they will change, and what impact this will have on their relationships. If your relationships are based on mutual respect and appreciation, then the impact is likely to be positive and rewarding. If, on the other hand, your relationships are fraying at the edges, or in any way unequal, then the training will probably help you to understand what is going on, and you may choose to repair, or end, that relationship. For some people, this may even include long-standing friendships. As Joanna said:

> I've lost some friends along the way. Not a huge amount but it's very significant for me because there's one friendship that I've had for twenty-odd years. I began to realize that my friend was so negative. She has had a tough time and I was always willing to listen to her woes and try to cheer her up. She always said she felt better for talking to me. But during the training I began to realize how much her misery was bringing me down, her negativity and self-centredness. The final straw was when I was having a difficult time and she phoned for a chat. I tried to tell her what was going on for me and she just wasn't able to hear me, just kept talking about herself. I realized that I wasn't really getting anything out of our friendship, so I stopped contacting her. It is a shame in some ways but I see life so differently now I don't want to go back to how things were. The friendships I have now I have because they are mutually beneficial and I feel enriched by them.

Changes may occur for a number of reasons. The first relates to how we talk with others.

'I can't talk like that any more'

Social chatting, or small talk, is important; in transactional analysis we call it pastiming (Berne, 1964) (see Glossary). Berne suggested that we all have a need for structure, and one type of structure is how we structure our time. He identified six patterns of time-structuring, which he called withdrawal, rituals, pastimes, activities, games and intimacy. The level of involvement with others, and that of unpredictability, increases with respect to the order shown. For example, someone who is in withdrawal will have little involvement with others, and, for that time, their life would be fairly predictable, whereas someone experiencing intimacy will have a high involvement with another, and the situation could be very unpredictable. Pastiming is a way for people to check each other out before deciding whether to become more involved. It is a way in which we can introduce ourselves to others that feels safe, using topics that are generally habitual, such as the weather, or the latest instalment of a TV show, a soap or drama series, or sports results. We may use pastiming to check in with colleagues at work/college after the weekend, e.g. 'Did you have a good weekend?'; 'How was the football match?' Sometimes we are interested in the answers, and sometimes not, depending upon our relationship with the other person. Pastiming is often preceded by rituals, e.g. 'Good morning!', 'Lovely day!', or 'How are you?' Have you ever been asked how you are, and then, when you answer with anything other than something like, 'I'm fine. How about you?' you get a strange look, or worse, your answer is ignored? It is because these routine phrases are a way of acknowledging another's presence, but without becoming emotionally involved. Often, this social chatting is used when there is a potential risk of shame or hurt; so, to reduce that possibility, the conversation is kept at a superficial level. Next time someone asks, 'How are you?', consider not giving your usual return phrase, and then see what happens.

There is nothing wrong with rituals or pastiming, per se. In fact, they are very useful as ways of communicating with others; but what happens during counselling and psychotherapy training is that you learn to focus on the essence of what is being said, on both the social level (the actual words used) and the psychological level (the hidden meaning), and also on what is possibly being avoided. A conversation may then begin to have a different meaning as you are likely to be increasingly drawn to the deeper and more intimate meanings of the relating with another person. Many trainees thoroughly enjoy this level of intimacy with their peers. As a result they feel less inclined to participate in pastiming; as Norman said:

> I just cannot be bothered with all that superficial stuff any more. I just want to get down to a real conversation with meaning.

Whereas Joanna said:

> I do struggle a little bit with the social chit chat, although to be truthful I haven't ever really enjoyed it that much. But the training has helped me to realize that most people don't know this stuff and they are doing the best that they can to get along with others.

Any change in how you communicate is liable to have an impact on your friends, colleagues and family. They may experience you as being distant, or somehow less supportive, and this may just be, perhaps, because you no longer want to gossip, or because you invite them to consider the issues from a different perspective. A common response from friends and family to the participants of my research was 'Don't use your psycho-babble on me!' or something similar, which can make this a challenging time for all concerned.

For some people, this newly learned ability to gain a deeper level of understanding and intimacy in their relationships is very welcome. As Paula said:

> For me, it's made me very grounded, and really in touch with myself. I look after myself and my family better because of all that training. So all in all, work and home life have really improved. My relationships are different now. I feel fortunate that the people who matter to me most were willing to go along this journey with me.

'I've discovered my Self'

During your training, and in accordance with the particular approach you are studying, you are likely to learn at least one theory of human personality, e.g. why people do what they do. There are so many different ways of looking at human behaviours, and the reasons for them, that training can be a fascinating time of self-discovery.

Whichever theory/theories you learn, you will inevitably apply them to yourself, your family and your friends, too. It is not only natural to do this, but you may find it unavoidable, because as a counsellor or psychotherapist it is crucial to know yourself very well in order to understand fully some of the powerful processes that occur in the therapy room.

The theories you learn during the training will underpin the approach you will use, both for yourself and for your clients. (Some of the different approaches are discussed in Chapter 2.) For the majority of my research participants, they felt that it was important that the theories worked for them personally, as well as professionally. You may wish to consider this for your own training because if the models do not fit well for you, then you may struggle to use them with clients. For example, a transactional analysis model uses many diagrams, some of which illustrate the dynamics of what happens in relationships. Similarly, the cognitive behavioural approach tends to focus on problem-solving, changing thinking processes, using action plans, homework and diaries. Some clients will find these diagrams or plans helpful as a visual representation, or structure, to understand how a process works, whereas others may experience this as too formulaic or rigid, and instead prefer a person-centred approach that does not rely on these methods, but favours the attitudes that are detailed below (Rogers, 1980). Although these attitudes refer to learning, they are equally applicable to the therapeutic relationship, and hopefully you will experience them in your own training.

> ***Realness in the facilitator of learning***
>
> Perhaps the most basic of these essential attitudes is realness or genuineness. When the facilitator is a real person, being what he or she is, entering into relationships with the learners without presenting a front or a façade, the facilitator is much more likely to be effective. This means that the feelings that the facilitator is experiencing are available to his or her awareness, that he or she is able to live these feelings, to be them, and able to communicate

them if appropriate. It means that the facilitator comes into a direct, personal encounter with the learners, meeting each of them on a person-to-person basis. It means that the facilitator is *being*, not denying him or herself. The facilitator is *present* to the students.

Prizing, acceptance, trust

There is another attitude that stands out in those who are successful in facilitating learning. I have observed this attitude . . . I think of as a prizing of each learner, a prizing of his or her feelings, opinions, and person. It is a caring for the learner, but a nonpossessive caring. It is an acceptance of this other individual as a separate person, a respect for the other as having worth in his or her own right. It is a basic trust – a belief that this other person is somehow fundamentally trustworthy. Whether we call it 'prizing,' 'acceptance,' 'trust,' or some other term, it shows up in a variety of observable ways. . . . What I am describing is a prizing of the learners as imperfect human beings with many feelings, many potentialities. The facilitator's prizing or acceptance of the learners is an operational expression of his or her essential confidence and trust in the capacity of the human organism.

Empathic understanding

A further element that establishes a climate for self-initiated, experiential learning is empathic understanding. When the teacher has the ability to understand the student's reactions from the inside, has a sensitive awareness of how the process of education and learning seems *to the student*, then, again, the likelihood [is] that significant learning is increased. . . .

This attitude of standing in the student's shoes, of viewing the world through their eyes, is almost unheard of in the classroom. But when the teacher responds in a way that makes the students feel *understood* – not judged or evaluated – this has a tremendous impact.

(Rogers, 1980: 271–273)

There is no right or wrong in terms of which theoretical approach to choose. What is important, though, is that the models or attitudes work for you. If they do, then you will be able to use them in a variety of ways; if not, it might feel like putting people into boxes, or reducing them to formulas, which is neither the intent nor the purpose and discounts the richness of the theories.

During the training course, you may begin to find new ways of understanding others. You may see how to make sense of their world, and, therefore, begin to help them move forward. If you are able to embrace the theories with an open mind you may also learn about your own inner world, something you may not have been fully aware of beforehand. With this new knowledge, you are likely to make some decisions about who you are and how you wish to live. This tends to be something of an organic process that can creep up on you, so you are not always fully aware of how you are changing.

For Emma, her experience was that, during her training, she was:

> Becoming somebody different and it felt much more of a social than a theoretical process. Expressing stuff that I'd never expressed before. I don't mean in terms of emotional stuff, but like expressing who I am, my identity, myself and the longer I stay in it [the training], the longer I engage with it, the more me I am.

'The training has been life-changing'

The power of learning and applying these theories is life-changing. Many people embark on counselling or psychotherapy training for one of two reasons. What did you write down as your answers to the eight questions above? The most commonly expressed reason is to help others, whereas the most common, underlying, often unconscious, reason is to find a way to help themselves, their family or their relationships. If you are entering training as a way of getting help for yourself then I invite you to consider having the therapy first, and then decide later if you really want to become a therapist. For some people this may be difficult, perhaps because of the stigma that still surrounds mental health issues. To embark on a counselling or psychotherapy course as a way of accessing therapy may work because most training courses will expect you to have some therapy, but I encourage you to consider whether this is really what you want. It may be, perhaps, that you want both the training and the therapy.

One of the common motivations that became evident during my research was the personal and professional curiosity that brought the participants into training: 'Why do I, or others, keep doing that?', 'Why do some people go from one abusive relationship to another?' or 'Why do I keep ending up in the same situations at work?' If this is the case for you, then you may find some of the answers while undertaking your training; although they may not be the answers you were hoping to find. Some trainees, and clients too for that matter, are seeking an external cause for their internal problems. Consider further your answers to the questions posed in Chapter 1 regarding your life script, or locus of evaluation, in addition to those at the start of this chapter. The knowledge we gain in our training may mean that we have to come to terms with different frames of reference. Perhaps we have to own our part in how we've constructed our difficulties, which can be very challenging, as well as rewarding. As Sophie put it:

> When I started training I was a very angry person. I was angry with my parents, my family and with the world in general. I didn't know why I was angry, just that I was. I wanted to know why I was so angry and why I didn't see the world like other people seemed to. What I learned during my training was liberating but tough too. I had to learn to accept that my parents did their best for me and that at times what they did was not okay but they had their own problems to deal with. I was the one who got into the bad relationships afterwards; it was me that decided to harm myself by eating and drinking too

> much. I was forced to take responsibility for myself and my actions. It was very painful at times but now I am so glad I did. I've learned to let go of the past and enjoy the present whilst looking forward to my future. I feel empowered. The training has been life-changing.

This brings us on to the role of personal therapy in training. Depending upon the route you take, you may be required at some stage to embark on some personal counselling or psychotherapy for yourself.

Personal therapy

Having personal therapy is a requirement on many courses, and the type and duration will vary according to the approach and level of study. Generally, psychotherapy training will require a substantial commitment to personal psychotherapy, whereas some counselling courses may require only a minimal amount of personal counselling, if indeed any at all.

For example, at the higher end of the spectrum, psychoanalytic psychotherapy training requires between three to five sessions of personal analysis per week and, usually, this must be in place for at least one year prior to joining the training programme and continue until qualification.

In the middle, the Humanistic and Integrative Psychotherapy College of the UKCP requires that registrants:

> must have an experience of psychotherapy congruent with the psychotherapy in which they are in training, a minimum of 40 hours per year for four years, and, normally, to be in psychotherapy throughout their training. This personal psychotherapy must normally be undergone with a UKCP registered psychotherapist, or equivalent.
>
> (UKCP, 2011: 16)

At the other end of the spectrum, many basic counselling courses require ten to twenty hours per year, and some do not expect any personal therapy at all. Table 4.1 shows the personal therapy requirements for the UKCP colleges, and Table 4.2 summarizes the personal therapy requirements of the BABCP, BACP, COSCA, IACP and ICP.

As you can see from Tables 4.1 and 4.2, 'personal self-awareness' and therapy requirements vary greatly. It will not always be easy to identify which part of your learning has come from training and which from personal therapy as the experiences occur concurrently. Further, how that learning takes place often depends upon the approach to learning offered by the training provider; for example, whether they offer student-centred or experiential learning, your learning style, and how much you have been able to take ownership of your learning experience, as well as the modality in which you are training.

How the approach views relationship dynamics can be an interesting way to consider how change may occur in a training group. In a psychoanalytic training,

Table 4.1 UKCP colleges' personal therapy requirements

UKCP college	*Personal therapy requirement*
College for Family, Couple, and Systemic Therapy (CFCST)	No college requirement. However, the college requires that trainees have the opportunity to develop their self-awareness and self-reflexivity in a variety of settings. These learning contexts will include the supervision process and personal and professional development groups and may include personal therapy and consultation. (UKCP CFCST, 2009)
College for Sexual and Relationship Psychotherapy	No college requirement.
College of Constructivist Psychotherapies (CCP)	Trainees are required to develop their capacity to identify and manage appropriately their personal involvement and contribution to the process of constructivist psychotherapy. The purpose of this is primarily to safeguard the client and secondarily to ensure that the therapist discriminates between the clients and the therapists own construing. For many practitioners the attainment and maintenance of this reflexivity is achieved partly through the experience of being a client in personal psychotherapy. Though a personal therapy requirement is not at present mandatory for trainees, a minimum of 250 hours of personal therapy or demonstrable personal self-reflective experience is required. Thus, trainees themselves, their tutors, supervisors and peers are all involved in the judgement that the candidate is able to function professionally, taking into account their own contribution to the psychotherapeutic process and without exposing clients to exploitation or abuse. (UKCP CCP, 2009)
College of Hypno-Psychotherapists (CH-P)	250 hours of personal development of which a minimum of 48 hours must be contracted psychotherapy, on an individual basis with a UKCP registered psychotherapist or equivalent. The purpose of all developmental processes, in this context, is as a support to the student as they progress towards the goal of being a psychotherapist. It may be equally concerned with development of resilience and awareness as with the resolution of personal issues, when this best supports the practitioner's development towards effective and ethical practice. (UKCP CH-P, 2008)

(continued)

Table 4.1 (continued)

Council for Psychoanalysis and Jungian Analysis (CPJAC)	Trainees should be in an appropriate psychoanalytically based psychotherapy for about twelve months before the commencement of the course, throughout the duration of the training and for as long as necessary after graduation. The rationale for this is that 'Trainee therapists need to obtain as full an understanding as possible of unconscious processes in order that they can be of greater value to their patients. . . . The requirements for personal therapy must, therefore, be appropriate to the aims of the course. . . . the frequency of a training therapy/analysis should be decided by the needs of the trainee and the appropriate approach. This may take the form of a prescribed frequency, of sessions of variable length or of varying frequencies. (UKCP CPJAC, 2012)
Humanistic and Integrative Psychotherapy College (HIPC)	Candidates must have an experience of psychotherapy congruent with the psychotherapy in which they are in training, a minimum of 40 hours per year for four years, and normally be in psychotherapy throughout their training. . . . This personal psychotherapy must normally be undergone with a UKCP registered psychotherapist, or equivalent. (UKCP, 2011)
Psychotherapeutic Counselling and Intersubjective Psychotherapy College (PCIPC)	The practitioner must normally address their personal development requirements in training through individual personal psychotherapeutic counselling or psychotherapy in line with their theoretical orientation of their training. A candidate for registration is expected to have completed 105 hours of personal therapy. . . . A minimum of 50 hours of therapy must be undertaken during training. . . . The therapy should normally be with a qualified registered UKCP psychotherapeutic counsellor or psychotherapist. The therapy should be in the theoretical orientation of the training. (UKCP PCIPC, 2008)

emphasis is placed on the transference and counter-transference phenomenon. Put simply, transference is a process whereby one person, in this case a trainee, projects someone from their past onto the trainer, and then thinks about, feels and behaves towards that person (the trainer) as if they were that person from the past. Parents or parent figures, such as teachers, aunts, uncles, grandparents, youth-workers, and sometimes siblings, may be projected onto the trainer, especially if

Table 4.2 Summary of therapy requirements for BABCP, BACP, COSCA, ICP and IACP

BABCP	No requirement. However therapists are to ensure that: 'they can identify and manage their personal involvement in the process of Cognitive and/or Behavioural Therapy appropriately. Therapists must have developed an ability to recognise when they should seek additional professional advice and supervision.' (BABCP, 2012: 3)
BACP	No requirement. Applicants for accreditation are expected to: 'Describe an experience or an activity which has contributed to your own self-awareness . . . Provide a reason(s) for choosing the experience or activity . . . Show how you use this self-awareness in your practice.' (BACP, 2013b: 3)
COSCA	No requirement but applicants are expected to demonstrate how they are reflective practitioners. (COSCA, 2012)
ICP	250 hours of personal psychotherapeutic experience, or equivalent in individual or group setting. (EAP, 2007: 3)
IACP	Minimum of 50 hours of personal therapy during training (IACP, 2013)

there are unresolved issues with that person. This is often why some trainees feel very close to, or alternatively feel some antipathy towards, their trainer at certain stages of their training. Counter-transference is the experience that the person who is being projected onto, i.e. the trainer, feels in response to the trainee. This is a fascinating and very informative process in terms of facilitating a trainee's progress. It can be transformative, as long-held unconscious beliefs, feelings, behaviours, frustrations and motivations are explored and processed by the trainee, either in their own therapy or during practical sessions on the course. This leaves the trainee increasingly able to individuate and become autonomous.

In some humanistic training programmes the phenomena of transference and counter-transference may not be addressed directly, yet an intense process of self-development may still be happening in other ways, such as participation in process groups (see Chapter 5 for more information about what this is, and how it works); by applying the theory to yourself and your relationships; by creating a community where group members are encouraged to relate congruently by being open, honest and transparent about their thoughts, feelings and experiences; through counselling practice triads, peer and tutor feedback and personal development assignments. You, as a trainee, are likely to engage in a process whereby you will come to know yourself well. No other profession asks for this significant personal development in their trainees. It could be argued that this pursuit of personal growth and knowledge could be experienced by some as overwhelming, but those who undertake the training appear to gain significantly from their experiences.

Freud summed up well the need for personal therapy or analysis. He wrote:

> But where and how is the poor wretch to acquire the ideal qualification which he will need in this profession? The answer is in an analysis of himself, with which his preparation for his future activity begins.
>
> (Freud, 1926: 126)

As Ann says of her experience:

> it was fantastic. I absolutely loved therapy. I found it life-changing. I think I was lucky that she [the therapist] was very good, or very good for me, you know; it's a very subjective choice and she worked for me.

Why is personal therapy important?

What would you think if you went to see someone who purported to be a doctor, but on meeting him you discovered that he looked rather unwell, was obese, and seemed to be suffering from various skin conditions? How would you feel having this person near to you? Would you trust their judgement? How would you feel if he told you that you needed to lose weight, and eat more fruit, and drink more water to sort out your skin condition?

Similarly, imagine you have a long journey to make to Tristan da Cunha, the most remote inhabited archipelago in the world, and while you are talking with a friend before the journey a stranger comes up to you and says that although they have never been there, they have read about it in a book, and so know how to get there. Would you blindly go off with them without asking any questions? Would you, therefore, consider undergoing personal counselling or psychotherapy with someone who has not been on their own personal journey or, as in the first scenario, someone who apparently knows all the right things to do but does not follow their own advice? Would you feel OK offering therapy to others having not done your own?

Whether the course *requires* personal therapy or not is a matter for the course managers to decide. 'Requiring' a trainee to be in personal therapy is an interesting idea. Historically, many people went into training as a result of their personal therapy. Certainly, in my research, a number of the participants who had undertaken their training some years ago had done so because of the significant benefits they had experienced through their own therapy, and they wanted to be able to offer this to others. So, the idea of now requiring trainees to have their own therapy appears to suggest that many trainees are coming into training in a different way. Of those I interviewed, 28 per cent went into training as a result of their personal therapy; the remainder either began training as part of their professional development in allied professions, e.g. social workers, probation officers or teachers, or because of a relationship with someone else who was undertaking the same, or similar, training.

Whether it is ethical to require someone to be in therapy is open to discussion. I have received numerous telephone calls over the years from new trainees at other establishments who contact me to say, 'I'm on a course, and I have to have 20 hours of therapy'. When I ask if they actually want therapy, the responses I get vary from 'No, not really' to 'I'm just doing it so I can see what I'm meant to do' to 'I do have some issues I want to address'. I invite you to be curious about the philosophy underpinning the need for therapy. Even those who have had a happy childhood may have some underlying issues that could get in the way of them working effectively with their clients.

In 1992, the Humanistic and Integrative Section (HIPS), as it was then called, of the UKCP, had the following therapy requirement:

> For membership of this Section, it is a requirement of a training course that Students have personal psychotherapy with an experienced psychotherapist as part of their training. This should be at least as intensive in terms of frequency and duration as the form of psychotherapy to be practised.
>
> (UKCP, 1992)

This seems fairly straightforward, with the expectation being that the students experience for themselves what they intend to offer to others. Later, in 1993, the requirements were that 'any training shall include arrangements to ensure that the Students can identify and manage appropriately their personal involvement in and contribution to the processes of the psychotherapies that they practice' (UKCP, 1993). These two extracts specify the underlying reasons for therapists having their own therapy. Tudor (2008a) explains it further, and states that the need for ongoing personal therapy:

> is generally viewed as providing a supportive framework within which the trainee psychotherapist can reflect on his or her own issues, which are often evoked by the process of training itself and by working therapeutically with clients, in the course of which he or she also learns about the process of critical self-reflection. Personal therapy also provides a space in which the trainee can expand his or her own awareness and develop empathy both for him or herself and for others. This self-exploration leads not only to greater understanding and sensitivity, but also to greater authenticity as a person and as a psychotherapist.
>
> (Tudor, 2008a: 1–3)

Tudor adds that:

> therapy is too important to be required or regulated and that, given all the information about UKCP requirements, trainees can and should make up their own mind about whether they want to commit to personal therapy – or

> not. If they do and they fulfil the requirements then, on qualification, their name may be forwarded to the UKCP. If they don't, they may qualify as psychotherapists but not be registered. This places the various responsibilities where I believe they belong: with the trainee, to decide about his or her own personal therapy.
>
> (Tudor, 2008b: 5)

Some writers and researchers (Atkinson, 2006; Daw and Joseph, 2007: Garfield and Bergin, 1971; Gray *et al.*, 2006; Grimmer, 2005; Grimmer and Tribe, 2001; Leader, 2006; Macaskill, 1988; Macran and Shapiro, 1998; Macran *et al.*, 1999; Norcross, 2005; Norcross *et al.*, 1988; Rake and Paley, 2009; Von Haenisch, 2011; Watts, 2006) discuss the experiences, benefits and drawbacks of mandatory therapy for trainees. Murphy (2005) has shown in his research that:

> The key findings suggest that personal therapy for trainees can be a positive experience and can enhance the process of becoming a professional counsellor. The findings are put forward in terms of a model illustrating how therapy can be of use to trainees. This involves the trainee experiencing the emergence of four key processes: reflexivity, growth, authenticity and prolongation.
>
> (Murphy, 2005: 27)

Similarly, Grimmer and Tribe's (2001) research with counselling psychologists states:

> The results indicate that mandatory personal therapy can lead to perceived positive outcomes in terms of professional development including: a sense of the self as a professional through developing reflexivity as a result of being in the role of client; socialization into a professional role through validational and normative experiences such as the therapist modelling good and poor practice; support during times of personal difficulty; and personal development that leads to a perceived improved ability for the participant to distinguish between personal issues and those of the client. An important effect for participants who did not have a previous substantial experience of personal therapy appeared to be the validation of therapy as an effective psychological intervention.
>
> (Grimmer and Tribe, 2001: 287)

The findings of the above pieces of research are also reflected in the experiences of the participants in my project. This means that if trainees are fully aware of their options, are acquainted with the available research into the experiences of other students who have undertaken personal therapy, and understand the terms and conditions of their training, and any subsequent accreditation or registration requirements, it is a personal matter for them to decide how they want to undertake personal therapy. When they eventually do so, it will more likely be from a place of autonomy rather than one of adaptation.

During my research, it became clear that for some participants the desire for their own therapy became evident during the training experience in various ways. For some, this was during the practice exercises, or group activities, and for others it was their relationships with their peers, or friends and family, that prompted the wish for therapy. Some participants also mentioned their frustration when a peer was not having therapy, and how, sometimes, that was confronted by the trainer. As Jane said:

> The tutor was very challenging to one of the people in the group, and that was important to me because I thought it needed to be done, and it felt containing to me, but, also, that training didn't need to be a nurturing soft option, you know, when the boundaries need to be put in place, and people needed to be challenged, that it could happen.

You may also find it helpful to be clear about any personal therapy requirements, if there are any, from the start of training, otherwise you may come unstuck. Sally found herself in difficulty at the end of her training:

> When I first started my training we were not told about the need for personal therapy as far as I remember. I didn't read the handbook properly because I thought we would be told if we had to do anything in addition to the training. I completed my four years of training and then thought I'd prepare for my final exam. I went to see a new supervisor to help me through that process and she confronted me about my lack of personal therapy. It then slowly dawned on me that because I hadn't done any personal therapy that I'd have to wait four more years before I could take my exam as I had to have a minimum of four years of personal therapy.
>
> I was so angry; not only with my tutor for not bringing this to my attention, but with myself for not reading the handbook and also, perhaps irrationally, with the new supervisor for pointing this out. I wish now that I had read the handbook as I would probably have found this out and could have taken my exam much earlier. I also wish my trainers had been more explicit about it too. Although I've completed the four years of therapy now I am beginning to feel it's too late for me to take the final exam. I've been out of formal training for so long it seems like such an effort to even think of going back into that way of working. I feel such an idiot; my own therapy has really helped me hugely and if I'd have done it during the training it would have made such a difference to me, the training and my client work.

Undertaking personal therapy is a very personal decision. I invite you to ponder on your own views of receiving personal therapy as a part of your training.

Reflective practice

The ability to be a reflective practitioner (Schön, 1999) is one of the key qualities for being an effective counsellor or psychotherapist. Schön's concern was to show 'how the professional–client contract may be transformed within a framework of accountability, when the professional is able to function as a reflective practitioner' (ibid.: 295). You may already be a reflective practitioner in your current job-role, especially if you work in the helping professions, as it is increasingly seen as essential to professional development. COSCA (2012) also sees this as a requirement for its accreditation scheme, stating:

> You must be a reflective practitioner.
>
> A reflective practitioner focuses on his/her own actions, emotions and thoughts in the counselling/therapy session as well as attending to the quality of the interactions between the client and him/herself.
>
> Being a reflective practitioner involves a willingness to be vulnerable and to be open to learning. It also involves examining one's actions, emotions and thoughts in order to further develop active and critical inquiry about one's own aware and unaware activity in the session. Personal insight and self-awareness on the part of practitioners is considered central to being a reflective practitioner.
>
> (COSCA, 2012: 14)

Similarly, the BACP (2013b) refers to self-awareness under a broader heading of reflective practice in their accreditation criteria. Applicants are required to describe an experience or activity that has contributed to their own self-awareness, and they need to provide reasons for choosing that experience, or activity, and show how they have used this self-awareness in their practice (BACP, 2013b: 3).

Different types of reflective practice are set out by Bager-Charleson (2010), who has developed Kondrat's (M.E. Kondrat, cited in Gardner, 2008) differentiation between reflective self-awareness, reflexive self-awareness and critical reflexivity, as follows:

- *Reflective self-awareness* involves the capacity to be aware of our own biases and preferences – for instance, through the choice of theory and way of relating to our clients. A guiding question here is to what extent we are congruent with our 'espoused theories'. Do we practise what we preach? If not, why not?
- *Reflective self-awareness* involves considering what impact our own personal history and culture have on the way we interact with others. How do your own experiences and environment affect your choice of modality and the way that you choose to approach therapeutic practice?
- *Critical reflexivity* concerns the link between us and our social structure. Bolton (in Gardner, 2008) emphasises that 'we all wear culturally tinted lenses through which we view the world'. This encourages us to think about how gender, race, religion and social expectations might have shaped our attitudes towards ourselves and other people.

(Bager-Charleson, 2010: 33)

You may wish to consider developing these key skills, if you don't already have them, as they will be of great benefit to you as a trainee, in both your personal and your professional development.

Personal involvement

The BABCP (2012b) have a slightly different requirement which is that:

> Therapists must have ensured and continue to ensure that they can identify and manage their personal involvement in the process of Cognitive and/or Behavioural Therapy appropriately.
>
> Therapists must have developed an ability to recognise when they should seek additional professional advice and supervision.
>
> (BABCP, 2012b: 3)

This is similar to some of the other requirements shown in Tables 4.1 and 4.2, but the advantage of this wording is that it is left for the therapist applying for accreditation to take responsibility for their own psychological processes, which is in keeping with the earlier comments. The disadvantage is that, often, the processes that may interfere with our work as a counsellor or psychotherapist are unlikely to be in our conscious awareness, and, therefore, it could be difficult to take responsibility for them. Sometimes the call for therapy may become apparent to others, such as the trainer initially, in training, and subsequently to the supervisor, in supervision, rather than arising in the trainee, or supervisee, directly. The trainer or supervisor can recommend that the student or therapist seeks therapy but, as mentioned earlier, it will be a personal decision as to when, or if, that happens.

It is not clear in the BABCP accreditation process how the therapist's ability to manage their personal involvement is actually assessed. Paradoxically, the ability to monitor personal involvement often requires a certain type of professional maturity on behalf of the trainee/therapist, a skill that is often learned in personal therapy and in supervision.

If you do decide to undertake personal therapy, you may want to consider taking some time to find the right therapist for you.

How do I find the right therapist?

If substantial therapy is your desire, or a requirement of your training, then it is worth considering that you are going to spend a lot of time and money seeing a therapist, so it is important that you find the right one for you. In addition, for some training courses you may be asked to see someone who is fully qualified in a particular field, and to a particular level, so you may want to check you have this information before beginning your search.

You may find it helpful to ask the tutors on your training course whether they have a list of approved counsellors or psychotherapists. If there is no approved list, then consider going to the accrediting or registering body that you intend to join, and use their 'Find a Therapist' service. So, for example, if you are planning on joining, or have joined, a course that leads to UKCP registration, either as a psychotherapeutic counsellor or as a psychotherapist, then go to the UKCP website and search their listings; and similarly for the BABCP, BACP, BPC, COSCA, IACP or ICP.

Consider identifying two or three therapists who you think may be appropriate for you, and have an assessment session with each of them. It may be tempting to pick the one that is nearest, or cheapest, but my research shows that actually, having to travel to see your counsellor or psychotherapist was experienced by a number of the participants as being very beneficial in terms of giving them time to plan beforehand, and then afterwards to process what had happened in the session before going back home or to work etc. All of the participants who commented on the cost of therapy and training said that at some point they realized that what they were paying for was an investment in themselves and their future, and as such was priceless.

Once you have identified a possible counsellor or psychotherapist, you may wish to ask them the following questions.

1 What are your qualifications?

The answer you are given may help you to know if they are qualified to at least the same level that you are intending to train.

If you see someone who has only a certificate level of training, they may not yet be fully qualified, but you may wish to ask what sort of training they have done, and when they completed it.

There are still a number of practising counsellors and psychotherapists who trained years ago, before the more formal qualifications existed, so on paper, although they may not appear to be 'qualified', they have 30 or more years of experience, which could mean they are very skilled and competent therapists, which some may consider is more important. As mentioned earlier, you may want to take into account the course, training, accreditation or registration requirements, and if you are unsure check with the course leader.

If your therapist is in a more advanced training to yourself, you may want to ask if they plan to use some material from your sessions for case studies or training. If so, do you feel comfortable about this, and how will your confidentiality be maintained?

2 Where did you do your training?

The answer to this question can be helpful in ascertaining whether they have done training with the same provider you are intending to go to; if so, you may want to ask them about their experience, which may give you a further insight into the course you are hoping to attend.

3 What is your view on the requirement for trainees to have their own therapy?

The answer you are given here may help you to identify their philosophy of therapy for trainees. They may well have been in the same position during their own training, and may share this with you.

4 What experience do you have of working with trainee counsellors or psychotherapists?

This may be helpful to know because the training is likely to bring up issues for you to work with, not least that therapy may be a course requirement and, if you weren't in training, you might not choose to engage in it. Few other client groups go for counselling or psychotherapy because they are 'required' to do so; this aspect of your therapy may well affect your experience in therapy from time to time. You may like to ask your therapist if they are likely to have anyone else in your training cohort as a client. If they have not, you may feel more secure with regard to your confidentiality, especially if you later have problems with some of your peers, or your trainers. (See Question 7, below, with regard to confidentiality.)

5 What arrangements do you have for supervision?

Supervision is a process whereby counsellors and psychotherapists go to see another therapist who is usually more experienced, and has additional supervision qualifications. During this meeting, the counsellor or psychotherapist will discuss their caseload. This process is confidential, and usually facilitates the counsellor or psychotherapist's work with you. How much supervision a counsellor or psychotherapist has is often determined by their professional body. The norm in the humanistic field is for a minimum of one-and-a-half hours per month. For some, there is a ratio of one supervision hour for every six client hours.

6 Which professional body, or bodies, do you belong to? Which ones are you accredited or registered by? How long have you been a member?

It may be important to you that your counsellor or psychotherapist belongs to a professional organization that has a code of ethics and professional practice requirements that specifically relate to counselling and psychotherapy. This could be valuable for three reasons:

i Your counsellor or psychotherapist may be acting as an exemplar for you in terms of 'this is how to work as a counsellor or psychotherapist'. As you explore the ethics and professional practice requirements of being a counsellor or psychotherapist, in your own training you may, inevitably, be looking to see if and how your therapist manages these qualities.

ii Accredited or registered members of a professional body of counsellors or psychotherapists usually complete an annual continuing professional development (CPD) return that is submitted to their professional body each year on renewal of their membership. The CPD requirements vary between the professional bodies, and they generally involve a minimum number of hours of supervision, attendance on training courses and an expectation that the therapist will keep up to date with professional issues.

iii The professional body will have a complaints process should you ever need it. If you decide that you wish to make a formal complaint against your therapist, then an organization that understands the psychological processes involved in counselling and psychotherapy is likely to be better equipped to support you.

7 What are the limits of my confidentiality?

Counselling and psychotherapy is broadly confidential, but there are a number of exceptions to that:

i If there was a serious risk of harm to you or someone else, the therapist might need to breach your confidentiality in order to prevent or minimize harm.

ii Your confidentiality is extended to include your therapist's supervisor(s). It is usually not necessary that the supervisor knows who you are, although often first names are used.

iii There are certain circumstances when a counsellor or psychotherapist is required to break your confidentiality. For example, in response to a court order, or by law. This is very rare, and your therapist will usually inform you about any such request.

iv As a trainee you may be asked to provide evidence that you have had a specific number of therapy hours; this is generally done via a letter from your counsellor or psychotherapist.

v Some training courses have a contract whereby your personal counsellor or psychotherapist and your course provider have an 'open door' policy, whereby they can share any concerns they may have, for example about your mental health and fitness to practise. Any such contract should be explicit, and is highly unlikely to happen without you being fully informed first, about what is to be said, and to whom, and why.

8 How do you work?

You may find it helpful, at least initially, to see someone who has trained in the same modality that you are considering training in, and as mentioned earlier (UKCP, 2007), this may even be a requirement. If that is not possible, then some other approach that is compatible would be the next best alternative. You may like to ask your trainer for guidance here.

9 What are your fees?

Some therapists offer a reduced fee for trainees.

10 Finally ask yourself, 'What does my instinct tell me?'

Do you feel comfortable with this person? Do you have any niggling doubts? This is probably *the* most important question to ask yourself.

Conclusion

In this chapter we have looked at the personal impact of undertaking counselling and psychotherapy training, including the influence on your relationships with friends and family. Further, the importance of having personal counselling or psychotherapy has been explored, whether as a requirement of your training or for your own personal development. Key questions to ask any potential counsellor or psychotherapist with whom you may work have been identified.

This chapter has focused on the developing relationship you will have with yourself. In the following chapter, we will discuss the nature of the relationship you may develop with your trainer and your peers, and the group dynamics and processes on your course.

Questions to ask friends and family

1. What do you think of me training to become a counsellor or psychotherapist?
2. I am told that people who train to become a counsellor or psychotherapist often change. Do you think our relationship is robust enough to sustain me changing?

Questions to ask training providers

1. What are the personal therapy requirements for this course?
2. Are there any specific requirements that my therapist will need to meet in order to be suitable to work with me?
3. If I cannot find a therapist who uses the same approach as the training course, what other approaches would be suitable?
4. Do you have a list of approved therapists that I can use to help me find a therapist?
5. Do you require any contact with my therapist, and, if so, what contract would you have with them in terms of the boundaries of such contact with respect to my confidentiality?

Chapter 5

Training relationships and group process

According to my research, the nature of various relationships developed on the course was significantly influential on the trainee's experience of their training. There were six main themes to come from this area of the research, and they were:

- the nature of the relationship with the trainer;
- the bond that developed between peers;
- how the training was transformational;
- the nature of the training group;
- the importance of ethics; and finally
- the sense of belonging that many of the participants experienced during the training and afterwards.

These themes are the focus of this chapter.

Relationship with the trainer

As has already been mentioned, many counselling and psychotherapy approaches now accept that the relationship clients have with their therapist is significant in terms of the outcome of that therapy (Asay and Lambert, 1999; Horvath and Luborsky, 1993; Lambert, 1986; Rogers, 1957; Strupp, 1977). My research suggests that this is also true of the counselling and psychotherapy training relationship, although the nature of that relationship is different because the focus is on training, and not on therapy. A number of writers discuss the values that are held in psychotherapy, and how they influence training (Bergin *et al.*, 1996; Carlsson and Schubert, 2009; Palmer and Barnes, 2001; Walsh *et al.*, 1999). Each member of a course, including the trainer and the training provider, will bring their own perceptions, standards, beliefs, morals and ethics into the training group. This can then generate an interesting mix of views and ideas, which, in turn, will produce a wonderful arena for learning, not only about the academic theories, but also about the exquisiteness of human nature.

The qualities of effective trainers

You can expect your trainers to be more experienced and qualified than you are, to have significant clinical practice experience, and to have a teaching qualification, such as a 'Certificate in Education' (graduate, or postgraduate), 'Preparing to Teach in the Lifelong Learning Sector' (PTLLS), a 'Certificate in Teaching in the Lifelong Learning Sector' (CTLLS) or a 'Diploma in Teaching in the Lifelong Learning Sector' (DTLLS). Some modalities also use an apprenticeship scheme for therapists who wish to become trainers.

Trainer qualities that helped trainees to resolve various difficulties that they faced, such as a lack of information, disputes about assignments, concern about the amount of work involved, or unhappiness about the way a trainer, or a peer, related to them, or to someone else, were the trainer's capacity for respectful relationships, their possession of a positive view of human nature, their ability to support and challenge, and their theoretical knowledge and ability to apply it to practice.

Walking the talk

One of the key qualities identified by the research participants was the ability of the trainer to 'walk the talk', and that they, themselves, demonstrate the ethics, relational qualities and skills that they are teaching. This links with Rogers' (1980) 'attitude of realness' in the facilitator of learning. For example, if you are undertaking a person-centred training that emphasizes the application of Rogers' six 'necessary and sufficient conditions of therapeutic personality change and for constructive personality change to occur' (Rogers, 1957), which include a demonstration of empathy, congruence and unconditional positive regard, and the trainer is bullying, judgemental or insincere, then, as a student, it is likely that you will have some concerns about how you can demonstrate these conditions, as they are not being demonstrated to you. Similarly, if you are on a gestalt training course where the central idea is that 'human beings are in constant development' and that 'the person is regarded as an exploring, adapting, self-reflecting being, in a process of continuous change' (Parlett and Denham, 2007: 229–230), and the trainer is not open to this experience and seems to be stuck in a specific frame of reference, you may question the reliability of the trainer. If your tutor embodies these qualities, then you will have a useful resource throughout your training.

As John put it:

> Our trainer was a really inspirational woman; she was kind, encouraging and supportive whilst at the same time robust and potent. We would challenge and confront what she would say and instead of shouting us down or getting on her high horse about it she would discuss and debate with us. Sometimes we changed her mind on things and other times we changed our minds, sometimes we just agreed to differ but each had respect for the other's views.

Similarly, Jennie said:

> I had experienced both trainers and really felt they were solid, safe and grounded. That is not to say they didn't make mistakes; they did but they had the qualities of people I respect. That, even if it all goes horribly wrong, they will be active, and come back, and do something about it. They were excellent role models. Also what I really appreciated was that I got from them a high level of respect, and sense that they, as the trainers, were mindful of meeting the needs of the group as a whole, as well as the individuals, rather than their own grandiosity of 'Look what a great trainer I am' type of thing.

Whereas Harry had a rather different experience:

> Our trainer, I finally realized, was quite self-obsessed and narcissistic. If one of us was to challenge her about what she was doing she would fly into a rage. But at the same time she could be very charming and lull you into a false sense of security. I felt as though I was walking on eggshells at times when I was around her.

Of course, trainers, like everyone else, will have good days and bad days. The difference between these experiences is that it appears that John and Jennie's trainers were each sufficiently grounded and stable as individuals, whereas Harry's trainer may have had some underlying problems. The above scenario also highlights the possibility for continued personal therapy throughout a career as a counsellor or psychotherapist, and then later on as a trainer.

Respect was recognized as being important for a positive experience. Hilary says of her trainer:

> I was very fond of him, and I respected him highly. Though I didn't have him up on a high pedestal but I probably had him on a low one. I respected the way he thought.

Having a trainer on a pedestal, whether big or small, can, initially, be very helpful in terms of knowing someone who has done what you are doing, and is now making a success of it. The relationship you develop with your trainer is likely to be important, so consider using them as a resource by asking questions to clarify your own thoughts and ideas about the theories that are being taught. You may even want to disagree with them when what they are suggesting does not work for you. An effective trainer will be able to explain their thoughts, ideas and views on the theories they are teaching, and give examples or illustrations to show how the theories work. Be prepared to challenge and be challenged!

My research has shown that most trainers appear to take great satisfaction in encouraging their students' unique way of practising and thinking about their practice. What they intend to do is to train people who will become effective, ethical and professional therapists in their own right, with their own set of values, principles and philosophy. Rose summed it up beautifully when she said:

> My training group was a hotbed of ideas. We would discuss, argue, challenge; best of all we would laugh, often at ourselves and some of the crazy ideas we may have had. It was a wonderfully enriching and rewarding process. I admired our trainer for keeping us in order from time to time as we were apt to digress. We were able to play with the theory, pull it apart and then put it back together again. We could take what we liked and throw away the rest. Our trainer wasn't at all precious about the theories. He knew what he liked and what worked well for him. He would offer us his thoughts and we could agree or disagree; in fact he was very encouraging if someone came up with a completely different take on how a piece of theory could be used and would say 'go on, say more' or 'that sounds really interesting, why don't you write that up?' I think we could do it in the way that we did because our trainer was solid, ethical and comfortable in his own skin. They really were the best of times with my training group.

It may be an idea to see if you can get to speak with past students of the course you are looking to join. Some training centres will have current or past students who are willing to come in on open or selection days to talk with new applicants about the course; this is usually done without the trainers present, so everyone can be candid.

'I had an absolute ball'

If you are undertaking a core training programme with one specific trainer or training provider, you may like to also seek out additional training days with other trainers. This will give you variety and differing viewpoints, which can be helpful. The wonderful thing about counselling and psychotherapy training is that there are often numerous ways to facilitate a client's process and progress. By seeking out training with other trainers, you are opening yourself up to augmenting your skills base and knowledge. This becomes increasingly important as your training develops, especially in your third and fourth years. The most effective therapists tend to be those who are open to different ideas and ways of doing things; there is often no clear right or wrong way of working with a client, per se; rather it is what works best for this client, with this issue, at this time.

If you do decide to broaden your training experiences, you may like to let your trainer know that this is what you are planning to do and see if they are supportive of the idea. If you are at the first stage of your training, they may suggest you wait until you have completed at least the first, and maybe the second year of training, so you have a good grounding in at least one theoretical approach. For many trainees this is easier because integrating new ideas into an existing knowledge base will feel more straightforward. Most trainers are likely to embrace this inclusivity, and may even ask you to present your thoughts to your training group after you have attended the additional training day. One good way to access such training is by going to conferences that are held by the main professional bodies. If you are training on a person-centred course, you may like to find out when the next person-centred conference is being held, or go for an allied approach, such as existential, gestalt or transactional analysis, or consider a more generic humanistic conference. You are bound to find some thoughts and ideas that you can connect with, and, perhaps, others that you do not. It is all part of the rich tapestry of the counselling and psychotherapy arena.

As well as thoroughly enjoying her training, Jennie also attended conferences and workshops. She said:

> I had an absolute ball. My trainers were great, very supportive and encouraging of me and my peers going off to do additional workshops. I managed to get to one conference and one extra training day per year. I found the national conferences the best as there were often a number of different workshops I could go to throughout the two or three days we were there. Initially, I went with a colleague of mine and we had a lot of fun and met some really interesting people. It was great going with Julie as we'd meet up at coffee and lunch breaks and exchange our experiences. Sometimes we went to the same workshop together but often we went to different ones as we have different interests and passions. What I found the most thrilling was attending some of the workshops that were run by the authors of books I had read; that was great seeing them in action. When I went back to my course after being at a conference or workshop my trainers would ask me to say something about what I'd found and learned. Some of my peers were rather envious but others were inspired and it actually prompted them to go too so we ended up going in a bigger and bigger group.

This brings us to the relationships that we may develop with our peers, which can be equally important.

Relationship with peers

All the participants in my research project made notable comments concerning the relationships they developed, and group dynamics they experienced, during their training. Their accounts included creating close bonds with some peers which matured into lifelong friendships, feeling challenged by the behaviour of some colleagues in the group, the re-experiencing of familial patterns from their childhood, and the often unexpected, but welcome, sense of belonging that many attained on achieving wider professional recognition.

While you are doing your training, your group may become as important to you as your family. You are likely to make some solid friendships that will last long after you have finished your training – and you may experience some of the most challenging relationships to date. This section explores and explains the nature and significance of this group cohesion, which, according to some trainees, has been essential in their successful completion of training: the sense of belonging that they experienced, coupled with personal therapy, facilitated a transformative experience and acted as a template for future training and professional and personal relationships.

'I'm as close to them as I would be to my twin sister, if I had one'

The training sessions often create a sense of intimacy and closeness, and, at times, your training group will become very important to you.

Helen described it well when she said:

> I've just had a great joyride working with those people because we're all so different. I'm as close to them as I would be to my twin sister, if I had one. We've gone through each other's troubled lives because people have trouble in their own personal lives, but we've all stood with it. It's been okay. So, I think, that would be the thing I treasure the most from my training.

Similarly, John said of his intense training weekends:

> They were always just stunning. A mixture of therapy, thinking, walking, talking, eating, drinking and laughing. It was something, I think, which we all looked forward to immensely. The group was on the one hand very challenging and on the other hand very supportive, which was a great combination.

Carly sums it up well:

> Looking back on it now I was rather naive when I joined my training group. I left school with some basic qualifications and although I'd done some courses through work I hadn't been in this type of education for years. During the first few weeks I felt OK but as time went on I began to feel as though I was falling back. Some of my peers seemed to be streets ahead of me, were quoting authors and what they'd written. I began to withdraw more and more as I felt increasingly inadequate.
>
> During one session we were doing skills practice and I got some great feedback from my tutor about how I was using my skills. He said I seemed to be a natural; my pacing was good, I conveyed empathy and acceptance toward my client and I had a relaxed style, I felt really pleased. Later that day in our process group I said how chuffed I felt getting the positive feedback about my skills and that I was struggling with the more academic side.
>
> Two of my peers invited me to join their reading group. They both said that they had felt overwhelmed by the reading and had got together to read chapters and discuss them as a way of getting started. I joined that group and

> the three of us would meet up every week and talk about what we had read. It was great! Not only did I get to learn the theories but I also made two really close friends too. We helped each other out with reading each other's assignments, preparing case studies and listening to tapes to find ones that would help us to pass the course. It really was a collaborative process. I am so glad I spoke out; I think if I hadn't done so I probably would have left the course.
>
> We still have our group, we meet monthly rather than weekly and although we don't do as much reading now, we focus on current issues, ethical dilemmas and have some peer supervision. I joined that group ten years ago and we're still going strong. I would highly recommend it.

Meeting up with peers in between training sessions can be very helpful, as Carly has mentioned. This can be especially important if your training group meets monthly rather than weekly. A number of the research participants said that having the additional contact, in between training days, could be especially helpful if they were feeling stuck, and wanted support before the next training session.

A transformational experience

My research agrees with Rogers' (1980) attitudes towards trainers as being central to the success of the training programme, and suggests that competent trainers possess the qualities of mutual respect, acceptance, congruence, integrity and an enquiring and reflective mind. This does not mean that everything runs smoothly or that you will always agree with your trainer or peers on every issue, but that a common willingness to learn, to impact on others and be impacted upon by others is essential. This fits in with the cognitive-gestalt (Burns, 1995; Dewey, 1938; Kelly, 1955; Piaget and Inhelder, 1969; Vygotsky, 1978; Wertsch, 1985) and humanistic approaches to learning (Kolb, 1984; Kolb and Kolb, 2006; Honey and Mumford, 1986, 1992; Maslow, 1987; Rogers, 1969; Rogers and Freiberg, 1994) mentioned in Chapter 1, and with reflective practice (Bager-Charleson, 2010; Schön, 1999), mentioned in Chapter 4, and reflective and transformational learning (Mezirow and Associates, 1990; Mezirow, 1991, 2000).

Mezirow and Associates (1990) suggest that the learner needs to take a critical reflection on their learning process:

> Perhaps even more central to adult learning than elaborating established meaning schemes is the process of reflecting back on prior learning to determine whether what we have learned is justified under present circumstances. This is a crucial learning process egregiously ignored by learning theorists.
>
> (Mezirow and Associates, 1990: 5)

He goes on to suggest that such reflection on assumptions and perceptions leads to transformative learning:

> Perspective transformation is the process of becoming critically aware of how and why our presuppositions have come to constrain the way we perceive, understand, and feel about our world; of reformulating these assumptions to

> permit a more inclusive, discriminating, permeable and integrative perspective; and of making decisions or otherwise acting on these new understandings. More inclusive, discriminating, permeable and integrative perspectives are superior perspectives that adults choose if they can because they are motivated to better understand the meaning of their experience.
>
> (Mezirow and Associates, 1990: 14)

This suggests that transformational learning takes place when the learner becomes aware of the significance of how they evaluate themselves, and their lives, in the light of their new learning experience. He goes on to say how one key element in the new experience impacts on the learner's frame of reference:

> Frames of reference are the structures of assumptions through which we understand our experiences. They selectively shape and delimit expectations, perceptions, cognition, and feelings. They set 'our line of action'.
>
> (Mezirow, 2000: 5)

> We transform our taken-for-granted frames of reference (meaning perspectives, habits of mind, mind-sets) to make them more inclusive, discriminating, open, emotionally capable of change, and reflective so that they may generate beliefs and opinions that will prove more true or justified to guide action.
>
> (Mezirow, 2000: 8–9)

I invite you to consider that your frame of reference will be challenged during your training, especially if you are on a well-run and robust course. (Chapter 4 gives more information about this experience.)

Mezirow suggested there are ten phases of transformational learning:

1. A disorienting dilemma;
2. Self-examination with feelings of guilt or shame;
3. A critical assessment of epistemic, socio-cultural, or psychic assumptions;
4. Recognition that one's discontent and the process of transformation are shared and that others have negotiated a similar change;
5. Exploration of options for new roles, relationships, and actions;
6. Planning of a course of action;
7. Acquisition of knowledge and skills for implementing one's plans;
8. Provisional trying of new roles;
9. Building of competence and self-confidence in new roles and relationships;
10. A reintegration into one's life on the basis of conditions dictated by one's new perspective.

(Mezirow, 1991: 168–169)

Mezirow acknowledges that these are rarely linear in their occurrence, and certain stages of transformation may be experienced multiple times within the

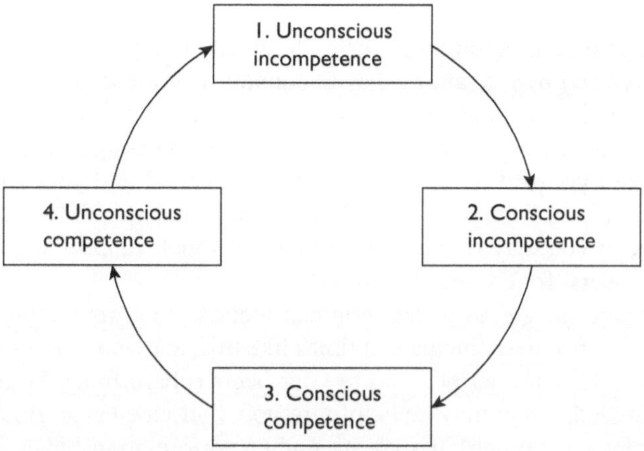

Figure 5.1 Unconscious competence model (Robinson, 1974)

transformation process. I like to link these stages with the 'unconscious competence' model, Figure 5.1 (Robinson, 1974, cited in Clarkson and Gilbert, 1991), as it can help to make sense of what is happening at each stage of learning.

People usually join a training course to learn, and one of the first things you may realize is just how much there is you need to discover. Learning to drive is a good analogy. At first, you sit behind the steering wheel, thinking, 'Great! Now I'm going to learn to drive.' You don't yet know what you don't know, and this is the stage of 'unconscious incompetence.' This first step reflects the initial stage of competency, and is commonly found in any new learning experience. Then, when you start the engine and put your foot on the accelerator, but don't move because the handbrake is still on, and then, even with the handbrake off, there is still no forward movement as there is no knowledge that a gear needs to be engaged, you begin to feel unsettled (phase one). Next, as you lurch forward in strange and nerve-racking jumps, you are beginning to realize that you have a lot to learn, and are now at the stage of 'conscious incompetence'. For some people, the feelings associated with this (phases two and three) are just too much to tolerate, and they give up, saying something like 'It's too hard, I'll never get the hang of it!'

Those with determination, and an understanding that others can drive (phase four), will continue and practise their driving regularly (phases five and six). They will concentrate hard, remember to use the 'mirror–signal–manoeuvre' sequence, position themselves in the road well, and generally move in the right direction (phases seven and eight). This group of learners has now reached the stage of 'conscious competence' and, as they are consciously aware of all the necessary skills required in driving, they will soon be able to apply for their driving test (phase nine).

Many years later, these drivers can drive their car without any problems (phase ten), and can't remember the crunched gears, 'kangaroo petrol' and awful hill-starts of their learning days. They have now achieved the stage of 'unconscious competence'.

When someone joins a training course, they will often go through these phases and stages over and over again as they encounter new pieces of theory, develop their therapy and academic skills, and experience personal and professional challenges. On such courses, you may be asked to write assignments, make presentations, record yourself working, and present yourself, and your work, to your training group. If you have been away from formal education for a while this may feel daunting, so you may find it helpful to get as much support as you can from your trainers, peers, friends and family.

Going through the stages of learning can feel exciting, rewarding and tough. Your self-confidence may fluctuate at times like this, and you may like to remember that you are in a similar position to your peers (phase four). Some will have skills and knowledge that may be helpful to you, and vice versa. Being cooperative, and helping each other out, may strengthen your relationships.

Group development

One model of understanding group processes and development was developed by Tuckman (1965). He named the stages as:

1 Forming
2 Storming
3 Norming
4 Performing
5 Adjourning or Mourning (added later by Tuckman and Jenson, 1977)

Tudor (1999: 28) states that Tuckman also acknowledged the existence of a pre-stage one (Shellow *et al.,* 1958). When you are fantasizing about how the training group will be, this is pre-stage one, where all your experiences of groups, good, bad or indifferent, are likely to influence the imago you develop for the course.

Once on your course the trainers, depending upon the theoretical orientation of the training, may help you form as a group through facilitating processes, usually called 'ice-breakers', that are used to help you and the other trainees interact with each other.

During stage one, 'forming', there is often a heavy reliance on the trainer to lead the group. It is a time when the group participants are getting to know each other.

The second stage, 'storming', can be an uncomfortable part of group development. This is when some members of the group may vie for leadership, there may be conflict between members, and cliques may form. It can be a time when the group struggles with the tasks in hand, and some members ask themselves, 'Do I really want to do this?', or, 'How can I do this?' This is a time when learning contracts can be very helpful to act as a support to help you through the rocky times, and it is also a time when, if you dislike conflict, and want everyone to be nice to each other, you may experience a bumpy ride. This is a stage where your tolerance and patience may well feel tested, as may your attitudes towards and beliefs about others. At the end of this stage, you are likely to have a new understanding about yourself, and to have developed some bonds with some your peers. As a group, you will have reached a point where members can work together to complete the task in hand. Despite its challenges, it is an essential part of group development. If a group doesn't negotiate this stage successfully, they cannot progress to 'norming', and they will continue to 'storm', perhaps for the duration of the group, or course, which can be an unproductive time for all concerned. During this stage, the trainer remains an important focus, as their task is to maintain boundaries with confidence, demonstrate potency by holding all as 'OK', and show acceptance of group members and their ideas, thereby offering permission to be different. As this happens, confidence develops and the focus will shift on to the responsibilities necessary to complete the course.

The third stage, 'norming', is a time when the group becomes more focused on the tasks in hand, and decisions are made by the group as a whole. It's a time when group members begin to feel more settled in themselves, and committed to their relationships with others in the group and to the course itself. The group discussions become more cooperative and less competitive.

The fourth stage in this process is 'performing'. Once the group achieves this stage, then it will be a robust and effective group. The group members are usually well motivated and focused, and are unselfconsciously developing their expertise and knowledge. During this phase, the group functions as a well-oiled machine.

Group development is not always a linear process, and it can move back and forth between stages as circumstances change. For example, if trainers or group members either leave or join the group, then it will usually revert to the earlier developmental 'storming' stage, and will then need to 're-norm' in order to process and accommodate the changes.

The final stage, 'adjourning', sometimes referred to as 'mourning', concerns the ending of the group as its task is now complete. Marking the end of a group is as important as any other stage of group development, and training courses often end with some form of celebration and expression of appreciation.

As Jan says of her training group, which revisited the 'storming' and 'norming' stages on a number of occasions:

> The main challenges were to do with other people in the group; the group dynamic. We had a group that went through a lot of change and had various, sort of, episodes within that, so there were outsiders who came into the group either from other training courses or were just with us for one weekend. It was great to meet new people and yet they were different to us somehow; I think we may have viewed them with some suspicion as well as awe as they had nearly finished their training whereas we were really only starting. There were some people who were very disruptive and a situation where two people in the group had an affair! All sorts of tricky issues, which, I think, must have been

> really difficult for our trainers to contain. But they did hold those processes very well. Once we had sorted ourselves out then the group process became smoother and felt calmer too. Although we did still, at times, have some rather uncomfortable periods, the end-of-course celebration was pretty good.
>
> Thinking back on it now in the disruptive times – I was, like, 'I like all these people, I want everybody to like each other', and it felt like 'This is not OK' and yet it was OK, but at times I found it very, very difficult to be a part of.

Jan is also referring here to the processes that go on when groups get together, and how these experiences may mirror your experience of your first group: your family. As Jan says, she wanted everyone to get on with each other, which probably links back to her experience as a child. I invite you to think about your early life and answer these questions. What were the dynamics in your family? Did you all have to get on? Did you fight? Was it generally fair, or unfair? Was there any competition between you and your siblings, or your parents? What did you have to do to get approval, or criticism, from your parents? What did you do to get attention? And how do these patterns continue for you today?

Attachment styles

The attachment patterns created during a trainee's earliest relationships influence the development of their life script, and impact on their ability to create relationships with their trainer and peers. There are three attachment styles – 'secure', 'insecure ambivalent/resistant', and 'insecure avoidant' (Ainsworth and Bell, 1970). Briefly, they can be summarized as:

Secure attachment

A child who has a secure attachment with their care-giver is likely to view their care-giver as a safe place from which they can explore the world around them. They are easily soothed by the care-giver, and will be more likely to develop trusting relationships, and have a good sense of their own self-worth.

A trainee with a secure attachment will build sound relationships with their trainer and peers based on mutual respect and are likely to get on well with their studies.

Insecure ambivalent/resistant attachment

A child who has an insecure ambivalent/resistant attachment style is clingy with and dependent on the care-giver, and is also likely to be resistant to interactions with the care-giver and can be difficult to soothe, and may resist comfort. They usually have a negative view of themselves, and tend to overreact to get attention.

A trainee with this attachment pattern may become the centre of attention in the training group; they may be critical of the trainer, the course or their peers, and refuse positive comments or feedback. For example, Ian said:

> There was someone in my training group who always seemed to want to find fault with the trainer or to spoil what was going on. At times his comments seemed to be ordinary questions but when the trainer answered his question he would then seem to be dissatisfied with the answer. It got to the point where my heart would sink every time he opened his mouth as I knew we were in for a bit of a process.

Insecure avoidant attachment

A child who has an insecure-avoidant attachment style will avoid or ignore the care-giver, and will not seek comfort when they are distressed. They can be seen as being physically and emotionally independent. They often view themselves as being worthless, having been rejected by the primary care-giver. A trainee with this attachment pattern may seem rather aloof in the training group. They may work hard and complete their tasks well, but will rarely seek support from the trainer if they get stuck. They are unlikely to be either the centre of attention in terms of putting themselves forward, or to join in with some of the social events that can occur on courses.

If, in our past, we have developed secure relationships with our parents, or care-givers, then there is a good chance that we will be able to repeat that experience with others. However, if our early relationships didn't meet our needs, then we will develop an insecure attachment style and may still be yearning for an idealized parent figure, seeking to find it in others.

Imagine you were a fellow student on John or Jennie's course, as mentioned earlier in the chapter. If you have a template of healthy, securely attached relationships with others then you are more likely to look for, and get, what you expect. If your relationship template is insecure then you may, initially, feel mistrustful of others. With support and encouragement from your trainers, peers and personal therapist, you may be able to create a new relational template based on mutual trust and respect.

Imagine, now, that you were on Harry's course. If your template is of healthy, securely attached relationships, and you experienced such a rage-fuelled outburst, you might well feel able to challenge the trainer. If, on the other hand, you have a template of an overbearing or abusive relationship, then this kind of behaviour may be the norm for you, and you may feel powerless to do anything about it in the here and now, just as you did as a child. As has already been mentioned, it is fairly common for some adults to project figures from the past onto current relationships in this way.

This does not just extend to those on your course, but can include virtually any relationship, for example work colleagues, employers or others in positions of authority. Consider, for a moment, your relationships with others – is there a pattern in terms of who you get along with, and who you don't? Is there any link between that current relationship and the one you had with your parents, care-givers or, perhaps, a teacher from the past? This transferential process (see Chapter 4 and

Glossary) is usually mentioned in reference to personal therapy, where it may be encouraged and used, for the benefit of the client, whereas in training this phenomenon, when present, needs to be addressed and processed (Blohm, 2006; Bonds-White, 2003; Hearst, 1990; Klain, 1975; Langs, 1992; Reiss, 1975; Rieken, 2003; Russell and Staszewski, 1988; Stauble, 1965).

Power

Transferential issues can translate into concerns about power, which can be played out in a multitude of ways. At times, both trainee and trainer can get locked into an unhelpful process where there are personal issues for each of them; in this situation, each may benefit tremendously from exploring the process within the training group. A trainer may also feel it is useful to occasionally return to personal therapy. Some trainers receive supervision on their training, and this would also be a good place for them to address problematic interpersonal dynamics. Should you find yourself locked in a difficult process with a trainer, you could seek support from your friends and family, explore it with your peers in your course process group (see later in this chapter), or in your personal therapy or you may want to ask the trainer concerned for a tutorial.

Whatever your early experience, whether it was in your family of origin, a foster or adoptive family, or an institution, you may like to consider that some of the processes you experienced may be replayed in your training group for you. For example, if you were competitive as a child, perhaps competing with siblings, then you may well experience this with one or more of your peers in the training group. This could be something that you create by yourself, or it may be co-created with someone else who is also competitive. Similarly, if you always felt unseen, or discounted, by some members of your family, then this may also be recreated in your group. The invitation, here, is to be curious about the part you may play to make this happen.

When such processes get acted out within a training group, it can feel very uncomfortable for all concerned.

As Michael says of his course:

> It was a bit of a disaster. We had two trainers and they fell out over something. There were different factions in the training group, some people were in supervision with one trainer and some the other and there were a few of us who didn't have supervision with either of them. I was on the outside so I didn't really know what was going on; it all became really uncomfortable.

It would probably have been more helpful, in this situation, for the trainers to have held a transparent and respectful discussion that was supported by the ethical principles mentioned in Chapter 3, where they disclosed as much about their differences as felt appropriate, and to have then facilitated a process whereby all group members could have explored the events in a similar way.

The ability of group members to process events on the course can release stuck and unprocessed emotion. An example of this working well was mentioned by Helen, who said:

> Our process group was amazing. I hadn't experienced anything like it before. We had two people on our course that fell out because they both went for placements with the same organization; one was offered a placement but the other was not. It was really awkward for a little while. I liked both of them and felt torn as I wanted to support them but felt invited to take sides. I decided during our process group time to say something. I felt uncomfortable as I wouldn't have normally spoken up but their friendship was important to me so I said what I was experiencing and asked them to find a way to resolve their difficulties. At first they both just looked at me, then one burst into tears shortly followed by the other. After a little while they were both able to say what had been going on for them and to take support from the others in the group. Although there were periods of discomfort for all of us I'm glad I spoke up as we ended up being really close friends.

The psychological filter

What Helen refers to as a 'process group', I like to think of as the 'psychological filter' for the training group. It is sometimes called a 'personal development group' or 'an encounter group' (Boyd, 1991; Egan, 1973; Hall and Hall, 1988; Hall *et al.,* 1997, 1999; McLeod, 2009; Rogers, 1971; Rose, 2004, 2008; Tudor, 1999). During these groups, you have an opportunity to explore some of your experiences on your course. A well-functioning process group supports a well-functioning training course. The process group's purpose is for group members to give and receive feedback about their experiences of each other and the course and will often, but not always, include trainers. Sometimes process groups are facilitated by someone who is not a tutor on the course, as this is seen as providing trainees with the option to share experiences more openly without fear of being 'judged' by their trainers, who may also be marking their assignments. It is debatable how external the tutor is if they are being paid by the training organization and may be asked to report back to the course leader. Under these circumstances, a specific confidentiality contract may need to be agreed – how much of what is said is confidential, and when would that be breached, e.g. what would happen if a trainee made an allegation against a trainer, or disclosed behaviour that could put themselves, or others, at risk?

You may like to use the process group as a place to ask for support, if you are struggling, and a space to share the highs and lows, the challenges and rewards of being on the course. It can be a time of intimacy, and is usually built on mutual trust, openness and respect.

A well-facilitated process group can be very beneficial to you, and it is possible that you will learn just as much about yourself in this environment as in your personal therapy. As Jennie says with regard to her training group:

> The process group was challenging and rewarding. I felt very exposed – well, vulnerable – at times and yet also very well supported. It was a unique experience. I think it was the process group that gave the group the cohesion and sense of us all being in it together.

Whereas Harry had a different experience:

> The process group was strange; we tended just to sit in silence for quite a while to begin with. It seemed as if each week one person would be 'it'. Once, in the third year, I was 'it'; I think it was because there was a lot of envy at the time. I was doing well with the course and seeing clients whereas some of my peers were yet to see their first client. The comments that were made towards me felt attacking rather than supportive or appropriately challenging. It wasn't a good experience for me.

Joy says of her experience:

> The process group was generally very good. I appreciated the openness and honesty that we usually shared as well as the support I had received. Although, for some reason, on one occasion our trainer wasn't there, I did think that was weird and one person in our group then began criticizing her. We let her speak for a while and then confronted her and suggested she take her grievances directly to the trainer.

In the last two examples, there may have been underlying script issues at work that caused the people concerned to behave in the way that they did by attacking a peer or trainer. This could be an example of transferential issues being played out in the training group. Joy experienced a positive transference when she joined the training group:

> When I met our trainer for the first time I thought she was lovely. She seemed interested in me; I hadn't had that before. I worshipped her for a while, hung onto her every word, I felt like a child every time I saw her and she became my 'mum' for a time. I used my journal to confide in her some of my darkest secrets that I hadn't told anyone before. She didn't seem to judge me and would write supportive comments that helped me to feel seen and heard. I needed to have that relationship with her. As time went on my confidence increased and I began to share more of myself with the training group, developing solid relationships with some of my peers. My need for my trainer lessened although she will always remain an important person in my therapeutic journey.

If you have any problems on your course, you may wish to consider taking them to your process group. There, you may have the chance to explore them directly, with the person concerned, and if you come from a place of mutual respect and ethical awareness you are more likely to be heard and the issue resolved, or, if the person is not there, to get some help and support from your peers, which may then facilitate you talking with the person directly.

The functions of, and requirements for, the process group are likely to vary between courses. One interesting point is when the group is held during the training day; whether it has a different room to the rest of the day, or whether it can be requested at any time. A number of my research participants mentioned having their process group in the early afternoon, which had benefits and drawbacks. As Sheila said:

> Our process group began straight after lunch. Frequently I would be involved but now and then not. Occasionally I saw it as an extension of lunch and stayed withdrawn. One day I even fell asleep! The other problem having it at that time was that if something happened later in the afternoon it was too late and I'd have to wait until next month before saying anything.

Other groups have process time at the start or end of the day, which may be disrupted if trainees are late, or a missed opportunity if they leave early. This may become a problem if the significance of the process group, as the psychological filter, is discounted.

'I wish they would do it properly'

Sometimes you may feel frustrated with yourself, or others, during your training. You may feel irritated with yourself because you don't understand a specific piece of theory, or a model, or perhaps because you are struggling with the skills practice, or because you keep falling into problem-solving rather than listening to your client. You may feel annoyed with your peers for the same reasons, or because they are not having therapy, or they are not keeping to the negotiated group guidelines. Perhaps they are being 'too nice', and giving you placatory feedback because they don't want to upset you, or alternatively they are being critical, rather than giving you constructive critique.

You may feel angry with your trainer because you experience them as not practising what they teach, or they may seem to be racing ahead with the next piece of theory or therapy intervention as you struggle to keep up. You may experience them as being too controlling, or not controlling enough.

Whatever the issue, there are numerous options for helping you to find a way to deal with it. You may wish to seek clarity and support from your process group, therapist, peers, friends or family. If your frustration is with someone else, it may be helpful to speak to the person with whom you have a problem, or work towards doing so. It may help to share what it is that's bothering you, and identify, specifically, what you would like the other person to do about it, if anything.

If you have an issue with a peer or a trainer, it may help to consider the problem in the light of the ethical principles that were discussed in Chapter 3. In the case of a fellow group member who is not in therapy, it might be appropriate in the first instance to speak directly to your peer. This would mean taking action underpinned by the principles of courage, honesty and integrity. Your peer may have a valid reason for not undergoing therapy at this time that has been agreed with the trainer. In any case, whatever the issue, it would be good practice to give your colleague the opportunity to put things right. If they choose not to, you may decide that it is necessary to speak with your trainer.

'I really appreciate the sense of belonging'

One significant theme that emerged in my research was the sense of belonging that trainees experienced, both during their training and, later, in the wider profession. It is for this reason that many go on to complete their final exams, professional registration or accreditation.

This is something that Fiona continues to appreciate about being a psychotherapist:

> I loved my training and made a few really good friends. I thoroughly enjoyed my final exams and getting my UKCP registration. Now what excites me is the annual conference. I really appreciate the sense of belonging I get when I'm there; I go to meet my friends and colleagues, whom I've got to know well over the last 15 years. We talk the same language, have great fun, learn new ways of doing things, catch up on each other's news and dance the evenings away. It is a highlight of my year.

Ruth, who is now a trainer, says:

> What I like best about what I do is that I can go anywhere in the world and meet up with friends and colleagues who work in a similar way to me. I just love that sense of belonging that I get when I go to international trainers' meetings or conferences. We may all work in different countries and in different fields but in essence there is a real cohesion, a sense of community that I haven't found elsewhere in my life. I wouldn't change it for anything. I feel very privileged too that I can do what I do.

Annie put it simply when she said:

> When I got my accreditation I felt as though I'd finally arrived. I could hold my head up high and say I am a counsellor and I've got a piece of paper to prove it! There was something more for me with my accreditation that I didn't get when I passed my diploma. I think it may be something to do with having some external recognition or validation, belonging to a profession.

Conversely, it could be a fear, either of achieving, or of not attaining, that sense of belonging, or acceptance, that prevents some people from reaching their potential.

Conclusion

In this chapter, we have looked at how the relationship you have with your trainer and peers is significant in terms of how you experience your training. Coupled with this is an opportunity for you to identify any unconscious processes that may have been formed in your relationships with figures from your past that may influence your training today; and further, for you to think about ways to help yourself, if these begin operating while you are training.

We have also looked at the various group dynamics and processes that are likely to be manifest in any counselling or psychotherapy training programme, and discussed the importance of ethical principles in structuring functional relationships in training programmes. Finally, we explored the sense of belonging that was important to many of my research participants, both during and after their training. In the following chapter we will consider some of the additional challenges of training, examinations and accreditation systems.

Here are some questions for you to ask your prospective trainers.

Questions to ask trainers

1. How do you monitor the training group's progress and process?

   One answer may be supervision, and, although there is often no professional requirement for supervision of training, it is certainly good ethical practice to do so. The frequency and type of supervision will vary. The important point here is that the trainer appreciates the benefits of having external supervision, meaning having supervision with someone who is not directly connected to the training establishment. Other ways may be regular team meetings, discussions with external examiners, feedback from the training group, coursework results and community meetings, and the process group.
2. How long have you been training?

   This will be helpful to know in terms of how experienced the trainer may be.
3. What qualifications do you have to teach?

   It is helpful if your trainer has some formal teaching qualification, or is presently undergoing training to achieve one. (See Chapter 3 for some information on likely qualifications.)
4. Do you have a clinical practice?

   If a trainer also maintains a clinical practice, they are still current in terms of their work.
5. Does the course have a process group?
6. Which ethical guidelines underpin the course?

Chapter 6

The challenges of training

One of the key themes that arose from my research was that at some stage in the training many trainees experienced some sense of disappointment, disillusionment or challenge that impacted on them significantly. These difficulties concerned four main areas:

- the training course itself;
- personal challenges;
- professional problems; and
- money.

This chapter discusses and explores these areas. If you have read some of the other chapters in this book, you will already be aware that counselling and psychotherapy training is unlike any other course you have attended. It involves the whole of you: mind, body and spirit; it is all-encompassing, and will impact on virtually every aspect of your life.

The training course

All of the participants I interviewed said that they had reached a stage during their training when they had begun to feel disillusioned with their course; this tended to happen somewhere between years two and three. Some of the common reasons cited by the research participants were: that the coursework was more demanding than they had imagined; that the programme was more like a full-time course than a part-time one; that they had difficulty finding a placement to get the clinical hours they needed; and that they had had a lack of knowledge regarding the requirements of the course.

Expectations

Sometimes, the disappointment is because of a mismatch between the course content and the expectations of the trainee. This happened to Vicky. She said:

> it left me feeling a little bit disillusioned because a lot of the material I was being taught I knew, because I'd already studied it in my degree.

Whereas for Ruth:

> I struggled with the coursework. I hadn't realized I would need to write assignments; I thought as it was a 'skills' course, it would be all practical.

Similarly for Dorcas:

> I was looking for a set of skills I could use with my probation work clients. I wanted to know how I could get them 'onside' in terms of complying with their probation orders. I did learn some useful listening skills and got a lot out of the personal development module, but I was also looking for help with goal-setting, action planning and time management and I thought the course would cover that too.

Having a clear idea about the course content and assessment methods is essential.

I invite you to be clear about what you are hoping to get out of your counselling or psychotherapy training, and to find out if that is going to be achievable in the course you have chosen. You can get lots of information by asking your trainer questions; you may like to use some of the ones posed at the end of this and other chapters. One great way to find out about a course is to consider speaking with other trainees who have just finished the training. You may also find it useful to speak with a couple of people who finished one or two years ago, to give you an idea of how their careers have developed for them since they completed their training. Any course literature you are given, especially the brochure, may help you to understand some of the academic requirements of the course. Most courses include all the relevant training requirements in the appropriate handbook, and it will be worth asking to see one. Or, if you are able to speak with a past trainee, you may consider asking to see their handbook, which will give you a good idea of the course requirements.

'I think some people enter the training for the wrong reasons'

Sometimes, people join training programmes for what could be seen as the wrong reasons. With regard to psychotherapy training, Steve's view was that:

> I think some people enter the training for the wrong reasons. Originally, psychotherapy training was an additional training for people who were already counsellors or psychiatrists. Now it's a whole training from the start and 'A', I think it's got a bit mixed up because it tries to do two things: to train people to be counsellors and psychotherapists in one go, and I don't think that is really possible, certainly not on these short courses of just two to three years.

> And 'B', people go in for three reasons: they have had therapy of some sort and decide they want to be a therapist, or they've never had therapy and decide they want to be a therapist. And I also think lots of people enter training the first year, the foundation year, for personal development. So, they're using it as therapy more than learning.

Incongruity

Sometimes, disillusionment concerns a relationship with a peer or trainer. This was often in the form of an attitude or behaviour that was incongruent with that of the course. Geoff found that there was a dissonance between the course philosophy and what was being taught, and he said:

> I was on a person-centred course and during one training day the tutor was showing us how to do 'two-chair' work [originally a gestalt technique] with the therapist directing the client. Although interesting it seemed out of step with what we were learning.

If the trainer has qualified in a different modality to the one being taught, some skills or attitudes being demonstrated may not fit with the course values or approach. Trainees may integrate these behaviours into their practice thinking they are being congruent with the course's core model, when, in reality, they are not. If these trainees then become trainers themselves, they may pass on this distorted practice to future generations of counsellors and therapists.

Congruence between the course tutor's attitude and behaviour and the philosophical beliefs and methodology of the core modality are essential if you are to get a genuine and reliable demonstration and integration of the approach being offered.

Academic work

Another common time for doubt is during assessments or examinations. You may be required to produce written assignments, case studies and video or audio tapes of your client work; to make presentations to your trainers and peers and to complete written and oral exams. Part of the learning is likely to involve developing specific academic skills, which may include comparing and contrasting models, making critical analysis, being able to synthesize approaches, applying theory to practice and learning to give and receive constructive feedback. This may well make demands upon your time and challenge you in a number of ways. As Pat said:

> Before starting my course I hadn't written an essay since leaving school 28 years ago. I hadn't got a clue what to do. I did submit something but when I got it back I found out that I hadn't answered the question. I was very disappointed

> as I'd spent so much time and worked so hard but the tutor gave me some helpful advice as did student services. A couple of peers let me read theirs and then I began to get the hang of it. I still need some help with grammar and punctuation but generally I think I do OK now.

Writing assignments, when you haven't done anything like it before, or for a long time, may feel daunting for some people. If this is the case for you, then you may like to find sources of help that can support you at this time (see, for example, Copus, 2009; Cottrell, 2011; Godfrey, 2009; Goodwin, 2009; Greetham, 2008; McMillan and Weyers, 2011; van Emden and Becker, 2010). As a trainer and examiner, I have read a number of excellent assignments that were well written in terms of the effective use of language, grammar and punctuation, that demonstrated the trainee's understanding of theory by the making of links to clinical practice, that were well referenced and proof-read. They were full of good ideas, such as comparing, contrasting and critiquing different models. In addition the candidates developed new ways of working with clients, showed curiosity about their own process in therapy and reflected competently on their practice. In spite of this, though, they had not explicitly answered the question, or met the learning outcomes or the assessment criteria. My invitation to you is to make it easy for your markers to pass you, and here are some tips that you may find useful:

1. Proof-read your assignment before submitting it. When we read over something we have written, we may unconsciously gloss over errors, and just 'fill in the gaps' because we know what we meant to write.
2. Find out if there are assignments from previous students which you can look at to get an idea of what is needed.
3. Develop a plan for the assignment. You may wish to check your understanding of the question(s); also have the assessment criteria available so you can then expand your plan to include how you intend to meet them. The whole document can then act as a guide for you while you are getting your thoughts and ideas together and researching your options; it can also help keep you focused while you are writing. You may also like to include some timescales in the schedule so that you can complete your assignment in time for the submission deadline.
4. Consider giving clinical examples to demonstrate your thinking and practice. Use transcripts, if you can, as these can really bring the work alive.
5. If you are going to use clinical material such as transcripts remember to get permission, and maintain your client's confidentiality. This can be done by changing the client's name and other relevant details so they cannot be identified.
6. Once you have written your assignment, you may find it helpful to go through the learning outcomes and assignment criteria, and mark on your draft where you think you have met them.
7. Consider asking someone to read through your work to see if they agree that you have answered the question(s) and met the learning outcomes and

criteria. It would be worth asking someone who will give you a clear and honest answer rather than someone who will want to avoid being critical in order to please you!

8 You may like to ask your trainer or supervisor to read your work and ask them for feedback before marking, if that is an option.
9 Consider using headings and sub-headings to guide the marker through your work and to help the flow of the work.
10 For most courses, even fairly basic ones, you are likely to be expected to use references throughout your work. This will help the markers to verify that you are acquainted with the sources of the theory you use. Many training-centre handbooks have information in them about referencing and will state what system they would like you to use. For example, the American Psychological Association (APA) and the Harvard referencing style both use a system of author and date in brackets, which is placed in the text; while other institutes prefer the Vancouver style of referencing, a system of numbered end-notes.

Learning how to study may be experienced as a challenge in its own right. Sam found the studying easier said than done. He said:

> I had left school with no qualifications nearly 30 years before joining the course and, although I was enjoying it, I found the whole reading and written work gruelling. I explained this to my tutor who suggested I went to student services for a dyslexia test. I completed the assessment and discovered that I was dyslexic. At first I felt embarrassed but the support worker was very kind and I got lots of advice, technical support and help. In fact without that help I don't think I would have passed the course. It has also helped make sense why I have struggled all my life with reading and remembering things particularly.

The purpose of coursework and assignments is to give you the opportunity to demonstrate what you know, to establish your strengths and to identify any areas for development, sometimes called 'learning edges'. Your trainer will give you constructive feedback on your coursework and assignments; this will include the presentation, how clearly you have conveyed your ideas, whether you have met specific learning outcomes, how well you demonstrated your understanding of theory through its application to your practice and some ideas for improvement. Some trainees tend to focus on the negative, and discount the positive; I invite you to read the comments carefully in order to enjoy and celebrate what you have done well, and to consider what you may like to do to help you with the areas for development.

Assignments and impending exams, particularly final exams, can be quite unsettling, and the cause of varying levels of anxiety for the trainees, sometimes coinciding with a revisit to the 'conscious incompetence' stage of learning (Robinson, 1974) mentioned in Chapter 5. For some trainees this may include the possibility of polarization, a form of black-and-white thinking where trainees think about themselves and their work only as good or bad, right or wrong, or in terms of passing or failing.

You may like to consider using your learning contract to specify in advance what help you will need, and how you will get it, during this stage of your training. Consider too that your trainers will probably have completed something similar during their training (phase four of transformational learning; see Chapter 5); so think about having a tutorial if you would like some additional support.

'We've got this enormous fairytale of ideas'

Final oral and written examinations are intended to assess you and your skills to see whether you are competent enough to work as an independent counsellor or psychotherapist. A number of my research participants had taken their qualifying examination over twenty years ago. They told me that they had had no preconceived ideas about what their exam experience would be like, beyond knowing the structure it would take. For example, Harriet said:

> I mainly heard a description about it. I didn't have any real positive or negative stories. Just more of a description of the basic process . . . nowadays there's a fantastic body of history into which people tap which engenders hopes, fears, fantasies, desires, excitements, etc., etc., you know, so we've got this enormous fairytale of ideas, and what have you, out of which people can construct narratives which frighten or encourage themselves. That wasn't there for us.

These stories have developed over time, and may dissuade a trainee from taking that final step; the tales get passed on like exaggerated anecdotes. Rose said:

> I've heard stories saying that the written exam is tough, that some people had to resubmit it and that the oral exam was quite traumatic for some people. I've seen some people get very stressed and heard that others were quite, well, felt quite unfairly treated, sort of, hidden process going on, examiners vying with each other or the process being a bit fuzzy, blurred, uncomfortable. The impression I got was that it's not a positive experience.

Rose's description was typical of some of the stories heard from the research participants about final exams. Whether a person chooses to take the final examination often has significant personal meaning. As Charlotte said:

> I was determined to get through. I found the coursework and especially the dissertation hard work as I hadn't done any research before but I wanted to prove to myself that I'm not stupid and I did that by getting my degree. I am very proud of what I have achieved.

What I discovered in my research was that the stories that people had heard about final exams usually did not reflect their own experiences. As Rose continues:

> I loved the oral exam, I had a great time, I had prepared well and I felt confident. I had a lovely board of examiners. I got high marks. I think it was a good experience because I had prepared well, and I was well supported by colleagues and friends.

John said:

> They only examined me on one tape. They asked me some interesting questions, you know, some that I really had not thought of . . . I was aware of finding it difficult at times . . . it was kind of challenging and in some ways I would have liked to have been more stretched.

Sue said:

> I didn't get a particularly high mark but I wasn't bothered with that. I passed and that is all that mattered to me.

For some people, the stories that surround final exams serve as a reason not to take them. Charlie says:

> I have probably been collecting the horror stories, rather than the success stories, to satisfy my need for not taking it because deep down I believe I'll never be good enough. I could see every reason why they would fail me, I wasn't looking at every reason why they would pass me but then I haven't put myself forward to be considered to take the exam.

Almost all of the participants in my research who did not take their final exams had, for various reasons, decided not to be a counsellor or psychotherapist. Although they had got a lot from the training a few of them recognized that they still held beliefs about their inability to succeed, which meant that they were holding themselves back in terms of fulfilling their potential. This highlights the influence of negative beliefs in someone's life script. You may choose to consider processing some of these areas in personal therapy in order to clarify how your life script may influence your thoughts and feelings towards any assessment processes, and your performances within them.

Personal challenges

During your training you may become very passionate about what you are learning, and this might be frustrating for friends and family who may not share your zeal and enthusiasm. One of the main challenges that the research participants commented on was that more personal change was involved than they had imagined. This may sound dramatic, but once you are on this road there is usually no turning back. You cannot un-experience what you have experienced, and you cannot unlearn what you have learned. Also, at times, our training may take us away from our family, and this may cause some difficulty for all involved.

Charlotte had to travel over 200 miles to her new training group, and this had an impact on her and her family. She said:

> Because my new training group was so far away I had to leave home the day before so I would be there for the Saturday morning. I didn't actually mind the travelling, in fact I found it really helpful in terms of giving me time to process the training weekend before I got home and had to be 'mum' again. I couldn't have done it without the support of my husband. I know he and the children hated me going. The children tended to play up when I was away and I'd get phone calls from them asking me go home. I used to feel very guilty leaving the family one weekend a month.

Fiona's marriage was affected by her training:

> I had been married for about 15 years when I started my psychotherapy training. I would have said our marriage was OK but as time went on I began to see the cracks in our relationship. We ended up separating as we couldn't seem to find a way to work together to make our marriage work.

Gerry's experience was helped by having a supportive partner. She said:

> I lapped up everything on my course, I just loved it all. Yes it got tricky at times but I have a good relationship with my partner which made it much easier. When I had assignments to write he would look after the children so I could study. He would read through my work and often come up with helpful ideas for punctuation and grammar. After each training day I would often come home to my dinner on the table; I felt well looked after. He was encouraging of me doing the training, he believed in me.
>
> The children were only babies when I started, so all the child development information was great. I could see how the children were going through their developmental stages. Sleepless nights, tantrums and squabbles played havoc with my intention to hold them with 'unconditional positive regard' at times. At first I would feel very critical of myself for not being able to be this calm, composed parent who didn't raise their voice but after a while I also realized that I am a human being and at times I do raise my voice, and that I will make mistakes.

The most significant outcome from my research was the recognition that all the participants I interviewed changed their lives as a direct result of undertaking the training.

Another cause of disillusionment can be the realization that training, counselling or psychotherapy isn't a panacea; it cannot solve every problem. We cannot fix our family, partner or parents, or, sometimes, not even ourselves. This is when the real underlying reason for starting the training in the first place can come to light. Have a look at the questions posed in Chapter 1, and at the start of Chapter 4, and see if you can clarify your underlying motivation.

Paula considered that her main difficulty was personal to her. She said:

> The biggest personal challenge – but it also made me want to keep being there – was that I was so shy, and so depressed, and so insecure, that I wouldn't get up and participate in the training, but I knew that my being there was helpful . . . but it was difficult for me to be there in that I was nervous and didn't want to be called on, or put on the spot about having to do something publicly.

Paula's experience was not uncommon; a number of the research participants admitted that they had felt a mixture of excitement and fear during their training, often feeling 'on the edge' in terms of their own comfort and possible exposure, and that, at times, this tension made the training quite exhausting. As Wendy said:

> I would often leave the training weekend 'brain-dead', there was so much going on. I could barely string a sentence together.

A number of research participants commented on how anger was addressed on their course. Jim talks about how he was confronted by a new trainer. He said:

> She [the trainer] said [to me], 'Your questions are really, really good. I've noticed that they all have an angry edge to them. Since you've never met me, it's unlikely that you're angry with me but you're clearly angry about something, or angry at somebody.' Nobody had ever pointed that out to me before, with such clarity; I thought, 'I'm going to learn how to do this.'

'I need a balance in my life'

Counselling and psychotherapy training is not something you can easily 'switch off' from in the way that you can with other types of courses. This is the time when the support of your friends and family, as well as your peers, can be so important. You may like to consider having an agreement with your partner, or family, about how much time this course is going to take up, and discuss how you will allow for taking time out and spending time with your partner, friends and family. For many, it is all too easy to say, 'Just another hour, and I'll join you', only to discover that three hours have passed, the dog hasn't been walked, the sun has set and you can't go out, you haven't spoken to your friend recently, the novel you wanted to read has gone unread, and your partner has gone to bed. As Toni put it:

> I neglected my husband and family. My course became everything for me. In the end my husband gave me an ultimatum: 'It's either me and the children or the

> course.' He shocked me; I hadn't realized how ignored and abandoned he felt. I regret that but thanks to him we found a way for me to complete the course by putting a boundary around college, placing a limit on how many evenings the studying took up; ensuring our weekend family time was protected and spending at least two evenings a week as a couple. I'm glad to say we're doing fine now.

But for Sandi:

> All I seemed to do was work; I went to work each day to do my paid job, then I also had two voluntary placements that I went to every week after work. What with supervision, training course meetings, home study groups and personal therapy there was no free time left at the end of the week. My friends gave up phoning me and asking me out. When the course finished I felt alone, bereft and depressed. What I learned from that whole experience is that I need a balance in my life of work and social time with friends.

'It is one hell of a lot of work!'

Finally, the amount of training, personal therapy and client hours, plus all the necessary coursework, is a significant undertaking. Counselling and psychotherapy training requires considerable resources in terms of time, money, commitment and 'head space'. Even the best informed of trainees may be unaware of the personal impact the training will have on them, and their family.

In essence, Greta summed up psychotherapy training when she said:

> It is a bloody long process, and you've really got to know that you want to do it. You have to be really motivated and dedicated to keep going. I think training to be a psychotherapist, in particular, is hard. It's not just the book learning, is it? It's all the other things, like the psychiatric placement, gaining all those clinical, supervision and therapy hours, and a lot of people have to do all this and a full-time job besides; that takes some stamina.
>
> It is one hell of a lot of work. It can take up to eight years to gain the final qualification and professional registration.

Professional development

One of the biggest frustrations that a number of the research participants experienced was the realization that there was no certainty of getting a job after they had completed their training. Paul's story was reflected by a number of research participants. He said:

> I was in year three when I realized how hard it was going to be to make a living out of this work. I went to a workshop being run by a local counselling organization and a number of the therapists there were talking about their difficulty in finding jobs and clients.

Paul did continue with his training, and he found work with a drugs and alcohol rehabilitation team. (See Chapter 7 for more information on employment opportunities.)

Some trainees felt tested when applying theory to practice. Robin said:

> I had no idea how difficult it would be to apply theory to my practice. Some of what I learned is only just starting to make sense to me now, a year after I finished my training.

Other participants said that applying theory to their practice was one of the more complex areas of training, and that they had learned this skill in their supervision sessions rather than on their training course. Claire said:

> Even though I finished my training three years ago I think only now do I really have a better handle on what I'm doing. For example, last session I was explaining to my supervisor about an experience I was having with a client: I felt angry with her because she was complaining about her job and not doing anything about it. Initially my supervisor and I explored my anger and what it may mean for me and then he said, 'Do you think others get angry with her?' I replied, 'Yes, I think so.' My supervisor then said, 'It sounds to me as though you may be experiencing what others feel when in contact with your client. So in the transference you feel angry and if you were to act it out with your client that would be your counter transferential response.' I suddenly understood transference and counter transference in a way I had not done so before.

'I don't know who was more nervous, me or my client'

Seeing your first client can be exciting and scary at the same time: exciting because you are now moving forward in terms of your professional development, and scary because you are fearful of making a mistake. Good support from your peers, trainers and supervisor, as well as friends and family, may help you at this time. You might like to do a grounding exercise before your first client session to settle yourself, and to be as fully present as you can be. Your client is likely to be nervous, too; the more grounded you are, the more relaxed they are likely to be.

Sally says of her experience with her first client:

> I don't know who was more nervous, me or my client. I was shaking with nerves beforehand; Jane, who runs the placement, took me into her office and we had a wide-ranging conversation about life, the universe and everything which settled me and I felt much more grounded after that although I think my hands were a little sweaty. I could see my client through the window in the door of the counselling room and then she came in. I could see she was nervous too, she kept twisting a tissue round and round and bits were dropping onto the floor. We said hello and our session began.

Placements usually offer a three- to four-hour block on the same day, at the same time each week, so you may consider accounting for this in your diary. Another aspect you may like to bear in mind is that sometimes clients will turn up, and sometimes they will not. Failure to attend occurs most frequently in a voluntary or NHS setting, or when working with the 14 to 25 years age group. It may be useful to have more than one placement so that you are more easily able to gain your clinical practice hours in order to qualify. Simon had one placement, and said:

> I used to get very frustrated when clients did not turn up, especially at the beginning and end of the course. At the beginning my frustration was about my need to 'get going' and later it was more about, 'I want to finish and get my diploma'.

You may find it helpful to take your difficult feelings to your supervisor, or to your therapist, and let them help you to process what you are experiencing. Expressing your annoyance or frustration with friends and family if a client does not attend (DNA) can relieve the stress, but bear in mind that you cannot go into any detail about that client because you would be breaking their confidentiality and breaching codes of ethics.

At various stages during your training, you will be asked to clarify how many clinical and supervision hours you have completed. In order to qualify and to gain accreditation or registration, you will be asked to produce this log, or information from it. You may like to consider starting one at the beginning of your placement and update it regularly. I offer some suggested templates in Appendix 3 that you may like to use. If you leave it until you are about to finish training, or applying for accreditation, you will have to wade through three or four, or more, years of diaries to collate your hours.

Money

Many research participants had a realization part way through their training that they would probably not earn the income they had hoped for when embarking on their course. The reality is that while many people do make a reasonable living out of their counselling or psychotherapy, some do not. A number of participants said that it took longer than expected to build up a thriving practice, that they had needed to stay determined and focused and to devote quite a lot of time and energy to marketing and networking. (See Chapter 7 for more information on setting up a private practice.) Charlotte said:

> I have a successful practice now but it has taken me a long time to feel confident that I will get enough clients. During the early years I would give talks to various organizations such as the WI [Women's Institute] and Mother's Union about the benefits of counselling and psychotherapy as well as offering free taster sessions for prospective clients at health and wellbeing fairs and networking with other therapists. I spent money on advertising, some

> of which worked, and developed a website which was effective. Being self-employed can be hard work at times but I do think it is worth it.

A few people had a different experience with obtaining work. As Janice put it:

> I think trainees need to have a bit more of a realistic idea of how therapists find work because that's something that took me a long time to find out. I think, initially, when people say, 'Well, okay. You're charging something like thirty pounds an hour for clients, and you can see up to twenty clients a week', and people go, 'Mmmmm. Thirty pounds an hour times twenty? This is how much income I can have', and my experience is nothing like that. I know of a number of my peers who, one after the other, have stopped working as a therapist because they can't make it work financially.

A number of others were able to get a paid job on the back of volunteering. Gary said:

> I undertook a placement with a drugs and alcohol charity. I worked with them for five years alongside my training course and day job as a theatre technician. It was hard work but it all paid off because a vacancy arose for a paid full-time counsellor at the centre and, I think partly because they knew me and my work, I got the job.

The majority of the people I interviewed who had been qualified for some time also undertook additional related work, such as offering supervision and training to supplement their income. One issue that was mentioned by some of the participants was the level of fees they could charge. In some areas, where the market is saturated with counsellors and psychotherapists, the thought was that fees needed to be kept lower. In some rural areas, the usual fees range from £25 to £35/€30 to €40 per hour (2014 prices), or, if working in a city, a therapist may be able to charge more, say £35 to £45/€40 to €50 as a newly qualified counsellor or psychotherapist. The other consideration you may wish to think about is that, for those who are self-employed, and certainly when setting out, therapy work is not usually a Monday-to-Friday, nine-to-five job. Some clients may be able to see you during the day but others may wish to attend after their work has finished. Further, because of the personal impact of the work, you may choose to limit the number of clients you see a day; a number of the research participants said they limited their practice to between four and six clients a day, on three or four days a week.

'Financially, I'm not sure if it's viable'

Finance clearly plays a significant part in trainees' expectations of training, their lifestyle and future plans. One of the commonly cited reasons for not continuing in training is the cost of doing the training plus the added expenses, for example, of personal therapy, supervision, books, exam preparation or accreditation workshops, continuing professional development, and insurance. This was sometimes accompanied by a perceived loss in quality of life due to reduced disposable income and uncertainty about whether it would be worth taking the necessary financial risk. Liz says:

> I have thought about going part-time from my day job, and seeing clients one day per week, but I'm worried that I won't have the same money. Financially, I'm not sure if it's viable.

There are few other professional training programmes that require such a significant financial input from the trainee with no guarantee of seeing a substantial financial return on their investment. Once in the profession, however, subsequent training and expenditure tends to be for the development of a niche, or specialism.

The costs make training, and psychotherapy training in particular, somewhat exclusive, with an absence of equality of opportunity, because only those who can afford it are able to train. This inequality is a political issue and is a source of concern. Is it acceptable that only those who are better off financially can afford to do this training? Is it fair that potential trainees with a wealth of life experience are denied the opportunity to train because they cannot afford it?

If you are keen to do the training but are financially challenged, you may like to find out whether your course provider operates a bursary scheme, or whether you can pay in instalments. Another option may be to go to your local public library and research the help that enables people to find funding. The following books are usually kept in the reference section and so cannot be borrowed, so you will need a pen and paper:

- *The Educational Grants Directory*, published by the Directory of Social Change (DSC)
- *A Guide to Grants for Individuals in Need* (DSC)
- *Directory of Grant Making Trusts* (DSC)
- *The Guide to the Major Trusts* (DSC, in two volumes)
- *Charities Digest*, published by Waterlow
- *The Grants Register*, published by Palgrave Macmillan.

There are also online services such as:

- The Charity Commission. Use the advanced search option to find charities who will give grants to individuals – www.charity-commission.gov.uk, and, for Northern Ireland, www.charitycommissionni.org.uk
- Turn2us – www.turn2us.org.uk
- Prospects – www.prospects.ac.uk/funding_postgraduate_study.htm
- GRANTnet – an online database – www.grantnet.org.uk
- Charity Choice – an online database – www.charitychoice.co.uk

- Philanthropy Ireland – an online service that offers funding, grants and links to various organizations. The grants tend to be only via charities and organizations, rather than directly to individuals, but this may be a good place to start your search for funding – www.philanthropy.ie/information/grant-seekers
- Studentfinance.ie – www.studentfinance.ie
- Citizens Information – www.citizensinformation.ie

When going through the directory and putting in any application, it is important that you are well informed about all the aspects of your course so that you can identify whether you, and the course you are proposing to take, meet the donating organization's eligibility criteria. Obtaining money through charitable trusts and grant-making organizations can be a long process, so you may like to start applying in plenty of time.

'Am I worth it?'

Money can be understood as a metaphor. If a person uses cost as a reason for not doing the training, it could be that they do not feel they are getting much value out of it; or it could be that as the journey of counselling and psychotherapy training tends to be a very personal one, they do not feel worthy enough to spend that amount of money on themselves. If you consider you are not getting value for money, then this is an issue that you may like to take up with the training provider. If you feel that you are not worth spending such sums of money on for your personal and professional development then you may choose to explore this in your therapy.

Conclusion

This chapter has focused on a number of the common challenges that some trainees may face when undertaking their counselling or psychotherapy training, including the impact on personal relationships, completing clinical placements, writing assignments, and undertaking final examinations, together with the influence of myths and stories on those processes. In the following chapter regulation, accreditation and employment opportunities are discussed and explored.

Here are some questions that may help you with some of the issues raised in this chapter.

Questions for you

1. What is your motivation, or inspiration, for doing the training? Could your motivation be hidden from you?
2. Have you calculated all the costs of the training, including course fees, personal therapy, supervision, books, travelling expenses, accommodation etc.?
3. In the light of all the costs that have been identified in this chapter, can you afford to do it?
4. Who will help and support you when the training starts to get challenging; when you start to question yourself, your motivation and your relationships?

5 Have you got the time to do the training – not just the attendance on the course, but all the extra requirements, like personal therapy, seeing clients, supervision, self-study and any peer or home study groups you may join?
6 How confident are you about writing assignments? If you are not confident, who can you ask for help?
7 Who will you ask to proof-read your assignments before you submit them?

Questions to ask your partner, family and friends

1 'Will you support me to do this training?'
You may find it beneficial to ask specifically for what you need, for example, looking after the children, making the dinner, doing the shopping, paying the bills or doing various jobs around the house.
2 'Will you help towards the costs?'
If you need to rely on someone else to support you financially, you may both find it helpful to have a clear and explicit agreement regarding how much money you will need.

A question to ask your employer

1 'Will you be supportive of me undertaking counselling or psychotherapy training? If so, will you be able to help me with fees, time off, or study leave?'
If you can show that your training will help you in your work, and your employer has a training budget, they may be willing to make a contribution towards your course costs. If they don't have such a budget, they may still be willing to let you have some time off, go to flexible working, or reduce your hours to help you complete the course.

Questions to ask the trainer

1 'Where did you do your training, and who were your trainers?'
The answer you get here may help you to find out whether the trainers on your course have completed a similar type and level of training.
2 'What are all the costs for the training, per year?'
They will be able to give you the course costs, and may then give you an idea of the additional costs.
3 'What financial help is there to support trainees who are financially challenged?'
They may have a list of local charities or organizations, as well as the ones mentioned in this chapter, which may be able to offer financial aid. Ask about paying in instalments and getting career development loans too.
4 'What is your policy with regard to tutorials? Are they per term, per module, or per year? Is there an additional cost? Is there any flexibility should I need more?'
5 'What examinations are there with regard to interim and final qualifications?'

Chapter 7

The outcomes of counselling and psychotherapy training

In this chapter, I will give you an idea of the employment opportunities that may be available once you have completed your training, and then I will introduce you to some of the relevant political issues that are currently evident in the profession. I will then give you details of some of the various accreditation and professional registration systems that may be open to you once you have qualified. The reason for including this information in the book is because the training course you choose may well dictate which accreditation or professional registration options you will have available to you. In turn, this may influence your opportunities for employment, and your eligibility to be on either an Accredited Voluntary Register accredited by the Professional Standards Authority for Health and Social Care (PSA), or, in the case of arts therapists, the statutory register held by the Health and Care Professions Council (HCPC).

Employment opportunities

Having spent a number of years in training, and invested quite a large sum of money on that training, and on personal therapy and supervision, it is important to know what employment opportunities exist for you post-qualification.

This will vary from region to region, but the blunt truth is that there are far more trained counsellors and psychotherapists than there are jobs available.

A 2012 review of national job vacancies within the NHS revealed just four jobs for counsellors and eight for psychotherapists, compared to 1,511 for nursing staff and 428 for consultants (NHS, 2012). This was much the same six months later, when there were five vacancies for counsellors and none for psychotherapists (NHS, 2013). A wider national search on the internet showed a further 23 vacancies for paid counsellors and psychotherapists, with the majority being part-time posts. There were, however, a number of vacancies for voluntary work, mainly for counsellors.

The best places to look for vacancies are:

The BACP Jobs Online facility – www.bacp.co.uk/jobs Here, you can view basic information as a member of the public, but you will need to be a BACP member to get fuller details. The vacancies advertised range from voluntary positions to self-employed and employed opportunities.

Therapy Today This is a BACP printed journal available free to members, or, otherwise, via a subscription.

NHS NHS vacancies are advertised at www.jobs.nhs.uk.

Local press Local media may also publish vacancies, so consider looking in your local newspaper, or listening to your local commercial radio station.

The Guardian *newspaper* The Wednesday edition, or its website (http://jobs.guardian.co.uk/jobs/social-care/counselling), nationally advertises jobs in the health and care sector.

Another option is to consider your local primary care (GP) counselling or psychotherapy service provider for any possible local vacancies. Having said that, in many areas, since the introduction of Improving Access to Psychological Therapies (IAPT), the range of counselling and psychotherapy available within the primary care service has been seriously reduced, with limited choice for patients, and restrictions on counsellors and psychotherapists who wish to work in the NHS. If you are looking to work within the IAPT system, then you may be better off training as a psychological well-being practitioner (PWP), although this will limit your options outside the NHS. The role of PWPs is fairly new in terms of its development, but it is worth considering as an option, especially if you do want to work in the NHS.

National Occupational Standards

In some areas of employment you may be expected to be able to demonstrate how you meet the national occupational standards (NOS) set by Skills for Health for cognitive behavioural therapy, family and systemic therapy, humanistic therapy and psychoanalytic/psychodynamic therapy. According to their website, the national occupational standards:

> describe the skills, knowledge and understanding needed to undertake a particular task or job to a nationally recognised level of competence. They focus on what the person needs to be able to do, as well as what they must know and understand to work effectively.
>
> They cover the key activities undertaken within the occupation in question under all the circumstances the job holder is likely to encounter.
>
> (Skills for Health, 2011)

Full details of the competencies can be found on the Skills for Health website (https://tools.skillsforhealth.org.uk). You may wish to bear these in mind when applying for posts.

What about private practice?

One option that increasing numbers of counsellors and psychotherapists consider is the setting up of a private practice. There are a number of authors (Bor and Stokes, 2010; Hodson, 2012; McMahon *et al.*, 2005; Warren, 2010) who offer advice and guidance in this area. This is an option for many, but be warned: some counselling courses only qualify you to work within an agency setting. One such example is the Counselling and Psychotherapy Central Awarding Body's (CPCAB) level four 'Diploma in Therapeutic Counselling' and level five 'Diploma in Psychotherapeutic Counselling'. You will need to be clear about this when choosing your course. The CPCAB are the only awarding body to clearly state that the qualification is for working within an agency, and the majority make no reference to any limits on practice post-qualification. This leads the potential student to think that there are no limits for them after training; but it is quite probable that there will be limits in a professional sense, even though the legal limitations are unclear. The professional limitations are especially applicable to some of the courses aimed at levels one to four. (For more information on the levels of training, see Chapter 1.)

Working in private practice does not suit everyone. In reality, it is unwise to consider setting up a private practice unless you have at least a few years of clinical experience under your belt. Many psychotherapy training programmes encourage trainees to set up a private practice during their training. Where psychotherapy training is a secondary qualification after counselling or other health/social-work training, this may not raise many concerns, but if the trainee has no clinical experience, then a placement within an organization would be the preferred option. This protects and supports not only the counsellor or psychotherapist but also, and more importantly, their clients. Most counselling trainings do not support the setting up of a private practice during training. Furthermore, if you are considering some form of accreditation or registration system, you need to be aware of the requirements of that system. (See later in this chapter for more information.)

Additionally, private practice can be a lonely and isolating experience; it is hard work, and can be very challenging, as well as rewarding. The BACP offers a range of information sheets, including *Practical aspects of setting up a counselling service* (BACP, 2010c: E1) and *Professional aspects of setting up a counselling and psychotherapy service* (BACP, 2008: P1).

You may wish to consider the following:

1 Where will you set up your practice, e.g. from home, or from rented rooms, or a therapy centre?
2 If you want to work from home, do you have a suitable room? How will having clients in the house affect you, and other members of your household? If you can have a separate entrance, that usually makes it easier. What about safety? Will you arrange for there to be someone else in the house while you are working? Lone-working is not ideal, and could be considered unwise. Do consider your own and your clients' safety. You may also wish to think

about having a contingency plan should you become ill or unable for work for an extended period of time. The BACP (2010e: P14) information sheet *The impact of personal crisis on independent therapists' practice – what is your contingency plan or plan B?* may be a helpful starting point.

3 If you want to work from a centre, find out about their fees, terms and conditions, and what days and times are available. You may wish to reflect on whether this will fit in with your 'day-job', if you have one. Again, take into account whether there will be anyone else in the building while you are working, as you may find this helpful from a safety point of view.

4 To work from home, you may want to see if your house insurance offers public liability protection, and, if so, you may decide to let your insurance company know that you will be seeing clients at home. Under these circumstances, some insurance companies will not insure you for theft, unless there is forced entry to the building. Others may put other exclusions or limitations on your insurance. There are specific policies available for people who work from home. If you work from a centre, the insurance may be provided by them.

5 Whether you work from home, or from a centre, it may be an idea to take out professional indemnity insurance. It is not compulsory, but you may find the benefits helpful should a client, or a third party, make a complaint against you. This can happen even to experienced and conscientious practitioners.

6 You may also wish to consider joining a professional body, which has its own codes of ethics and professional practice. Accredited registration may also help you to obtain clients. Being a member of a body can be useful in terms of having access to continuing professional development (CPD) training events and networking opportunities, as well as keeping abreast of events in the wider counselling and psychotherapy arena.

7 How and where you market your counselling or psychotherapy service, if you choose to do so, will be important. Where and how will you find your clients? Do you want to set up your own website? Where do you plan to advertise? Will you advertise, or hope to have referrals only by personal recommendation? The BACP (2010b: A3) information sheet *Getting the best out of your directory entries and websites* provides some helpful information, offering hints and tips and advice on advertising and marketing.

8 If you are going to set yourself up as self-employed, you may wish to contact the Inland Revenue for guidance and advice on what records you will need to keep, and on how you go about registering as self-employed. You may also wish to speak with a certified accountant who will also be able to offer you useful guidance.

9 It is useful to undertake some market research to see if there is a demand for what you offer, and to find out what is already available nearby. This is time-consuming, and you may not like what you find out, but you may also be pleasantly surprised. This question may help you focus your marketing: what is your unique selling point (USP)?

10 Your market research will help you to identify what other therapists in the local area charge for their services, and this could help you in deciding your own scale of fees. The BACP (2010d: P2) information sheet *Charging for therapy in private practice – pitfalls and ethical issues* may also be helpful to you in deciding on your fees.

Can I work with children or young people?

Trainees commonly ask this question. The quick answer to this query is that there is nothing to stop you doing so, but, unless your training course specifically included training to work with children, or young people, you may not feel ethically competent enough to do so.

Working with children is specialized; it is not at all the same as working with adults as there are different ethical, legal, and, in some cases, training implications (Daniels and Jenkins, 2010; UKCP, 2008b, 2008c, 2008d) that are worth considering. As a minimum, anyone wishing to work with children would find it helpful to have been trained in a range of child-development theories, including psychological, cognitive and emotional developmental stages, and the growing field of neuroscience (Geldard and Geldard, 2007, 2009; Hughes, 2006; Hughes *et al.*, 2012; Perry, 2009; Sunderland, 2007; Tudor, 2007). Without this training, you may not be able to determine whether the behaviours you are seeing in the child are normal, healthy child-developmental stages, or whether there are issues that need to be addressed within the therapy. Theories of attachment, and how changes in a child's life can impact on them (Cozolino, 2006; Howe, 2005, 2011; Schore, 2012; Urwin and Sternberg, 2012; Wilkinson, 2010), will help a practitioner understand how well a child is relating, or attached, to their parents. Through this type of training, you will learn how to recognize developmental deficits, and how to use therapeutic play methods. Most basic (levels one to four) counselling courses will not contain this type of information. Many psychotherapy courses will provide some information on child development and theories of attachment, but are unlikely to include therapeutic play methods (Axline, 1990; Ray, 2011; Sunderland, 2001; Tait, 2012) unless they are primarily aimed at working with children.

Working with teenagers may be possible, depending upon the age and maturity of the client, but, even with teenagers, some training in the ages and stages of psychological, cognitive and emotional development can help you to recognize the difference between the normal challenges of being a teenager and what may actually need therapeutic input.

If these areas were not covered in your core training, you may wish to undertake a specific course that will train you to work with children and young people.

The UKCP has established the Faculty for the Psychological Health of Children, and holds a register of psychotherapists who have undergone a further accreditation process to demonstrate their ability to work with this client group.

The BACP has a Counselling Children and Young People (CCYP) division which publishes its own journal, runs CPD training days and offers a wealth of information and reading material specific to working with children and young people, while COSCA also provides a range of resources concerning working with children and young people. Whether you can work with children or young people is really a matter for your own ethical stance, the advice of your supervisor, and whether you consider that you have the necessary competence to work with this, or, indeed, any other client group.

What about other client groups?

Most counselling training courses, unless they state otherwise, are likely to train you to work with adults who have 'mild-to-moderate' mental health problems. Psychotherapy training will help you to develop your knowledge and skills to work with clients who have 'moderate-to-severe' and 'enduring' problems. If you complete a generic level four counselling diploma course you are likely to feel, and to be, competent to work with clients with mild symptoms of depression, anxiety, worry and stress, or relationship difficulties. If you complete a level five or six course, then you are probably going to be able to work with the same issues, but to a more moderate level. If you have current experience of working with a specific client group then you may feel confident working therapeutically with them once you have completed your training. As with working with children and young people, it is a matter for your own ethical stance whether you feel competent to work with any client.

Politics and counselling and psychotherapy

For a profession that claims to facilitate health and well-being, and personal growth and development, there are significant political problems that can cause difficulties in the provision of services. For example, the European Association for Psychotherapy (EAP) recognizes 21 different theoretical approaches, the BACP accredits courses reflecting 18 modalities (see Table 2.3) and the UKCP recognizes nearly 40 (Table 2.1). Within these different approaches, the respective therapists and professional bodies have a vested interest in wanting the public to see their approach as being the one that will help them with their problem(s). On the other hand, the policies of statutory bodies restrict client access to a handful of approaches, and agree a limited number of sessions for a limited range of issues.

The National Institute for Health and Clinical Excellence (NICE) guidelines promote cognitive behavioural therapy (CBT), and its variations, for a range of mental health problems, but CBT does not suit everyone. No one approach will suit every client, or address every issue. Research carried out by CBT practitioners into their work has given sufficient evidence to suggest their models work, but this does not mean that any other approach will not work equally well, or maybe even better. Some research (Elliott and Freire, 2011) suggests that person-centred therapy has similar success to CBT provided it is undertaken by properly trained person-centred therapists. Similarly, Widdowson (2012) has published interesting research into the use of transactional analysis for clients suffering from depression.

Alternatively, Asay and Lambert (1999) attribute the improvements from therapy to their being a result of four variables: expectancy, or hope, 15 per cent; the therapeutic relationship, 30 per cent; client variables and events external to the therapy, e.g. life events, 40 per cent; and therapist model and technique factors, only 15 per cent. This would suggest that it is the therapeutic relationship that is more significant in the successful outcome of therapy than the modality or techniques.

You may find it helpful to be aware of the politics that structure the relationships between the different modalities and professional organizations, such as how joining one organization may preclude you from joining another. For example, the British Association for Behavioural and Cognitive Psychotherapies (BABCP) does not recognize UKCP registration as a Psychotherapeutic Counsellor, or as a Psychotherapist, as evidence of a core profession, although they will accept members of the Association of Counsellors and Psychotherapists in Primary Care (CPC), an organizational member of the UKCP. This seems inconsistent, and rather arbitrary.

For the benefit of clients, and the future of counselling and psychotherapy, what is apparent is a clear need for well-planned and executed research into the effectiveness of all the theoretical approaches across a wide range of issues. When you approach a training provider, you may wish to ask about their own research: what do they do, how do they do it, and what are their findings? You might like to enquire about the possibilities of undertaking research yourself, which can be very rewarding and exciting. Alternatively, if your course does not offer the opportunity to do some research while you are training, you may consider doing some after you have qualified, or join in with a current research project. If you end up working within the NHS, you will fill in numerous forms for each of your clients that will constitute research into the effectiveness of the services you are providing.

Statutory regulation

In 2007, the UK government published a White Paper called *Trust, Assurance and Safety – The Regulation of Health Professionals in the 21st Century*. They wanted to bring in statutory regulation for 'applied psychologists, several groups of healthcare scientists, psychotherapists and counsellors and other psychological therapists' (Department of Health, 2007: 11). This would have brought counselling and psychotherapy into line with other allied professions, e.g. arts therapists, who have been regulated since 1997 (BAAT, 2012), and psychologists, who have been regulated since 2009 (British Psychological Society, 2011). This process was halted for counsellors and psychotherapists in the UK in May 2010, when there was a change of government. Discussion about statutory regulation in the Republic of Ireland is still ongoing.

The counselling and psychotherapy professional bodies did not complete the process of statutory regulation before the change of government due to their inability to agree on various issues. These included: the suitability of the Heath and Care Professions Council (HCPC) as the regulatory body; the definition of protected titles (e.g. 'counsellor', 'psychotherapist'); the creation of a core curriculum, or academic levels of training; the imposition of statutory regulation, and the impact on therapeutic work. There were also significant divisions in the counselling and psychotherapy community as a whole, with some bodies and groups generally in favour of statutory regulation, e.g. BACP and UKCP, and others vehemently opposed to it (Bates and House, 2004; Hogan, 1979, 2003; House, 1995, 2003; House and Totton, 1997; Mowbray, 1995; Musgrave, 2009; Parker, 1999; Parker and Revelli, 2008; Postle, 2007; Samuels, 2009). Many practitioners were fearful of what would happen to their jobs, and their clients, if regulation were to be imposed. Some argue that state regulation will not protect the public from abuse, but it will reduce autonomy in terms of client choice, and it 'medicalizes' the profession. Others view therapy as an art, rather than a science, and believe that regulation will not take into account the diversity of the work, the clients and the therapists, and that it will stifle creativity (Postle and House, 2009). Postle (2007) cautions that if the profession becomes too tightly bound by regulation, the very nature of the process of psychotherapy will become lost.

Thorne (2009) sums up the argument against regulation by stating that the proposals for it were:

> ill-conceived, based on paltry evidence, threaten creativity in a field which has been notably creative and responsible, will diminish rather than extend sources of help for the vulnerable and, in any case, must fail to achieve the very objectives they are intended to accomplish. For me, however, all these valid arguments tend to pale into insignificance beside the high probability that if these proposals enter the statute book, they will constitute yet another powerful encouragement for individuals to be wary of their fellows and to assume that trustworthiness is in short supply and can only be uneasily 'guaranteed' by state certification.
>
> (Thorne, 2009: 7)

Musgrave (2009) went further by stating that there would be 'unintended side effects' if state regulation went ahead, including:

- Course innovation will be constrained.
- Critical reflection, an activity that lies at the heart of good counselling and psychotherapy, will be inhibited as trainees are increasingly encouraged to rely on 'evidence based' guidelines, the justification for which is often tendentious and mostly poorly understood.
- Once counselling and psychotherapy are formally redefined as health interventions there will be increased reliance on flawed science and an over valuing of evidence from randomised controlled trials. This will eventually have the effect of restricting the range of therapies available.

- There will almost certainly be fewer volunteer counsellors.
- For similar reasons there will probably be fewer part-time, self-employed counsellors working just occasionally.
- There will be a corresponding increase in the number of hours more established counsellors work.
- People from black and minority ethnic communities are underrepresented in the field of counselling and psychotherapy. The costs of regulation will strengthen this bias within the field.

(Musgrave, 2009)

In February 2011, the government published a command paper entitled *Enabling Excellence: Autonomy and Accountability for Health and Social Care Staff* (Department of Health, 2011). This paper suggested that statutory regulation was not necessarily the way forward for many professions, and that 'assured voluntary registration' (AVR) would be more appropriate. Counselling and psychotherapy are not specifically mentioned in the paper, but it supersedes the earlier White Paper. When this paper was published, there were many who were temporarily relieved, although some (e.g. Postle, 2013) are not convinced that the proposed AVR is the way forward, either.

Others (Cooper and McLeod, 2010; Samuels, 1997; House and Totton, 1997; Tudor, 2011) advocate pluralism. According to Samuels:

> Pluralism is an attitude to conflict which tries to reconcile differences without imposing a false resolution on them or losing sight of the unique value of each position.
>
> (Samuels, 1997: 135)

Cooper and McLeod state that:

> a pluralist holds that there can be many 'right' answers to scientific, moral or psychological questions which are not reducible down to any one, single truth. Central to this standpoint is also the belief that there is no one, privileged perspective from which the 'truth' can be known.
>
> (Cooper and McLeod, 2010: 7)

> pluralistic working relied on a practical appreciation of the nature of collaboration, which is understood as a principled, ethical commitment to the valuing of human connectedness and community.
>
> (ibid.: 146)

Pluralism would certainly seem to be more in keeping with the counselling and psychotherapy field, which, in general, promotes acceptance, appreciation of difference and mutual respect. For the time being, AVR is the path being followed in the UK, but what may happen in the future is open to debate. What this does mean is that Arts Therapists, who are statutorily regulated, have protected titles, meaning that only those people who are properly qualified and registered with the HCPC can call themselves 'art therapists', 'drama therapists' or 'music therapists'. As counselling and psychotherapy are not statutorily regulated, then anyone can call themselves a 'counsellor' or 'psychotherapist', no matter what level of training they have; if, indeed, they have any at all.

Statutory regulation in the Republic of Ireland

In the Republic of Ireland, statutory regulation is still under discussion. If it is implemented, and you want to work there, then you may wish to consider whether you meet all the necessary requirements. Martina Vaughan, Chair of the Irish Council for Psychotherapy (ICP), gave me the following information:

> In regards to statutory regulation in Ireland the process is continuing at present with a Forum called the Psychological Therapies Forum meeting three to four times a year in order to bring all the agencies and representative bodies into some form of readiness for the eventual process of regulation. This is a slow process and there are many players and stakeholders involved so nothing is happening at speed.
>
> All training standards for psychotherapy in Ireland are set with reference to the EAP Training Standards Document (latest version July 2012). Graduates from these trainings then gain accreditation through one of the five Modalities of Psychotherapy which are Section Members of the umbrella body ICP.

The names of the five modalities are:

> Constructivist Psychotherapy
> Humanistic and Integrative Psychotherapy
> Cognitive Behavioural Psychotherapy
> Couple and Family Therapy
> Psychoanalytic Psychotherapy
>
> (Vaughan, M., Personal Communication, 4 October 2012)

Professional recognition

Some trainees have a clear idea of where they would like to work, which professional organization(s) they would like or need to join, or to which professional body, or bodies, they would like to align themselves. When considering which training course(s) to undertake, you may find it helpful to have an idea of what you would like to accomplish professionally, which could mean working in a particular field, or organization, or to achieve specific professional recognition. Once you know, you can then devise a path from where you are now to where you want to get to, and you will have an idea of what you need to do in order to achieve your goal. For example, if you think you would like to achieve BACP accreditation, you may choose to complete a BACP accredited training course, or one that meets the BACP training criteria for accreditation. Similarly, if you wanted to achieve UKCP registration you would then, in most cases, need to choose a programme that is run by an association that is an organizational member of a UKCP college. Later in this chapter, you will read that some of the accreditation or professional registration requirements are similar, but that others are quite different. You may find it useful to know this information at the start of your training, as otherwise it might come as an unwelcome surprise later on.

What is assured voluntary registration?

Assured voluntary registration (AVR) means that the Professional Standards Authority for Health and Social Care (PSA), previously called the Council for Healthcare Regulatory Excellence (CHRE), has expanded its role to include the setting of standards for organizations that hold voluntary registers for practitioners. These include counsellors, and psychotherapists, who provide health or social care services, but who are not required to be registered by law. Now that the standards have been set, the holders of a voluntary register can apply to the PSA for accreditation. Once approved, the register becomes known as an accredited register, and this recognition would then inform employers, commissioners and the public that anyone on the accredited register will have been assessed as having met the standards set by the register-holding organization, and that they follow a particular code of conduct. According to the PSA, the purpose of the scheme is to:

> enhance public protection and raise professional standards. The Authority sets high standards for organisations holding voluntary registers and accredited registers require their registrants to meet high standards of personal behaviour, technical competence and, where applicable, business practice.
>
> (PSA, 2013)

There are two main differences between assured voluntary registration and statutory regulation. The first is that assured voluntary registration is, as its name suggests, voluntary and not mandatory; counsellors and psychotherapists can choose whether to be on the register without this affecting their ability to practise, although it may affect their employability, as employers may choose to consider only applicants who are on the register. The second is that if someone is removed or struck off from a voluntary register, then that does not necessarily prevent them from continuing to see clients, even though they may have been subjected to disciplinary proceedings via their professional body, or to legal proceedings, or been referred to the Disclosure and Barring Service (DBS) (in England, Wales and Northern Ireland), the Protecting Vulnerable Groups (PVG) Scheme (in Scotland) or the Garda Central Vetting Unit (in the Republic of Ireland).

The development of the assured voluntary registration system for counselling and psychotherapy is still relatively recent, but it is likely to impact on newly qualified counsellors and psychotherapists in terms of the standards that the PSA sets for the organizations who wish to hold an accredited register. You may like to check whether the professional organization that you intend to join holds an accredited register.

Accreditation and registration systems

Whether you are for or against assured voluntary registration or statutory regulation, you may wish to keep up to date with other forms of accreditation or professional registration, some of which are more formalized than others.

If you are going to invest a significant amount of time, money and effort into your training, then you are likely to want to reap the rewards of all your hard work, and to be recognized by other professionals, potential employers and the general public. As statutory regulation of counselling and psychotherapy is not in place, at least for now, becoming accredited will distinguish you from another practitioner who is not so recognized, and to some it may demonstrate that you have a professional and ethical attitude to your work. Increasingly, employers are looking for counsellors or psychotherapists who are accredited, or registered, primarily with the BACP or UKCP in England and Wales, COSCA in Scotland, and IACP or ICP in the Republic of Ireland. In the UK, with assured voluntary registration, the practitioner may need to be on an accredited register that is recognized by the PSA, as employers may seek out the guarantee of a more professional standard of therapist. Certainly, by being on the accredited register you will be demonstrating a commitment to your profession.

There are a large number of different professional bodies in the UK and the Republic of Ireland, but there is not enough space in this chapter to outline all of them, or to detail their various requirements. The following organizations have been chosen because, between them, they hold the majority of memberships for counsellors and psychotherapists. The organizations are the BACP, BABCP, COSCA, IACP, ICP and UKCP. (See Table 7.1 for summaries of the training, supervision, and clinical practice requirements for accreditation or registration.) They all have one register for their members, except for the BABCP, which has three, and the UKCP, which has two. (In addition, the UKCP has different requirements for each college, as shown in Table 7.1.)

BABCP

The British Association for Behavioural and Cognitive Psychotherapies (BABCP) has three accreditation schemes, one each for Provisional, Full and PWP accreditation.

Provisional Accreditation requires the practitioner to be qualified and accredited in a core profession, e.g. psychology, psychiatry, nursing, counselling, occupational therapy, social work or education, prior to CBT training. The following

Table 7.1 Summary of accreditation requirements

	Hours of training	*Supervision*	*Clinical practice*
BACP (2013b)	450	150 hours 1.5 per month	450 At least 150 post-qualification
BABCP Provisional (2012b)	450, of which 200 are contact teaching hours	40 hours	200 hours
BABCP Full (2012d)	Additional 30 hours of CPD	1 hour per month	None stated
BABCP PWP (2012c)	Accredited course of 45 days or equivalent	25 clinical supervision 25 case management supervision	80 hours Min 6 months
COSCA (2012)	300 + 54 CPD (average of 18 per year)	Ratio 1:12	450 2 years post-qualification min of 60 hours per year
IACP (2013b)	450	Ratio of 1:8 during training and 1:10 or monthly afterwards	450 Min 100 during training
ICP (EAP, 2007)	500 to 800	150	300 to 600 hours
UKCP CCP (2009)	500	150	500 hours 200 during training
UKCP CFCST (2009)	450	1.5 per month for first three years the 12 hours per year	Not stated
UKCP CPJAC (2012)	Introductory year + 250 + 500 Tutorials	Included in training hours	Not stated but there must be at least two supervised training patients or groups or couples of not less than 18 months. The frequency of sessions needs to be congruent with training
UKCP CH-P (2008)	625 with a min of 500 classroom contact hours	Ratio 1:6	450 hours
UKCP HIPC (UKPC, 2011)	900, of which 600 are core training hours	Ratio 1:6	450 hours
UKCP PCIPC (2008)	450	Ratio 1:6	450 hours 100 during training

minimum standards are required, and are in addition to the number of training, supervision and clinical practice hours, as shown in Table 7.1:

> Half of the overall formal CBP training must focus on CBP skills development . . .
>
> A minimum of eight cases undertaken during training, covering at least three different problems types . . .
>
> Four of these cases written up and assessed as case studies (2000–4000 words).
>
> Three of these cases must have been closely supervised, using live (in vivo, video audio) assessment.
>
> (BABCP, 2012b)

Full accreditation needs to be completed 12 months after provisional accreditation has been awarded, and it requires a further 30 hours of continuing professional development training, with a minimum of one hour of clinical supervision per month.

With regard to PWPs, there are two routes to accreditation:

Route A For those PWPs who have graduated from an accredited, full, low-intensity (PWP) training course, the training based on a modular structure of four modules delivered over 45 days in total.

Route B For those who have sufficient previous training in a relevant, recognized core profession for PWP, and have also completed an accredited PWP top-up training consisting of modules one and two of the IAPT PWP National Curriculum. Applicants also have to demonstrate that they have met the competences for some of the essential core learning objectives as specified in the IAPT PWP National Curriculum for Modules three and four.

For both routes, in addition to the training, PWPs applying for accreditation need to have met the following criteria:

1. Have been accountable for their own professional practice to a senior member of the IAPT or equivalent service whilst working as a PWP continuously for the last six months.
2. Provide evidence of successfully completing training as a Psychological Wellbeing Practitioner on an Accredited Full PWP Course (*Route A*), or provide evidence of having a relevant recognised Core Professional Training, plus evidence of successfully completing top-up training on an Accredited PWP Course (*Route B*).
3. Evidence at least 80 hours of direct PWP clinical practice using the range of PWP assessment and intervention techniques.
4. Evidence at least 25 hours of Clinical Skills Supervision, and 25 hours of Clinical Case Management Supervision.
5. Sign a statement of intent to submit an application for re-accreditation in three years, and to sustain commitment to the theory and practice of PWP

working, Continuing Professional Development, Clinical Skills Supervision with a regular live element and Case Management Supervision.

6 Demonstrate knowledge and understanding of the therapeutic relationship and competence in the development, maintenance and ending of such relationships, evidenced through the Supervisor's Report.

7 Adhere to the BABCP Standards of Conduct, Performance and Ethics for members and be willing to be scrutinised in this adherence as required.

(BABCP, 2012c)

More information can be found on the BABCP website at www.babcp.com.

BACP

The BACP holds one accreditation register for both counsellors and psychotherapists, with no differentiation between the roles. Their standard for accreditation is for applicants 'to demonstrate the capacity for independent, competent, ethical practice' (BACP, 2013b: 2).

Therapists can only apply for accreditation if they have been in practice for at least three years.

The accreditation criteria, which are in addition to the number of training, supervision and clinical practice hours, as shown in Table 7.1, are that you need to be:

1 A member of BACP.
2 Covered by professional indemnity insurance.

When you submit your application you must be

3 Practising counselling or psychotherapy

and

> have an ongoing contract for counselling/psychotherapy supervision for a minimum of 1½ hours per month for each month in which practice is undertaken.
>
> (BACP, 2013b: 2–3)

Further criteria include your ability to convey your experience, knowledge and understanding through reflecting on your practice, to apply supervision to practice, and to demonstrate self-awareness and a commitment to continuing professional development via accounts of your clinical practice and the application of supervision.

Please note that the BACP does not accept home-study or distance learning courses to meet the training requirement.

The BACP also states in its criteria for accreditation of training courses that students need to have been in a supervised placement as part of their training, and, further, that they do not consider private practice appropriate for inexperienced students (BACP, 2009b).

More information on BACP accreditation can be found on the BACP website at www.bacp.co.uk/accreditation.

COSCA

Similarly, Counselling and Psychotherapy in Scotland (COSCA) also has its own accreditation system for both counsellors and psychotherapists. The requirements to become a Practitioner Member, in addition to the number of training, supervision and clinical practice hours, as shown in Table 7.1, are that:

> The cohesive core of the training needs to take place within a period of five years . . . . Additional training needs to be in substantial and planned blocks, and a clear progression from the core training.
>
> Practitioner Members are required to have a cumulative practice base of 200 hours, with an average of two hours per week; a supervision ratio of 1:12 and have achieved 54 cumulative hours of continuing professional development with an average of 18 hours per annum over the last three years.
>
> Applicants need to abide by COSCA's Statement of Ethics and Code of Practice and reflect knowledge of the statement throughout their application.
>
> (COSCA, 2012)

Application for recognition as a Practitioner Member can only be undertaken after a minimum of two years post-qualification. Additional training, clinical practice and supervision hours, similar to those laid down by the BACP, are required for full accreditation. More information on COSCA accreditation can be found on the COSCA website at www.cosca.org.uk.

IACP

In the Republic of Ireland, the Irish Association for Counselling and Psychotherapy (IACP) has its own accreditation system with very similar requirements to that of the BACP. It requires that, in addition to the number of training, supervision and clinical practice hours, as shown in Table 7.1, an applicant will:

> Have completed a Core Counselling Course, a minimum of at least two years' full- or part-time duration, which satisfies the criteria for course recognition by IACP including the following:
>
> A detailed study of at least one major school of counselling/psychotherapy with an introduction to other schools/models of counselling/psychotherapy for comparison and contrast.

A minimum of 50 hours of personal therapy during training.
Assessment of applicants for suitability before being selected onto a course.
Certification of having satisfactorily completed course.

After training an applicant will have completed [the following]:

- at least 75 percent [of their supervision] will have been in one-to-one supervision with a supervisor who didn't supervise the candidate during training and who wasn't a core trainer or assessor on the core course . . .
- [The clinical practice experience] needs to cover a variety of presenting problems.
- Supervision needs to take place at least once a month when the counsellor/psychotherapist is actively seeing or available to see clients.
- Have been in ongoing supervision in Ireland with the same supervisor for one year immediately preceding application.
- Supervisor's report/reports on all work covering the 450 hours will be submitted with the application.

Choose a supervisor who is

- an IACP Accredited Supervisor
- a BACP Accredited Supervisor or
- an IAHIP Accredited Supervisor.

The 450 hours of practice need to be carried out over a minimum of two years and a maximum of five years after the successful completion of a counselling or psychotherapy training.

In special circumstances an applicant may apply in writing to have their application for accreditation considered where more than five years have elapsed, but this will be at the discretion of the Accreditation Committee.

(IACP, 2012)

More information on accreditation with IACP can be found on their website at www.irish-counselling.ie.

ICP

The Irish Council for Psychotherapy acts as an awarding body on behalf of the European Association for Psychotherapy, conferring the European Certificate of Psychotherapy (ECP) in the Republic of Ireland. (See later in this chapter for more information on the ECP.)

UKCP

The United Kingdom Council for Psychotherapy (UKCP) holds two registers, one for psychotherapists and one for psychotherapeutic counsellors. Within the UKCP there are nine colleges. A college is a:

> collection of members – organizational and individual – who share a philosophy of psychotherapy. The college holds standards for education, training and practice that are both compatible with UKCP generic standards, and individual to the college's philosophy. Colleges are responsible for accepting members into full membership of UKCP and all existing members must belong to a college.
>
> (UKCP, 2013b)

In addition to the minimum standards of education and training, each of these colleges has additional, and varying, standards required for registration (see Table 7.1). To give you a flavour of the requirements, the Humanistic and Integrative Psychotherapy College (HIPC), at present one of the largest colleges, calls for the following minimum requirements for accreditation and registration, in addition to the number of training, supervision and clinical practice hours, as shown in Table 7.1:

> The supervised hours will need to focus on client work that reflects the approach to be practised and demonstrates that the trainee has the appropriate experience and competence for the model of psychotherapy that they will be practising . . . .
>
> In addition candidates will need to show that they have established themselves in practice with substantial experience in the kinds of psychotherapy that they intend to offer; and to have demonstrated their competence in their supervised psychotherapy practice for a minimum of a two-year period.
>
> For solely long-term modalities – a regular caseload including at least two long-term contracts to demonstrate the ability to manage closure.
>
> For solely time-limited modalities – completion of at least 12 cases is required, with evidence of efficacy and appropriate use of their model and its frameworks.
>
> It is recommended that candidates have experience of working with clients in both long-term and time-limited psychotherapy contracts.
>
> Training shall include arrangements to ensure that candidates can identify and manage appropriately their personal involvement in, and contributions to, the processes of the psychotherapy approach they practise.
>
> Candidates must have an experience of psychotherapy congruent with the psychotherapy in which they are in training, a minimum of 40 hours per year for four years, and normally be in psychotherapy throughout their training. This personal psychotherapy must normally be undergone with a UKCP registered psychotherapist, or equivalent.
>
> (Humanistic and Integrative Psychotherapy College, 2011)

Candidates also need to have completed a Mental Health Familiarization Placement (MHFP) (see Chapter 3 for more information on the MHFP), and to have met all the UKCP training requirements, including the criterion of it being at postgraduate level, and it having particular assessment processes, entry requirements, qualification and registration requirements, and continuing professional development.

More information can be found on the HIPC website at www.hipcollege.co.uk/page/training+standards.

The Psychotherapeutic Counselling and Intersubjective Psychotherapy College (PCIPC) of the UKCP has similar requirements to HIPC, but requires 450 hours of training and 105 hours of personal therapy. As with HIPC, there are further requirements concerning the training course, assessment processes, entry requirements, qualification and registration, and continuing professional development.

More information can be found on the college website at www.pc-college.co.uk.

IPN

One of the less well-known accrediting organizations, and one that may appeal to practitioners who don't want to join an organization with a prescribed numbers of hours of training, supervision and clinical practice, is the Independent Practitioners Network (IPN). The IPN offers:

> an authentic model of best practice accountability through open, committed relationships with peers. We are a nationwide network of practitioners of equal status rather than a hierarchical organisation. We work together in linked groups to offer each other mutual support and challenge. We believe that high-quality ethical practice is grounded in honesty, integrity and transparency. We welcome counsellors, psychotherapists, educators, growth workers and allied practitioners.
>
> (IPN, 2009)

The IPN is a peer network that has groups throughout the country. Each group has a minimum of five, but fewer than ten members, and these members are willing to stand by each other's work, a process in keeping with the practice of pluralism that was mentioned earlier in the chapter. More information about IPN can be found at http://i-p-n.org.

Whatever your preference, you may wish to consider joining at least one organization that can accredit you, and your work. Whichever one you choose will depend upon the training you have successfully completed, and your personal preference for the systems used.

European Certificate for Psychotherapy (ECP)

In 1997, the European Association for Psychotherapy (EAP) established a European Certificate for Psychotherapy (ECP). Their main goal is to create mutual recognition and equal conduct of psychotherapy across Europe, and, according to their website:

> The EAP represents 128 organisations (28 National Umbrella Associations (NUA), 17 European-wide associations for psychotherapy) from 41 European countries that amounts to more than 120,000 psychotherapists. Membership is also available for individual psychotherapists.
>
> Based on the 'Strasbourg Declaration on Psychotherapy of 1990', the EAP represents high training standards for a scientifically based, free and independent practice of psychotherapy.
>
> (European Association for Psychotherapy, 2012)

The UKCP is the National Umbrella Organization (NUO) for England, Wales, Scotland and Northern Ireland, and the ICP represents Ireland.

The criteria for the award of the ECP are:

> The total duration of the training will not be less than 3,200 hours, spread over a minimum of seven years, with the first three years being equivalent to a relevant university degree. The latter four years will be in a specific psychotherapy training.
>
> This includes:
>
> Personal Psychotherapeutic Experience or equivalent: to include training analysis, self-experience, and other methods involving elements of self-reflection, therapy and personal experience (not less than 250 hours).
>
> Theoretical Study: There will be a general part of university or professional training and a part which is specific to psychotherapy.
>
> Practical Training: This will include sufficient practice under continuous supervision appropriate to the psychotherapeutic modality and will be at least two years in duration.
>
> Placement in a mental health setting, or equivalent professional experience: The placement needs to provide adequate experience of psycho-social crisis and of collaboration with other specialists in the mental health field.
>
> (European Association for Psychotherapy, 2012)

The ECP may well be of interest to you if you are thinking of moving to live and work in the Republic of Ireland, or elsewhere in Europe. Depending upon the modality of the training course you complete, you may also be able to apply for the ECP via one of the 17 European-wide accrediting organizations, e.g. European Association for Body-Psychotherapy, European Association for Gestalt Therapy, European Association for Integrative Psychotherapy, European Association for

Transactional Analysis, etc., or via one of the European accredited psychotherapy training institutes. The EAP website has more information – www.europsyche.org.

You may wish to bear in mind that you will also have to comply with any other national regulations that may apply in the country to which you are moving, or in which you are intending to work.

With a growing trend to comply with European standards, it may be worth considering these requirements when you are choosing your training course.

Conclusion

In this chapter we have been looking at the various employment opportunities that may be available to you after you have completed your training, as well as information regarding a number of professional accreditation and registration schemes that are currently available, as well as the situation with assured voluntary registration and statutory regulation. In the final chapter I will bring the themes of the book together.

Questions to consider

1 Is the course you are interested in accredited, or recognized, by any professional body? If the course is recognized, or accredited, you may wish to go to that professional body's website and research their current accreditation criteria. This will enable you to be fully aware of all the requirements, including those involving the actual training course, e.g. the number of hours of training, personal therapy, clinical placement and supervision needed, the number of clinical hours that are pre- and post-training, time limits, assessment and qualification processes.

2 Does the professional body hold an accredited register with the PSA? Is this important to you?

3 Do you meet all the entry requirements, if there are any, for the accreditation, or registration, you intend to seek post-qualification? If not, is there any additional training or other requirement you may need to fulfil before starting on any training course? For example, some psychodynamic or psychoanalytic psychotherapy training courses require a minimum of one year of between two to five times weekly personal therapy before embarking on the academic training. Training providers usually inform you of any pre-course or entry requirements, but if they don't, then you may want to ask.

4 Do you live in the Republic of Ireland, or are you thinking of moving there, or elsewhere in Europe? If so, then you may wish to consider a training course that will help you to achieve the ECP. You may also wish to find out what the current situation is for statutory regulation, and whether this will have a bearing on the training course you choose.

Chapter 8

Bringing it all together

This chapter gathers together the themes, issues and ideas from previous chapters, and then offers you food for thought when planning your entry into counselling or psychotherapy training.

Plan of action

The following steps will help you decide whether to undertake training, and then, if you decide to go ahead, to find the most appropriate course to help you achieve your goals.

Step 1

The first and most important stage is to ask yourself, 'Why do I want to do this training?' and 'What are the *real* reasons?' Consider using the questions posed in Chapters 1 and 4 to help you.

Step 2

Speak with your partner, family and friends, as you may find it helpful to share and explore the pros and cons of the training that you are considering. Invite them to ask questions, and let them know what support you will need from them. Consider asking them to read Chapter 4, and then have a frank discussion about your plans and the possible impact this may have on your relationship. You may find the questions at the end of that chapter useful in those discussions.

Step 3

Consider the learning theories posed in Chapter 1. How you do learn? What is you preferred learning style? How familiar are you with student-centred and experiential learning? Would these methods suit you? Will you need any help with the academic aspect of the training? If so, how, and where, will you get that help?

Step 4

The next question to ask yourself is, 'What would be the right academic level for me?' You could read Chapter 1 again, reflect on the different levels of entry that are available, and then decide where would be the best starting point for your training in terms of your current level of academic achievement.

Step 5

Which modality do you think will suit you? You could read Chapter 2 again, and see if any of the approaches outlined there appeal to you; you could also undertake a one- or two-day taster course to further help you decide. An alternative would be to contact a number of training centres or professional bodies and ask them about their courses.

Step 6

Research whichever professional registering or accrediting body you would like to be associated with, post-qualification. This may be relevant if you are hoping to work within a specific organization, for example the NHS. You may consider checking to see if the accrediting body is registered, or in the process of being registered, with the Professional Standards Agency (www.professionalstandards.org.uk). You could also verify the accreditation or registration requirements so that you know these from the outset. (See Chapter 7 for more information on accreditation and registration systems.)

Step 7

Once you have identified your academic level of entry, the modality, and a professional registering or accrediting body, you are ready to find a course, and there are various places you can go to find information. One is the website for the accrediting or registering body that you are interested in joining, where there may be a list of training courses that they approve or accredit, or a list of organizations that run training or accreditation systems that meet their requirements. Alternatively, you may prefer to look at the website of the professional body for the specific modality that interests you. (See those listed in Appendix 2.) They may also have details of training courses or organizations that meet their standards.

Some courses are run as evening sessions, and others are one full day a week, or one weekend a month. The option you choose will depend upon your availability. Many trainees work full-time, so they appreciate the opportunity to train at weekends. For others, regular weekly sessions work better. What would be best for you?

Step 8

Once you have identified two or three training providers who offer the level and type of course you are seeking, decide whether you meet their entry requirements.

If you do not, is there anything you can do to enable you to meet them? Is there a 'non-standard' entry route you can take? Can you make use of an APL application with respect to previous training or experience either to meet the requirements or to enter the training at a later stage in the programme? You may like to read Chapter 3 again, for more information on entry requirements and APL processes.

You may consider going to visit the training providers, having prepared yourself beforehand, with a list of questions that are important to you. You could use the questions listed throughout the book. You may like to speak with the trainers, or, as already mentioned, attend a taster course, which will help you to get a sense of the trainer's teaching style. This could help you decide whether this will be the right course for you.

If you do visit the training provider, and meet the trainers, take notice of your own internal voice: does this experience feel right for you; do you have any niggling doubts; does this seem like a good match? Your instinct is very important, so do listen carefully to your response. As you visit, you may find it helpful to write down the answers you have been given to your questions so you can refer back to these later. You could also make a note of your impressions, and these may be in the form of words, pictures or feelings.

Step 9

When you have visited all the training providers that you think will meet your training needs, be curious about whether there is one to which you are particularly drawn. You may find it useful to reflect on why you are drawn to that course. This can involve pondering on the answers that they gave to your questions, whether they meet some or all of the training requirements set by the professional body, and if the key curriculum elements mentioned in Chapter 3 are present. If you are happy with what is being offered, then it looks like you have found yourself a course.

Choosing a course is not a wholly conscious process. There may be an unconscious element involved, so you may want to check out further why you feel drawn, or even why you feel indifferent, to a particular course. For example, does one of the tutors remind you of someone from your past who impacted on you in either a positive or a negative way? Do you feel uneasy about the promises that were made? Are they realistic? Do you have doubts about whether you will be able to achieve what you want to achieve? Is this feeling generated by unnecessary self-doubt? Do you need more information from the training establishment to settle you, or do you have an intuitive feeling that this course is not for you? In order to establish what is going on for you at an unconscious level, it can help to talk your feelings through with others.

Step 10

If you have found a course that ticks all the necessary boxes, then you may want to consider looking for a counsellor or psychotherapist with whom you can work.

You may find it very supportive to start this process early, and, particularly, to explore any unconscious factors, as mentioned above, that may be influencing you, before making a final decision. It may be useful to ensure that the therapist meets the requirements of your training course, and the relevant professional registration or accreditation bodies. You may wish to read Chapter 4 again, for ideas about how to choose a therapist and the questions you may like to ask of them.

Step 11

Placements are usually necessary from the second or third year of training onwards. Securing one can be quite competitive, so you may find it useful to begin looking for yours at this early stage. Initially, you may like to familiarize yourself, and build a relationship with your intended placement organization, by working for them in a non-clinical role on a voluntary basis.

Another option may be to ask your current employer if they could provide you with a placement. For example, if you are a social worker, there may be an opportunity for you to offer counselling or psychotherapy to the clients of another department. If you work with children, schools and families, could you offer your counselling or psychotherapy skills to the adult social care section?

Step 12

If you have read all the other chapters in this book, then, by now, you may realize that counselling and psychotherapy training is a very personal and unique experience, and this is by far the most significant aspect of the training. Are you ready for that challenge? What will you need to help and sustain you? Where will you get that help? How will you keep a balance between home, work and study?

Concluding comments

The purpose of this book has been to give you a clear idea of the nature of, and requirements for, training as a counsellor or psychotherapist, and to guide you through the process of selecting the most appropriate course for you depending upon your personal, academic and professional needs. If you decide to continue into training, then I hope you have a very rewarding and enlightening experience.

Appendix 1

UK main professional accrediting/ registering bodies

British Association for Behavioural and Cognitive Psychotherapies* (BABCP)
www.babcp.com
Telephone: 0161 705 4304
Email: babcp@babcp.com

British Association for Counselling and Psychotherapy* (BACP)
www.bacp.co.uk
Telephone: 01455 883300
Email: bacp@bacp.co.uk

British Psychoanalytic Council (BPC)
www.psychoanalytic-council.org
Telephone: 020 7561 9240
Email: mail@psychoanalytic-council.org

The BPC is the professional registering body for the following organizations:

- The Association for Psychodynamic Practice and Counselling in Organisational Settings
- Association of Medical Psychodynamic Psychotherapists
- Association of Psychodynamic Counsellors
- British Psychoanalytic Association
- The British Association of Psychotherapists
- British Psychoanalytical Society and the Institute of Psychoanalysis
- The London Centre for Psychotherapy
- North of England Association of Psychoanalytic Psychotherapists
- Northern Ireland Association for the Study of Psychoanalysis
- The Society of Analytical Psychology
- The Scottish Association of Psychoanalytical Psychotherapists
- Severnside Institute for Psychotherapy
- British Society of Couple Psychotherapists and Counsellors

The Tavistock and Portman NHS Foundation Trust
Tavistock Society of Psychotherapists
Foundation for Psychotherapy and Counselling

Counselling and Psychotherapy in Scotland* (COSCA)
www.cosca.org.uk
Telephone: 01786 475140
Email: info@cosca.org.uk

Health and Care Professions Council (HCPC)
www.hpc-uk.org
Telephone: 0845 300 6184

The HCPC is the professional registering body for the following:

- Arts psychotherapists, e.g. art, drama and music therapists;
- Practitioner psychologists, including registered psychologists, clinical psychologists, counselling psychologists, educational psychologists, forensic psychologists, health psychologists, occupational psychologists and sport and exercise psychologists.

Professional Standards Authority for Health and Social Care (PSA)
www.professionalstandards.org.uk
Telephone: 020 7389 8030
Email: info@professionalstandards.org.uk

The PSA sets standards for organizations that hold voluntary registers for people working in counselling and psychotherapy, as well as a variety of health and social care occupations.

United Kingdom Council for Psychotherapy (UKCP)
www.psychotherapy.org.uk
Telephone: 020 7014 9955
Email: info@ukcp.org.uk

The UKCP is the professional registering body for the following organizations:

Association for Group and Individual Psychotherapy
Association for Cognitive Analytic Therapy
Association for Counsellors and Psychotherapists in Primary Care
Association for Family Therapy
The Association of Independent Psychotherapists
Arbours Association
Association of Jungian Analysts

Bath Centre for Psychotherapy and Counselling
The Berne Institute
The Bowlby Centre
British Association for Psychoanalytic and Psychodynamic Supervision
British Psychodrama Association
Cambridge Body Psychotherapy Centre
Cambridge Society for Psychotherapy
Canterbury Consortium of Psychoanalytic and Psychodynamic Psychotherapists
The Caspari Foundation for Educational Therapy and Therapeutic Teaching
Centre for Counselling and Psychotherapy Education
Centre for Freudian Analysis and Research
Centre for Transpersonal Psychology
Chiron Association for Body Psychotherapists
Chiron Centre for Body Psychotherapy
College of Sexual and Relationship Therapists
Confederation of Analytical Psychologists
Forum for Independent Psychotherapists
Foundation for Psychotherapy and Counselling
Gestalt Centre, London
Gestalt Psychotherapy Training Institute
Group Analysis South West
Guild for Analytical Psychology and Spirituality
Guild of Psychotherapists
Hallam Institute of Psychotherapy
Institute of Group Analysis
The Independent Group of Analytical Psychologists
Institute of Family Therapy
Institute of Psychosynthesis
Institute of Psychotherapy and Disability
Institute of Psychotherapy and Social Studies
Institute for Arts in Therapy and Education
Karuna Institute
Liverpool Psychotherapy Organisation
London Association of Primal Psychotherapists
London School of Biodynamic Psychotherapy
Matrix College of Counselling and Psychotherapy Ltd
Metanoia Institute
Minster Centre
NAFSIYAT
Neuro-Linguistic Psychotherapy Counselling Association
North West Institute for Dynamic Psychotherapy
Northern Guild Psychological Solutions

PCP Education and Training
Philadelphia Association
Psychosynthesis and Education Trust
Research Society for Process Oriented Psychology UK
Re-Vision
Royal College of Psychiatrists
Scarborough Psychotherapy Training Institute
School of Psychotherapy and Counselling Regent's College
Sherwood Psychotherapy Training Institute
Site for Contemporary Psychoanalysis
Society for Existential Analysis
South Trent Training in Dynamic Psychotherapy
Spectrum
Tara Rokpa Therapy Association
Temenos
Terapia
United Kingdom Association for Transactional Analysis
United Kingdom Association of Humanistic Psychology Practitioners
Universities Psychotherapy and Counselling Association
West Midlands Institute of Psychotherapy
Westminster Pastoral Foundation

Ireland

The Irish Association for Counselling and Psychotherapy* (IACP)
www.irish-counselling.ie
Telephone: 01 2723427
Email: iacp@iacp.ie

The Irish Council for Psychotherapy (ICP)
www.psychotherapy-ireland.com
Telephone: 01 902 3819
Email: via form on website

The ICP is the professional registering body for the following organizations:

The Family Therapy Association of Ireland
The Irish Analytical Psychology Association
The Irish Association of Humanistic and Integrative Psychotherapy
The Irish Constructivists Psychotherapy Association
The Irish Forum for Psychoanalytic Psychotherapists
The Irish Forum for Child and Adolescent Psychotherapy
The Irish Group Analytic Society
The Irish Psychoanalytic Association

The National Association for Cognitive Behavioural Therapists
The Northern Ireland Institute of Human Relations

Note

* These organizations accredit therapists via individual member applications. They also accredit specific courses with various training providers. (See websites for more information.)

Appendix 2

Relevant professional organizations

UK

Arbours Association
www.arboursassociation.org
Telephone: 020 8340 7646, 020 8348 6466
Email: info@arboursassociation.org

Association for Cognitive Analytic Therapy
www.acat.me.uk
Telephone: 0844 800 9496
Email: admin@acat.me.uk

Association for Family Therapy and Systemic Practice
www.aft.org.uk
Telephone: 01925 444414

Association for Group and Individual Psychotherapy
www.agip.org.uk
Telephone: 020 7272 7013
Email: office@agip.org.uk

The Association for Person Centred Therapy Scotland
www.pctscotland.co.uk
Telephone: 0870 765 0871
Email: info@pctscotland.co.uk

Association of Counsellors and Psychotherapists in Primary Care
www.cpc-online.co.uk
Telephone: 01243 870701
Email: cpc@cpc-online.co.uk

Association of Independent Psychotherapists
www.aip.org.uk
Telephone: 020 7700 1911
Email: training@aip.org.uk

Association of Jungian Analysts
www.jungiananalysts.org.uk
Telephone/Fax: 020 7794 8711
Email: aja@dircon.co.uk

British Association for Behavioural and Cognitive Psychotherapies
www.babcp.com
Telephone: 0161 705 4304
Email: babcp@babcp.com

British Association for Counselling and Psychotherapy
www.bacp.co.uk
Telephone: 01455 883300
Email: bacp@bacp.co.uk

British Association for Music Therapy
www.bamt.org
Telephone: 020 7837 6100
Email: info@bamt.org

British Association for the Person Centred Approach
www.bapca.org.uk
Telephone: 01989 763 863

British Association of Art Therapists
www.baat.org
Telephone: 020 7686 4216
Email: info@baat.org

The British Association of Dramatherapists
www.badth.org.uk
Telephone: 01242 235515
Email: enquiries@badth.org.uk

British Autogenic Society
www.autogenic-therapy.org.uk
Telephone: 07534 539425
Email: baspromotions@googlemail.com

British Psychoanalytic Council
www.psychoanalytic-council.org
Telephone: 020 7561 9240
Email: mail@psychoanalytic-council.org

British Psychodrama Association
www.psychodrama.org.uk
Telephone: 07582 842231
E-mail: administrator@psychodrama.org.uk

British Psychological Society
www.bps.org.uk
Telephone: 0116 254 9568
Email: enquiries@bps.org.uk

Cambridge Society for Psychotherapy
www.cambridge-psychotherapy.org.uk
Telephone: 01223 510229
Email: info@cambridge-psychotherapy.org.uk

Centre for Counselling and Psychotherapy Education
www.ccpe.org.uk
Telephone: 020 7266 3006
Email: info@ccpe.org.uk

Centre for Freudian Analysis and Research
www.cfar.org.uk
Telephone: 0845 838 0829
Email: admin@cfar.demon.co.uk

Centre for Transpersonal Psychology
www.transpersonalcentre.co.uk
Telephone: 01727 751420
Email: enquiries@transpersonalcentre.co.uk

Chiron Association for Body Psychotherapy
www.body-psychotherapy.org.uk
Email: admin@body-psychotherapy.org.uk

College of Sexual and Relationship Therapists
www.cosrt.org.uk
Telephone: 020 8543 2707
Email: info@cosrt.org.uk

The Council for Psychoanalysis and Jungian Analysis
www.cpja.org.uk
Email: via form on the website

Counselling and Psychotherapy in Scotland
www.cosca.org.uk
Telephone: 01786 475140
Email: info@cosca.org.uk

Federation of Drug and Alcohol Professionals
www.fdap.org.uk
Telephone: 0207 234 9798
Email: office@fdap.org.uk

Forum for Independent Psychotherapists
www.fip.org.uk
Telephone: 020 8367 4359
Email: via form on website

The Gestalt Centre London
www.gestaltcentre.co.uk
Telephone: 020 7247 6501
Email: jacqueline@gestaltcentre.co.uk

Gestalt Psychotherapy and Training Institute
www.gpti.org.uk
Telephone: 01225 482135
Email: admin@gpti.org.uk

Guild of Analytical Psychology and Spirituality
www.gaps.co.uk
Telephone: 0118 922 2993
Email: admin@analyticalpsychology.org

Guild of Psychotherapists
www.guildofpsychotherapists.org.uk
Telephone: 020 7401 3260
Email: admin@guildofpsychotherapists.org.uk

Hallam Institute of Psychotherapy
www.hallaminstitute.org
Email: via form on website

Health and Care Professions Council
www.hpc-uk.org
Telephone: 0845 300 6184

Institute for Arts in Therapy and Education
www.artspsychotherapy.org
Telephone: 020 7704 2534
Email: info@artspsychotherapy.org

Institute of Family Therapy
www.instituteoffamilytherapy.org.uk
Telephone: 020 7391 9150
Email: training@ift.org.uk

Institute of Group Analysis
www.groupanalysis.org
Telephone: 020 7431 2693
Email: iga@igalondon.org.uk

Institute of Psychosynthesis
www.psychosynthesis.org
Telephone: 020 8202 4525
Email: institute@psychosynthesis.org

Institute for Psychotherapy and Disability
www.instpd.org.uk
Telephone: 01652 648335
Email: angela@instpd.org.uk

Institute of Psychotherapy and Social Studies
www.ipss-psychotherapy.org
Telephone: 020 8363 2777
Email: info@ipss-psychotherapy.org

London Association of Primal Psychotherapists
www.lapp.org
Telephone: 0207 267 9616
Email: info@lapp.org

Neurolinguistic Psychotherapy Counselling Association
www.nlptca.com
Telephone: 0870 241 3276
Email: enquiry@nlptca.com

Northern Ireland Group for Art as Therapy
www.nigat.org
Email: info@nigat.org

Psychosynthesis and Education Trust
www.psychosynthesis.edu
Telephone: 020 7403 2100
Email: enquiries@petrust.org.uk

Research Society for Process Oriented Psychology in the UK
www.rspopuk.com
Telephone: 020 8579 5123
Email: anup.karia@btinternet.com

School of Infant Mental Health
www.infantmentalhealth.com
Telephone: 020 7433 3112
Email: enquiries@infantmentalhealth.com

Society for Existential Analysis
www.existentialanalysis.co.uk
Email: via form on website

The United Kingdom Association for Transactional Analysis (formerly the Institute of Transactional Analysis)
www.uktransactionalanalysis.co.uk
Telephone: 01954 212468
Email: admin@ uktransactionalanalysis.co.uk

United Kingdom Association of Humanistic Psychology Practitioners
www.ahpp.org
Telephone: 08457 660326
Email: admin@ahpp.org

The United Kingdom Council for Psychotherapy
www.psychotherapy.org.uk
Telephone: 020 7014 9955
Email: info@ukcp.org.uk

Ireland

The Association for Psychoanalysis and Psychotherapy in Ireland
www.appi.ie
Telephone: 086 784 9145
Email: adminatappi@gmail.com

The Family Therapy Association of Ireland
www.familytherapyireland.com
Telephone: 01 2722105
Email: via form on website

Gerda Boyesen International Institute of Biodynamic Psychology and Psychotherapy Ltd
www.biodynamic.org
Telephone: 096 32285
Email: gbii@biodynamic.org

The Irish Analytical Psychology Association
www.jungireland.com
Email: jungireland@gmail.com This email address is being protected from spambots. You need JavaScript enabled to view it.

The Irish Association for Cognitive Analytical Therapy
www.icat.ie

The Irish Association for Counselling and Psychotherapy
www.irish-counselling.ie
Telephone: 01 2723427
Email: iacp@iacp.ie

The Irish Association for the Person Centred Approach
www.iapca.ie
Telephone: 087 1442 776
Email: info@iapca.ie

Irish Association for Psychotherapy in Primary Care
www.iappcare.com
Telephone: 091 565814
Email: info@iappcare.com

Irish Association of Creative Arts Therapists
www.iacat.ie
Telephone: 087 992 1746
Email: info@iacat.ie

The Irish Association of Humanistic and Integrative Psychotherapy
www.iahip.org
Telephone: 0 1 284 1665
Email: info@iahip.org

The Irish Constructivist Psychotherapy Association
www.irishconstructivists.org
Telephone: 01 272 2105
Email: amdps@indigo.ie

The Irish Council for Psychotherapy
www.psychotherapy-ireland.com
Telephone: 01 902 3819
Email: via form on website

The Irish Forum for Psychoanalytic Psychotherapists
www.ifpp.ie
Telephone: 091 452013
Email: amdps@indigo.ie

The Irish Gestalt Centre
www.irishgestaltcentre.com
Telephone: 09 1553548
Email: admin@irishgestaltcentre.com

The Irish Group Analytic Society
www.igas.ie
Email: askigas@gmail.com
(For training enquiries email: tsop@ucd.ie)

Northern Ireland Group for Art as Therapy
www.nigat.org
Email: info@nigat.org

Appendix 3

Log book templates

Client log book:

Client reference no.	*Length of session*	*Individual/couple*	*Taken to supervision*
01/2014	1 hour	Individual	06/01/14
02/2014	1 hour	Couple	
01/2014	1 hour	Individual	
02/2014	1 hour	Couple	04/02/14
01/2014	1 hour	Individual	04/02/14
02/2014	1 hour	Couple	

Training log book:

Date	*Where*	*Subject*	*Trainer*	*No. of hours*
11/01/2014	College	Ethics	Cathy McQuaid	6 hours
12/01/2014	College	Building the therapeutic relationship	Cathy McQuaid	6 hours
08/02/2014	College	Child Development 1	Sue Parker	6 hours
09/02/2014	College	Clinical Placements	Sue Parker	3 hours
09/02/2014	College	Skills Practice	Sue Parker	3 hours

Supervision log book:

Date	*Supervisor*	*Length of session*	*Clients/issues taken*
06/01/2014	Sarah Smith	1 hour	01/2014 – concern re boundaries.
04/02/2014	Sarah Smith	1 hour	01/2014 – feedback re boundaries. Feeling ineffective. 02/2014 – couple dynamics.

Appendix 4

Personal learning contract

Student name:	Year of study:
Module/area for development:	Target date for accomplishment:
Signed by student:	Signed by trainer/supervisor:

The knowledge, skills, attitudes and values to be acquired by the learner (learning objectives)	*How these objectives are to be accomplished (learning resources and strategies)*	*What evidence will be presented to demonstrate that the objectives have been accomplished*	*How this evidence will be judged or validated*
To learn how to use reflecting, paraphrasing and summarizing in counselling practice	To watch the tutor demonstrating these skills and to practise with peers (Reflector and Activist skills)	A 20-minute video of me working with a peer demonstrating these skills (Activist skills)	With my tutor, we will discuss the skills I use to assess, together with my application of these skills (Reflector skills)
To have a basic understanding of Rogers' six necessary and sufficient conditions for therapy	To read the *Carl Rogers Reader* (Theorist skills)	A 500-word written paper outlining my understanding of these conditions (Theorist skills)	I will ask a peer for feedback, and then submit the paper and feedback to the tutor (Reflector skills)

Glossary

activities One of the six patterns of time structuring (Berne, 1964), where the focus is on the achievement of goals. Work, sport and hobbies are activities.

congruence One of Rogers' Core Conditions (Rogers, 1957), essential for effective therapy. When someone is being congruent, they are being real and authentic, saying what they are thinking, feeling and experiencing. There is no facade, or defence system, in place.

counter-transference Originally described as the therapist's reaction to the transference of the client (the projection onto the therapist of a significant figure from the client's past). Awareness of counter-transference yields important insights. If it is missed by the therapist, then the client and therapist can be drawn into a replay of the original situation with the parent or other projected figure. This is often the cause of therapy becoming unstuck, and it is usually addressed in supervision. Counter-transference is also used to describe a therapist's transference onto the client.

discount Discounting is an internal mechanism which involves a person minimizing, or ignoring, some aspect of himself, others or the reality of the situation. Discounting is an important process in maintaining the Script and Frame of Reference (Schiff *et al.*, 1975). Discounting is not operationally observable; however, external manifestations of discounting can be observed. Discounting can be manifested by passive behaviours, re-defining, ulterior transactions and behaviours from the Drama Triangle (Karpman, 1976), e.g. Persecutor, Rescuer and Victim.

empathy One of Rogers' core conditions (Rogers, 1957), empathy is the ability to understand another's feelings without losing your own perspective. The therapist has a responsibility to be sensitive, supportive and enquiring of the client's experiences, and to relay that understanding back to the client.

games One of the six patterns of time structuring (Berne, 1964). Games are repetitive patterns of behaviour which lead to a well-defined payoff (Berne, 1966).

'I'm OK, you're OK' A life position (Berne, 1976). When in this position, I accept myself, unconditionally, as I am, and I accept you, unconditionally, as you are. This is the healthy position, enabling the person to be autonomous, and to form relationships that are balanced and rewarding. When confronted with a problem, 'I will get-on-with others' to solve the problem.

individuation The psychological process that makes of a human being an 'individual' – a unique, indivisible unit, or 'whole man'. In the past, it has been generally assumed that consciousness – or the sum total of representations, ideas, emotions, perceptions and other mental contents which the ego acknowledges – is equal to the psychological 'whole' of an individual (Jung, 2004).

injunctions An important negative script element held in the Child ego-state (Goulding and Goulding, 1972, 1976). The Gouldings identified 12 injunctions in all: 'Don't Be' ('Don't Exist'); 'Don't Be You'; 'Don't Be a Child'; 'Don't Grow Up'; 'Don't Make It'; 'Don't Be Important'; 'Don't Belong'; 'Don't Be Close'; 'Don't Be Well' ('Don't Be Sane'); 'Don't Think'; 'Don't Feel' (this may specify certain feelings to be excluded, or may be a total ban); 'Don't Do Anything' (it will be wrong, or dangerous).

intimacy One of the six patterns of time structuring (Berne, 1964). Berne (1966) defined intimacy as 'A game-free exchange of affective expression without covert exploitation.'

locus of evaluation Rogers (1951) defined locus of evaluation as 'The extent to which [one's] values and standards depend upon the judgments and expectations of others, or are based on a reliance on [one's] own experience' (p. 156). He went on to say that

> An internal locus of evaluation, within the individual himself, means that he is the center of the valuing process, the evidence being supplied by his own sense. When the locus of evaluation resides in others, their judgment as to the value of an object or experience becomes the criterion of value for the individual.
>
> (Rogers, 1959: 210)

narcissism Investment of psychological energy in the self. This may be positive and helpful, e.g. healthy self-respect. Over-valuation of the self is a defence, often, against the trauma of early loss of relationship. Rejecting and abusive behaviour towards the child inflicts a narcissistic wound.

pastimes One of the six patterns of time-structuring (Berne, 1964) in which there is talk about a topic, but no action is taken concerning it. Pastimes give considerable freedom without having to undertake a commitment to action. They constitute a large part of social activity, and, besides filling time, they provide a milieu in which people can safely check each other out before becoming more involved.

permissions An important positive script element held in the Child ego-state – the opposite to an injunction.

physis Berne introduced the concept of 'physis' as being 'the force of nature which strives to make things grow and to make growing things more perfect (Berne, 1968).

rituals One of the six patterns of time-structuring (Berne, 1964), where stylized, or predictable, exchanges occur with others which follow an agreed pattern, e.g. 'How are you?'; 'I'm fine.'

script 'An ongoing program, developed in early childhood under parental influence, which directs the individual's behavior in the most important aspects of his life' (Berne, 1975: 418).

self-actualization A natural tendency or drive towards health and to realize potential (Rogers, 1961).

stroke A stroke is a TA term meaning a unit of recognition. There are 'positive' and 'negative' strokes, 'verbal' and 'non-verbal', and 'conditional' and 'unconditional'. An example of a positive verbal unconditional stroke would be 'I love you', and a conditional stroke would be 'I love you when you work hard.' It does not matter what the sender of the stroke means; it is the recipient who decides on the meaning. Any stroke is better than no stroke at all (Berne, 1964).

supervision Supervision is a working alliance between two professionals, where supervisees offer an account of their work, reflect on it, receive feedback, and receive guidance, if appropriate. The object of this alliance is to enable the worker to gain in ethical competency, confidence and creativity, so as to give the best possible services to clients (Inskipp and Proctor, 2001).

transference Unawarely transferring attitudes, beliefs and feelings relating to a significant person in the past on to a person in the present, such as a therapist.

unconditional positive regard This involves showing complete acceptance and support, or even prizing, of another person, even though you may not agree with what they say or do. Carl Rogers believed that unconditional positive regard was an essential requirement for therapists to offer to their clients in order that they can learn to understand and accept themselves (Rogers, 1959).

withdrawal One of the six patterns of time-structuring (Berne, 1964). When in withdrawal, someone will not make contact with others, but may fantasize about doing so, or being elsewhere (Berne, 1966).

Bibliography

ABC Awards (2013a) *Level 3 Certificate in Counselling Skills: Units and Rules of Combination.* Nottingham: ABC Awards.

ABC Awards (2013b) *Level 4 Diploma in Therapeutic Counselling: Units and Rules of Combination.* Nottingham: ABC Awards.

AFT (2013) *Training Overview.* Online. Available at: www.aft.org.uk/training/view/training-overview.html (accessed 6 January 2013).

Ainsworth, M.D.S. and Bell, S.M. (1970) Attachment, exploration, and separation: illustrated by the behavior of one-year-olds in a strange situation. *Child Development*, 41: 49–67.

Aronowitz, S. (1981) Politics and higher education in the 1980s. In Giroux, H.A., Penna, A.N. and Pinar, W.F. (eds) *Curriculum and Instruction Alternatives in Education*, Berkeley: McCutchan Publishing.

Aronowitz, S. (1994) A different perspective on educational equality. *Review of Education/Pedagogy/Cultural Studies*, 16(2): 135–151.

Asay, T.P. and Lambert, M.J. (1999) The empirical case for the common factors in therapy: quantitative findings. In Duncan, B.L., Miller, S.D., Wampold, B.E. and Hubble, M.A. (eds), (2009) *The Heart and Soul of Change: What Works in Therapy.* Washington, DC: American Psychological Association Press, pp. 23–55.

Ashworth, M., Kordowicz, M. and Schofield, S. (2012) 'PSYCHLOPS' (Psychological Outcome Profiles): an outcome measure. *Integrating Science and Practice*, 2: 36–39.

Ashworth, M., Shepherd, M., Christey, J., Matthews, V., Wright, K., Parmentier, H., Robinson, S., and Godfrey, E. (2004) A client-generated psychometric instrument: The development of 'PSYCHLOPS'. *Counselling and Psychotherapy Research: Linking Research with Practice*, 4(2): 27–31.

Atkinson, P. (2006) Personal therapy in the training of therapists. *European Journal of Psychotherapy and Counselling*, 8(4): 407.

Axline, V.M. (1990) *Dibs in Search of Self: Personality Development in Play Therapy.* London: Penguin Books.

Baardseth, T.P., Goldberg, S.B., Pace, B.T., Wislocki, A.P., Frost, N.D., Siddiqui, J.R., Lindemann, A.M., Kivlighan, D.M., Laska, K.M., Del Re, A.C., Minami, T. and Wampold, B.E. (2013) Cognitive-behavioral therapy versus other therapies: redux. *Clinical Psychology Review* 33(3): 395–405.

BAAT (2011) *What Is Art Therapy?* Online. Available at: www.baat.org/art_therapy.html (accessed 24 April 2012).

BAAT (2012) *A Career in Art Therapy?* Online. Available at: www.baat.org/career.html (accessed 3 January 2013).

BABCP (2012a) *Minimum Training Standards for The Practice of Cognitive Behavioural Psychotherapy.* Bury: British Association for Behavioural and Cognitive Psychotherapies.

BABCP (2012b) *Cognitive Behavioural Psychotherapist (CBP) Provisional Accreditation.* Online. Available at: www.babcp.com/Accreditation/CBP/CBP-Provisional-Accreditation.aspx (accessed 21 August 2012).

BABCP (2012c) *Psychological Wellbeing Practitioner (PWP) Accreditation.* Online. Available at: www.babcp.com/Accreditation/PWP/PWP-Accreditation.aspx (accessed 21 August 2012).

BABCP (2012d) *Criteria and Guidelines for Full Accreditation as a Behavioural and/or Cognitive Psychotherapist.* Online. Available at: www.babcp.com/files/Accreditation/CBP/Full/CBP-Full-CriteriaGuidelines-V3-1012b.pdf (accessed 21 August 2012).

BACP (2008) *Professional Aspects of Setting Up a Counselling and Psychotherapy Service: Information Sheet P1.* Lutterworth: BACP.

BACP (2009a) *BACP Response to HPC Consultation.* Online. Available at: www.bacp.co.uk/news/index.php?newsId=1603 (accessed 1 December 2013).

BACP (2009b) *Accreditation of Training Courses.* Online. Available at: www.bacp.co.uk/accreditation/ACCREDITATION%20(FOR%20TRAINING%20COURSES)/index.php (accessed 21 August 2012).

BACP (2010a) *What is Counselling and Psychotherapy?* Online. Available at: www.bacp.co.uk/crs/Training/whatiscounselling.php (accessed 3 January 2013).

BACP (2010b) *Getting the Best Out of Your Directory Entries and Websites.* Information Sheet A3. Lutterworth: BACP.

BACP (2010c) *Practical Aspects of Setting Up a Counselling Service.* Information Sheet E1. Lutterworth: BACP.

BACP (2010d) *Charging for Therapy in Private Practice – Pitfalls and Ethical Issues.* Information Sheet P2. Lutterworth: BACP.

BACP (2010e) *The Impact of Personal Crisis on Independent Therapists' Practice – What Is Your Contingency Plan or Plan B?* Information Sheet P14. Lutterworth: BACP.

BACP (2013a) *Ethical Framework for Good Practice in Counselling and Psychotherapy.* Lutterworth: BACP.

BACP (2013b) *Counsellor/Psychotherapist Accreditation Scheme Standard for Accreditation.* Lutterworth: BACP.

BACP (2013c) *Accreditation of Training Courses.* Lutterworth: BACP.

BADTH (2011) *Dramatherapy.* Online. Available at: http://badth.org.uk/dtherapy (accessed 23 April 2012).

Bager-Charleson, S. (2010) *Reflective Practice in Counselling and Psychotherapy.* Exeter: Learning Matters Ltd.

Bambling, M., King, R., Raue, P., Schweitzer, R. and Lambert, W. (2006) Clinical supervision: Its influence on client-rated working alliance and client symptom reduction in the brief treatment of major depression. *Psychotherapy Research*, 6(3): 317–331.

Bandura, A. (1977) *Social Learning Theory.* New York: General Learning Press.

Barkham, M., Mellor-Clark, J., Connell, J. and Cahill, J. (2006) A core approach to practice-based evidence: a brief history of the origins and applications of the CORE-OM and CORE system. *Counselling and Psychotherapy Research*, 6(1): 3–15.

Barnett, R. and Coate, K. (2005) *Engaging the Curriculum in Higher Education.* Maidenhead: Society for Research into Higher Education and Open University Press.

Bates, Y. and House, R. (eds) (2004) *Ethically Challenged Professions.* Ross-on-Wye: PCCS Books.

Beck, A.T., Steer, R.A. and Brown, G.K. (1996) *Manual for the Beck Depression Inventory-II.* San Antonio, TX: Psychological Corporation.

Bennett-Levy, J. (2006) Therapist skills: a cognitive model of their acquisition and refinement. *Behavioural and Cognitive Psychotherapy*, 34: 57–78.

Bennett-Levy, J., Turner, J., Beaty, Y., Smith, T., Paterson, B. and Farmer, S. (2001) The value of self-practice of cognitive therapy techniques and self reflection in the training of cognitive therapists. *Behavioural and Cognitive Psychotherapy*, 29: 203–220.

Bergin, A.E., Payne, R.I. and Richards, P.S. (1996) Values in psychotherapy. In Shafranske, E.P. (ed.), *Religion and the Clinical Practice of Psychology.* Washington, DC: American Psychological Association, pp. 297–325.

Bernard, J.M. and Goodyear, R.K. (2009) *Fundamentals of Clinical Supervision.* Fourth Edition. Upper Saddle River, NJ: Merrill.

Berne, E. (1964) *Games People Play.* New York: Grove Press.

Berne, E. (1966) *Principles of Group Treatment.* New York: Grove Press.

Berne, E. (1968) *A Layman's Guide to Psychiatry and Psychoanalysis.* Third Edition. New York: Simon and Schuster.

Berne, E. (1975) *What Do You Say After You Say Hello?* London: Corgi.

Berne, E. (1976) Classification of positions. *Transactional Analysis Bulletin* selected articles from Volumes 1–9. San Francisco: TA Press (original work published 1962).

Biddle, F. (2013) *College of Hypno-psychotherapists.* Online. Available at: www.psychotherapy.org.uk/hypno_psychotherapy.html (accessed 26 May 2013)

Blohm, F. (2006) The Analytic Triad – indirect countertransferences in the psychotherapeutic process and training. *Forum der Psychoanalyse: Zeitschrift fur klinische Theorie und Praxis*, 22(4): 358–373.

Bondi, L. (2004) *Counselling and Psychotherapy: COSCA's Description.* Stirling: COSCA. Online. Available at: www.cosca.org.uk/docs/86.doc (accessed 25 November 2013).

Bonds-White, F. (2003) Anatomy of a training group. *Transactional Analysis Journal*, 33(4): 344–349.

Bor, R. and Stokes, A. (2010) *Setting Up in Independent Practice: A Handbook for Counsellors, Therapists and Psychologists.* Basingstoke: Palgrave Macmillan.

Boyd, R.D. (1991) *Personal Transformations in Small Groups: A Jungian Perspective.* London: Tavistock/Routledge.

British Psychological Society (2011) *Regulation of Psychology.* Online. Available at: www.bps.org.uk/what-we-do/bps/regulation-psychology/regulation-psychology (accessed 20 August 2012).

Burns, R. (1995) *The Adult Learner at Work.* Sydney: Business and Professional Publishing.

Butler, A.C., Chapman, J.E., Forman, E.M. and Beck, A.T. (2006) The empirical status of cognitive-behavioral therapy: a review of meta-analyses. *Clinical Psychology Review.* 26(1): 17–31.

Carlsson, J., and Schubert, J. (2009) Professional values and their development among trainees in psychoanalytic psychotherapy. *European Journal of Psychotherapy and Counselling*, 11(3): 267–286.

CCPE (2012) *Professional Courses.* Online. Available at: www.ccpe.org.uk (accessed 07 January 2013)

Centre for Transpersonal Psychology (2011) *Transpersonal Psychology.* Online. Available at: www.transpersonalcentre.co.uk/index.php/transpersonal-psychology (accessed 24 April 2012).

Clarkson, P. and Gilbert, M. (1991) The training of counselling trainers and supervisors. In Dryden, W., and Thorne, B., *Training and Supervision for Counselling in Action.* London: Sage.

Cooper, M. (2008) *Essential Research Findings in Counselling and Psychotherapy: The Facts Are Friendly.* London: Sage.

Cooper, M. and McLeod, J. (2010) *Pluralistic Counselling and Psychotherapy.* London: Sage.

Cooper. M., Watson, J.C. and Holldampf, D. (eds) (2010) *Person-Centred and Experiential Therapies Work: A Review of the Research on Counselling, Psychotherapy and Related Practices.* Ross-on-Wye: PCCS Books.

Copus, J. (2009) *Brilliant Writing Tips for Students.* Basingstoke: Palgrave Macmillan.

COSCA (2007) *Statement of Ethics and Code of Practice.* Stirling: COSCA.

COSCA (2011) *COSCA's Counselling Skills Certificate Developing Helping Relationships.* Online. Available at: www.cosca.org.uk/new_documents.php?headingno=16&heading =Counselling%20Skills%20Courses (accessed 19 June 2013).

COSCA (2012) *COSCA Accreditation Counsellors and Psychotherapists Guidelines, Criteria and Application. Diploma Route*, Stirling: COSCA.

COSCA (2013) *Diploma Courses in Counselling/Psychotherapy Validation and Revalidation Guidelines and Procedures.* Stirling: COSCA.

COSRT (2012) *Processes and Criteria for Approval of 2-year Diploma Level Sexual and Relationship Therapy Training Courses*, doc. ref. CA3. Online. Available at: www.cosrt.org.uk/courses-approval (accessed 1 December 2013).

COSRT (2013) *About COSRT.* Online. Available at: www.cosrt.org.uk/about.asp (accessed 26 May 2013).

Cottrell, S. (2011) *Critical Thinking Skills: Developing Effective Analysis and Argument.* Basingstoke: Palgrave Macmillan.

Cowmeadow, P. (1994) Deliberate self-harm and cognitive analytic therapy. *International Journal of Short-Term Psychotherapy*, 9: 135–50.

Cozolino, L. (2006) *The Neuroscience of Human Relationships: Attachment and the Developing Social Brain.* New York: W.W. Norton & Co.

CPCAB (2012) *Qualification Document Level 4 Diploma in Therapeutic Counselling (TC-L4).* Online. Available at: www.cpcab.co.uk/public_docs/tc-l4_qual_doc (accessed 1 December 2013).

CPJA (2012) *About CPJA.* Online. Available at: www.cpja.org.uk/site/aboutcpja.html (accessed 24 April 2012).

Daniels, D. and Jenkins, P. (2010) *Therapy with Children: Children's Rights, Confidentiality and the Law.* London: Sage.

Daw, B. and Joseph, S. (2007) Qualified therapists' experience of personal therapy. *Counselling and Psychotherapy Research: Linking Research with Practice*, 7(4): 227–232. Hove: Routledge.

Department of Health (2007) *Trust, Assurance and Safety – the Regulation of Health Professionals in the 21st Century.* London: HMSO.

Department of Health (2011) *Enabling Excellence: Autonomy and Accountability for Health and Social Care Staff.* London: HMSO.

Dewey, J. (1916) *Democracy and Education: An Introduction to the Philosophy of Education.* New York: Macmillan.

Dewey, J. (1938) *Experience and Education.* New York: Macmillan.

Duncan, B.L., Miller, S.D., Wampold, B.E. and Hubble, M.A. (2009) *The Heart and Soul of Change: Delivering What Works in Therapy.* Second Revised Edition. Washington, DC: American Psychological Association.

Egan, G. (1973) *Encounter: Group Process for Interpersonal Growth*. Monterey: Brooks/Cole.

Elliott, R. and Freire, E. (2011) *Person-Centred/Experiential Therapies Are Highly Effective: Summary of the 2008 Meta-analysis*. Online. Available at: www.pce-world.org/about-pce/articles/102-person-centredexperiential-therapies-are-highly-effective-summary-of-the-2008-meta-analysis.html (accessed 22 June 2013).

Elliott, R., Mack, C. and Shapiro, D. (1999) *Simplified Personal Questionnaire Procedure*. Online. Available at: www.experiential-researchers.org/instruments/elliott/PQ Procedure.doc (accessed 20 June 2013)

European Association for Pyschotherapy (EAP) (2007) *TAC Accreditation of Training Institutes for ECP Award: Questionnaire and procedures*. Online. Available at: www.psychotherapy-ireland.com/professional-development (accessed 28 May 2013).

European Association for Psychotherapy (2012) *European Association for Psychotherapy*. Online. Available at: www.europsyche.org (accessed 22 August 2012).

Evans, H.J. and Ryan, A. (2012) Addictions as a defence against relationship? Relationship as an antidote to addictions? A phenomenological exploration of the significance of relationship in recovery. *European Journal for Qualitative Research in Psychotherapy* 6: 20–28.

Fellows, J.L., Watters, C. and Gatherer, A. (2012) Clients' experience of psychodynamic therapies: a phenomenological study. *European Journal for Qualitative Research in Psychotherapy*, 6: 8–20.

Fonagy, P. (ed.) (2010) *Digest of National Occupational Standards for Psychological Therapies*. Bristol: Skills for Health.

Fortino, A. (2012) Education versus training: selecting the right lifelong learning experience. Paradigm Research International. Online. Available at: www.evolllution.com/opinions/education-versus-training-selecting-the-right-lifelong-learning-experience/ (accessed 22 May 2013).

Foulkes, S.H. (1948) *Introduction to Group-Analytic Psychotherapy: Studies in the Social Integration of Individuals and Groups*. London: Maresfield Reprints.

Foulkes, S.H. and Anthony, E.J. (1957) *Group Psychotherapy: The Psychoanalytic Approach*. Harmondsworth: Penguin.

Freire, P. (2003) From *Pedagogy of the Oppressed*. In Darder, A., Baltodano, M. and Torres, R.D. (eds) *The Critical Pedagogy Reader*. New York: Routledge Falmer.

Freud, S. (1920), *Beyond the Pleasure Principle*. London: International Psycho-Analytical Press.

Freud, S. (1923) *The Ego and the Id*. In J. Strachey (ed. and trans.) *The Standard Edition of the Complete Psychological Works of Sigmund Freud*, vol. 19, pp. 1–66. London: Hogarth Press.

Freud, S. (1926) Analysis terminable and interminable. In J. Strachey (ed. and trans.) *The Standard Edition of the Complete Psychological Works of Sigmund Freud*, vol. 23, pp. 216–253. London: Hogarth Press.

Galovski, T.E., Elwood, L.S., Blain, L.M. and Resick, P.A. (2013) Changes in anger in relationship to responsivity to PTSD treatment. *Psychological Trauma: Theory, Research, Practice, and Policy*, February 25.

Garfield, S. and Bergin, A. (1971) Personal therapy outcome and some therapist variables. *Psychotherapy: Theory, Research and Practice*, 8(3): 251–253.

Gardner, F. (2008) Using critical reflection in research and evaluation. In White, S., Fook, J. and Gardner, F. (eds) *Critical Reflection in Health and Social Care*. Maidenhead: Open University Press, pp. 156–172.

Geldard, K. and Geldard, D. (2007) *Counselling Children: A Practical Introduction.* London: Sage.

Geldard, K. and Geldard, D. (2009) *Counselling Adolescents: The Proactive Approach for Young People.* London: Sage.

Godfrey, J. (2009) *How to Use Your Reading in your Essays.* Basingstoke: Palgrave Macmillan.

Goodwin, J. (2009) *Planning your Essay.* Basingstoke: Palgrave Macmillan.

Goulding, R. and Goulding, M. (1972) in Sager, C.J. and Kaplan, H.S. (eds) *Progress in Group and Family Therapy.* New York: Brunner/Mazel.

Goulding, R. and Goulding, M. (1976) Injunctions, decisions and redecisions. *Transactional Analysis Journal*, 6(1): 41–48.

GPTI (2010) *GPTI Codes of Ethics and Professional Practice.* Online. Available at: www.gpti.org.uk/pdf/codeofethics2010.pdf (accessed 4 May 2013).

Gray, J., Keemar, K., Monach, J., Raido, C., Smith, L. and Shapiro, D. (2006) The influence of the psychotherapist's own psychotherapy on their practice of psychotherapy with clients. Paper presented at the Conference of the Society for Psychotherapy Research, Edinburgh.

Greetham, B. (2008) *How to Write Better Essays.* Second Edition. Basingstoke: Palgrave Macmillan

Grimmer, A. (2005) Personal therapy: Researching a knotty problem. *Therapy Today*, 16(7): 37–40.

Grimmer, A. and Tribe, R. (2001) Counselling psychologists' perceptions of the impact of mandatory personal therapy on professional development: an exploratory study. *Counselling Psychology Quarterly* 14(4): 287–301.

Group Analytic Society (2013) *About Us.* Online. Available at: http://groupanalyticsociety.co.uk (accessed 27 May 2013).

Hall, E. and Hall, C. (1988) *Human Relations in Education.* London: Routledge.

Hall, E., Hall, C., Biddulph, M., Duffy, T., Harris, B. and Hay, D. (1997) Group work in counsellor training: an evaluation. *Counselling Psychology Review* 12(4): 179–186.

Hall, E., Hall, C., Harris, B., Hay, D., Biddulph, M. and Duffy, T. (1999) An evaluation of the long-term outcomes of small-group work for counsellor development. *British Journal of Guidance and Counselling*, 27(1): 99–112.

Hearst, L.E. (1990) Transference, countertransference and projective processes in training course block sessions. *Group Analysis*, 23(4): 341–346.

Hess, A.K., Hess, K.D. and Hess, T.H. (eds) (2008) *Psychotherapy Supervision: Theory, Research, and Practice.* Second Edition. Hoboken, NJ: Wiley.

Hodson, P.L. (2012) *The Business of Therapy: How to Run a Successful Private Practice.* Maidenhead: Open University Press.

Hofmann, S.G., Asnaani, A., Vonk, I.J., Sawyer, A.T. and Fang, A. (2012) The efficacy of cognitive behavioral therapy: a review of meta-analyses. *Cognitive Therapy and Research*, 36(5): 427–440.

Hogan, D.B. (1979) *The Regulation of Psychotherapists.* Volume 1. Cambridge, MA: Ballinger Publishing Company.

Hogan, D. (2003) Professional regulation as facilitation not control. In Bates, Y. and House, R. (2003) *Ethically Challenged Professions.* Ross-on-Wye: PCCS Books.

Holloway, E.L. and Neufeldt, S.A. (1995) Supervision: its contributions to treatment efficacy. *Journal of Consulting and Clinical Psychology*, 63: 207–213.

Honey, P. and Mumford, L. (1986) *The Manual of Learning Styles.* Maidenhead: Peter Honey.

Honey, P. and Mumford, A. (1992) *The Manual of Learning Styles.* Third Edition. Maidenhead: Peter Honey.

hooks, b. (1994) *Teaching to Transgress: Education as the Practice of Freedom.* New York: Routledge

Horvath, A.O. and Luborsky, L. (1993) The role of the therapeutic alliance in psychotherapy. *Journal of Consulting and Clinical Psychology*, 61: 561–573.

House, R. (1995) The dynamics of power: why Mowbray is right about professionalization. *Counselling News*, 20: 24–25.

House, R. (2003) *Therapy Beyond Modernity: Deconstructing and Transcending Profession-Centred Therapy.* London: Karnac.

House, R. and Totton, N. (eds) (1997) *Implausible Professions: Arguments for Pluralism and Autonomy in Psychotherapy and Counselling.* Ross-on-Wye: PCCS Books.

Howe, D. (2005) *Child Abuse and Neglect: Attachment, Development and Intervention.* Basingstoke: Palgrave Macmillan.

Howe, D. (2011) *Attachment Across the Lifecourse: A Brief Introduction.* Basingstoke: Palgrave Macmillan.

Hughes, D. (2006) *Building the Bonds of Attachment: Awakening Love in Deeply Troubled Children.* Second Revised Edition. New York: Jason Aronson.

Hughes, D., Baylin, J. and Siegel, D.J. (2012) *Brain-Based Parenting: The Neuroscience of Caregiving for Healthy Attachment.* New York: W.W. Norton & Co.

Humanistic and Integrative Psychotherapy College (2011) *Training Standards of the Humanistic and Integrative Psychotherapy College (HIPC) of UKCP.* Online. Available at: www.hipcollege.co.uk/page/training+standards (accessed 21 August 2012).

IACP (2010) *What Is Counselling/Psychotherapy?* Co. Wicklow: IACP.

IACP (2012) *Information and Application Forms.* Co. Wicklow: IACP.

IACP (2013a) *Code of Ethics and Practice for Counsellors/Psychotherapists* Online. Available at: www.irish-counselling.ie/iacp-code-of-ethics (accessed 6 May 2013).

IACP (2013b) *Criteria and Guidelines for Courses Seeking Accreditation.* Online. Available at: www.irish-counselling.ie/course-accreditation-criteria (accessed 19 June 2013).

Inskipp, F. and Proctor, B. (2001) *The Art, Craft and Tasks of Counselling Supervision: Part 1: Making the Most of Supervision.* Third Edition. Twickenham: Cascade.

Institute of Group Analysis (2013) *The Institute of Group Analysis National Training Prospectus.* London: IGA.

IPN (2009) *IPN Home.* Online. Available at: http://i-p-n.org/home.htm (accessed 21 August 2012).

Jung, C. (2004) *The Meaning of Individuation.* Online. Available at: www.cgjungpage.org/index.php?option=content&task=view&id=526 (accessed 26 May 2013).

Karasu, T.B. (1986) The specificity versus nonspecificity dilemma: toward identifying therapeutic change agents. *American Journal of Psychiatry*, 143: 687–695.

Karpman, S. (1976) Fairy tales and script drama analysis. *Transactional Analysis Bulletin*, 7(26): 39–43.

Kelly, G. (1955) *The Psychology of Personal Constructs.* New York: W. W. Norton.

Klain, E. (1975) Transference situation in the educative group. *Psihijatrija Danas*, 7(2–3): 173–179.

Knowles, M.S. (1950) *Informal Adult Education.* Chicago: Association Press.

Knowles, M.S. (1975) *Self-Directed Learning: A Guide for Learners and Teachers.* Chicago: Association Press.

Knowles, M.S. (1978) *The Adult Learner: A Neglected Species.* Second Edition. Houston: Gulf Publishing Company, Book Division.

Knowles, M.S. (1984) *Andragogy in Action: Applying Modern Principles of Adult Education.* San Francisco: Jossey-Bass.

Knowles, M.S. (1986) *Using Learning Contracts.* San Francisco: Jossey-Bass.

Knowles, M.S. (1990) *The Adult Learner: A Neglected Species.* Fourth Edition. Houston: Gulf Publishing Company, Book Division.

Kolb, A.Y. and Kolb, D.A. (2006) Learning styles and learning spaces: a review of the multidisciplinary application of experiential learning in higher education. In Sims, R. and Sims, S. (eds) *Learning Styles and Learning: A Key to Meeting the Accountability Demands in Education.* Hauppauge, NY: Nova Publishers.

Kolb, D.A. (1984) *Experiential Learning: Experience as the Source of Learning and Development.* Upper Saddle River, NJ: Prentice-Hall.

Kroenke, K., and Spitzer, R.L. (2002) The PHQ-9: A new depression diagnostic and severity measure. *Psychiatric Annals*, 32: 509–515.

Kroenke K., Spitzer, R.L. and Williams, J.B.W. (2001) The PHQ-9: validity of a brief depression severity measure. *Journal of General Internal Medicine*, 16(9): 606–613.

Laird, D. (1985) *Approaches to Training and Development.* Reading, MA: Addison-Wesley.

Lambert, M.J. (1986) Implications of psychotherapy outcome research for eclectic psychotherapy. In Norcross, J.C. (ed.) *Handbook of Eclectic Psychotherapy.* New York: Brunner Mazel.

Lambert, M.J. and Ogles, B.M. (1997) The effectiveness of psychotherapy supervision. In Watkins, C.E., Jr. (ed.) *Handbook of Psychotherapy Supervision*, pp. 421–446. New York: Wiley.

Langs, R. (1992) Boundaries and frames: non-transference in teaching. *International Journal of Communicative Psychoanalysis and Psychotherapy*, 7(3–4): 125–130.

Leader, D. (2006) To what extent is personal therapeutic experience and external validation essential in therapeutic training? *European Journal of Psychotherapy and Counselling*, 8(4): 387–391.

Lindgren, O., Folkesson, P. and Almqvist, K. (2012) Renewing experience. *European Journal for Qualitative Research in Psychotherapy*, 6: 1–7.

Llewelyn, S. (1988) Psychological therapy as viewed by clients and therapists. *British Journal of Clinical Psychology*, 27: 223–238.

Longman Dictionary of Contemporary English (2009) Fifth Edition. Harlow: Pearson Education Ltd.

Macaskill, N. (1988) Personal therapy in the training of the psychotherapist: Is it effective? *British Journal of Psychotherapy*, 4(3): 199–226.

Macran, S. and Shapiro, D.A. (1998) The role of personal therapy for therapists: a review. *British Journal of Medical Psychology*, 71: 13–25.

Macran, S., Stiles, W. and Smith, J.A. (1999) How does personal therapy affect therapist's practice? *Journal of Counseling Psychology*, 46(4): 419–431.

Markowitz, J.C. and Weissman, M.M. (eds) (2012) *Casebook of Interpersonal Psychotherapy.* New York: Oxford University Press.

Maslow, A. (1987) *Motivation and Personality.* Third Edition. New York: Harper and Row.

McLeod, J. (2008) *Counselling in the Workplace: A Comprehensive Review of the Research Evidence.* Second Edition. Lutterworth: BACP.

McLeod, J. (2009) *The Counsellor's Workbook: Developing a Personal Approach.* Maidenhead: Open University Press.

McLeod, J. (2013) *An Introduction to Counselling*. Fifth Edition. Maidenhead: Open University Press.

McMahon, G., Palmer, S. and Wilding, C. (2005) *The Essential Skills for Setting Up a Counselling and Psychotherapy Practice*. London: Routledge.

McMillan, K. and Weyers, J. (2011) *How to Write Essays and Assignments*. Second Edition. Harlow: Prentice Hall.

Mellor-Clark, J., Barkham, M., Connell, J. and Evans, C. (1999) Practice-based evidence and need for a standardised evaluation system: informing the design of the CORE System. *European Journal of Psychotherapy, Counselling and Health*, 3: 357–374.

Mezirow, J. (1991) *Transformative Dimensions in Adult Learning*. San Francisco, CA: Jossey-Bass.

Mezirow, J. (2000) Learning to think like an adult: core concepts in transformation theory. In Mezirow, J. (ed.), *Learning in Transformation: Critical Perspectives on a Theory in Progress*, pp. 3–33. San Francisco: Jossey-Bass.

Mezirow, J. and Associates (1990) *Fostering Critical Reflection in Adulthood*. San Francisco: Jossey-Bass.

Moritz, S., Schroder, J., Meyer, B. and Hauschildt, M. (2013) The more it is needed, the less it is wanted: attitudes toward face-to-face intervention among depressed patients undergoing online treatment. *Depression and Anxiety*, 30(2): 157–167.

Mowbray, R. (1995) *The Case Against Psychotherapy Registration: A Conservation Issue for the Human Potential Movement*. London: Trans Marginal Press.

Murphy, D. (2005) A qualitative study into the experience of mandatory personal therapy during training. *Counselling and Psychotherapy Research: Linking Research with Practice*, 5(1): 27–32.

Musgrave, A. (2009) Unintended negative side effects of HPC regulation. *eIpnosis*. Online. Available at: http://ipnosis.postle.net/pages/AMusgrave2HoL.htm (accessed 25 May 2013).

NCHP (2013) *Training to be a Hypno-psychotherapist*. Online. Available at: www.hypnotherapyuk.net/prospectus/course-structure.aspx (accessed 26 May 2013).

Newton T. (2003) Identifying educational philosophy and practice through imagoes in transactional analysis training groups. *Transactional Analysis Journal*, 33(4): 321–331.

NHS (2012) *NHS Jobs*. Online. Available at: www.jobs.nhs.uk/index.html (accessed 20 August 2012).

NHS (2013) *NHS Jobs*. Online. Available at: www.jobs.nhs.uk/index.html (accessed 24 February 2013).

Norcross, J.C. (2005) The psychotherapist's own psychotherapy: educating and developing psychologists. *American Psychologist*, 60(8): 840–850.

Norcross, J.C., Strausser-Kirtland, D. and Missar, C. (1988) The processes and outcomes of psychotherapists' treatment experiences. *Psychotherapy*, 25(1): 36–43.

O'Hara, D. and Schofield, M.J. (2008) Personal approaches to psychotherapy integration. *Counselling and Psychotherapy Research*, 8 (1): 53–62.

Palmer, S. and Barnes, S. (2001) *Values and Ethics in the Practice of Psychotherapy and Counselling*. Maidenhead: Open University Press.

Parker, I. (1999) *Deconstructing Psychotherapy*. London: Sage.

Parker, I. and Revelli, S. (eds) (2008) *Psychoanalytic Practice and State Regulation*. London: Karnac.

Parlett, M. and Denham, J. (2007) Gestalt therapy. In Dryden, W. (ed.) *Dryden's Handbook of Individual Therapy*. Fifth Edition, pp. 227–255. London: Sage.

Peeters, F., Huibers, M., Roelofs, J., van Breukelen, G., Hollon, S.D., Markowitz, J.C., van Os, J. and Arntz, A. (2013) The clinical effectiveness of evidence-based interventions for depression: a pragmatic trial in routine practice. *Journal of Affective Disorders*, 145 (3): 349–355.

Perry, A. (ed.) (2009) *Teenagers and Attachment: Helping Adolescents Engage with Life and Learning*. Richmond: Worth Publishing.

PET (2012a) *What Is Psychosynthesis?* Online. Available at: http://psychosynthesis.edu/about/psychosynthesis (accessed 1 December 2013).

PET (2012b) *Training*. Online. Available at: http://psychosynthesis.edu/training (accessed 6 January 2013).

Piaget, J. and Inhelder, B. (1969) *The Psychology of the Child*. New York: Basic Books.

Pinar, W.F. (1981) The reconceptualization of curriculum studies. In Giroux, H.A., Penna, A.N. and Pinar, W.F. (eds) *Curriculum and Instruction Alternatives in Education*. Berkerley: McCutchen Publishing.

Postle, D. (2007) *Regulating the Psychological Therapies: From Taxonomy to Taxidermy*. Ross-on-Wye: PCCS Books.

Postle, D. (2013) State regulation-lite? *eIpnosis*. Online. Available at: http://ipnosis.postle.net/pages/Feb2013PSALaunch.htm (accessed 25 May 2013).

Postle, D. and House, R. (eds) (2009) *Compliance? Ambivalence? Rejection? Nine Papers Challenging the Health Professions Council Proposals for the State Regulation of the Psychological Therapies*. London: Wentworth Learning Resources.

PSA (2013) *Voluntary Registers FAQs*. Online. Available at: www.professionalstandards.org.uk/voluntary-registers/about-accreditation/voluntary-registers-faqs (accessed 28 May 2013).

QAA (2011) *Qualifications Can Cross Boundaries – A Rough Guide to Comparing Qualifications in the UK and Ireland*. Online Available at: www.qaa.ac.uk/Publications/InformationAndGuidance/Documents/Quals_cross_boundaries.pdf (accessed 24 April 2012).

QAA (2013) *Subject Benchmark Statement: Counselling and Psychotherapy*. Gloucester. QAA. Online. Available at: www.qaa.ac.uk/Publications/InformationAndGuidance/Documents/Subject-benchmark-statement-counselling-psychotherapy.pdf (accessed 23 June 2013).

Rake, C. and Paley, G. (2009) Personal therapy for psychotherapists: the impact on therapeutic practice. A qualitative study using interpretative phenomenological analysis. *Psychodynamic Practice: Individuals, Groups and Organisations*, 15(3): 275–294.

Ray, D. (2011) *Advanced Play Therapy: Essential Conditions, Knowledge, and Skills for Child Practice*. Hove: Routledge.

Regent's School of Psychotherapy and Psychology (2012a) *Advanced Diploma in Existential Psychotherapy*. Online. Available at: www.regents.ac.uk/study/postgraduate-study/programmes/advanced-diploma-existential-psychotherapy.aspx (accessed 1 December 2013).

Regent's School of Psychotherapy and Psychology (2012b) *MA/Post-Graduate Diploma in Psychotherapy and Counselling: Course Structure*. Online. Available at: www.regents.ac.uk/study/postgraduate-study/programmes/ma-psychotherapy-counselling.aspx (accessed 1 December 2013).

Reiss, N.B. (1975) Problems in the teaching of psychotherapy. *Psychotherapy: Theory, Research and Practice*, 12(3): 332–335.

Rice, C.D. (2004) *Enlightened Universities: Beyond Political Agendas*. Edinburgh: Policy Institute Series: Society No. 4.

Rieken, B. (2003) Counter-transference problems, analysis of relationship, and self-disclosure in the shadow of psychotherapy training. Examples and reflections in individual psychological view. [German]. *Zeitschrift fur Individualpsychologie*, 28(4), 332–353.

Robinson, W.L. (1974) Conscious competency – the mark of a competent instructor. *Personnel Journal*, 53: 538–539.

Rogers, A. (1996) *Teaching Adults*. Second Edition. Buckingham: Open University Press.

Rogers, C.R. (1951) *Client-Centred Therapy*. Boston: Houghton-Mifflin.

Rogers, C.R. (1957) The necessary and sufficient conditions of psychotherapeutic personality change. *Journal of Consulting Psychology*, 21: 95–103.

Rogers, C.R. (1959) A theory of therapy, personality, and interpersonal relationships as developed in the client-centered framework. Reprinted in Kirschenbaum, H. and Henderson, V. (eds) *The Carl Rogers Reader* (1989). Boston: Houghton Mifflin.

Rogers, C.R. (1961) *On Becoming A Person: A Therapist's View of Psychotheraphy*. Boston: Houghton Mifflin.

Rogers, C.R. (1969) *Freedom to Learn*. Columbus, OH: Merrill.

Rogers, C.R. (1971) *Encounter Groups*. Harmondsworth: Penguin.

Rogers, C.R. (1974) In retrospect: forty-six years. *American Psychologist*, 29(2): 115–118.

Rogers, C.R. (1979) Foundation of the Person-Centred Approach. *Education*, 100(2): 98–107.

Rogers, C.R. (1980) *A Way of Being*. New York: Houghton-Mifflin.

Rogers, C.R. and Freiberg, H. J. (1994) *Freedom to Learn*. Third Edition. Columbus, OH: Merrill/Macmillan.

Rose, C. (2004) The personal development group. *Counselling and Psychotherapy Journal*, 14 (5): 13–15.

Rose, C. (2008) *The Personal Development Group: The Student's Guide*. London: Karnac.

Russell, R.L. and Staszewski, C. (1988) The unit problem: some systematic distinctions and critical dilemmas for psychotherapy process research. *Psychotherapy: Theory, Research, Practice, Training*, 25(2): 191–200.

Samuels, A. (1997) Pluralism and the future of psychotherapy. In Palmer, S. and Varma, V. (eds) *The Future of Counselling and Psychotherapy*, pp. 132–152. London: Sage.

Samuels, A. (2009) HPC regulation: more harm than good? *Therapy Today*, 20(5): 41.

Schiff, J.L., in collaboration with Schiff, A.W., Mellor, K., Schiff, E., Schiff, S., Richman, D., Fishman, J., Wolz, L., Fishman, C. and Momb, D. (1975) *Cathexis Reader: Transactional Analysis Treatment of Psychosis*. New York: Harper & Row.

Schön, D.A. (1999) *The Reflective Practitioner: How Professionals Think in Action*. Aldershot: Ashgate.

Schore, A. (2012) *The Science of the Art of Psychotherapy*. New York: W.W. Norton & Co.

Shellow, R.S., Ward, J.L. and Rubenfeld, S. (1958) Group therapy and the institutional delinquent. *International Journal of Group Psychotherapy*, 8: 256–275.

Shor, I. (1992) *Empowering Education: Critical Teaching for Social Change*. London: University of Chicago Press.

Skills for Health (2011) *Competences/National Occupational Standards (NOS) FAQ*. Online. Available at: www.skillsforhealth.org.uk/about-us/competences%10national-occupational-standards/competences%10national-occupational-standards-%28nos%29-faq (accessed 5 July 2013).

Skinner, B.F. (1965) *Science and Human Behaviour*. New Edition. New York: The Free Press.

Smith. J.A. (1995) Semi-structured interviewing and qualitative analysis. In Smith, J.A., Harre, R. and Van Langenhove, L. (eds) (1995) *Rethinking Methods in Psychology*. London: Sage.

Spitzer, R.L., Kroenke, K., Williams, J.B.W. and Lowe, B. (2006) A brief measure for assessing generalized anxiety disorder: the GAD-7. *Archives of Internal Medicine*, 166(10): 1092–1097.

Stauble, W.J. (1965) Training group psychotherapists. *The Canadian Psychiatric Association Journal/La Revue de l'Association des psychiatres du Canada*, 10(3): 216–222.

Stiles, W., Barkham, M., Mellor-Clark, J. and Connell, J. (2008) Effectiveness of cognitive-behavioural, person-centred, and psychodynamic therapies in UK primary-care routine practice: replication in a larger sample. *Psychological Medicine*, 38 (5): 677–688.

Stiles, W.B., Barkham, M., Twigg, E., Mellor-Clark, J. and Cooper, M. (2006) Effectiveness of cognitive-behavioural, person-centred and psychodynamic therapies as practised in the UK National Health Service settings. *Psychological Medicine*, 36: 555–566.

Strupp, H.H. (1977) A reformulation of the dynamics of the therapist's contribution. In Gurman, A.S. and Razin, A.M. (eds) *Effective Psychotherapy*. Oxford: Pergamon Press.

Sunderland, M. (2001) *Using Story Telling as a Therapeutic Tool with Children*. Milton Keynes: Speechmark Publishing Ltd.

Sunderland, M. (2007) *What Every Parent Needs to Know: The Incredible Effects of Love, Nurture and Play on Your Child's Development*. London: Dorling Kindersley.

Sweeney, B. (2010) *Contructivist and Existentialist College: Philosophical Position*. London: UKCP. Online. Available at: http://www.psychotherapy.org.uk/constructivists.html (accessed 26 May 2013).

Tait, A. (2012) *Direct Work with Vulnerable Children: Playful Activities and Strategies for Communication*. London: Jessica Kingsley Publishers.

Thorne, B. (2009) Foreword. In Postle, D. and House, R. (eds) *Compliance? Ambivalence? Rejection? Nine Papers Challenging the Health Professions Council July 2009 Proposals for the State Regulation of thePsychological Therapies*. London: Wentworth Learning Resources.

Tolin, D.F. (2010) Is cognitive-behavioral therapy more effective than other therapies? A meta-analytic review. *Clinical Psychology Review*, 30(6): 710–720.

Tuckman, B. (1965) Developmental sequence in small groups. *Psychological Bulletin*, 63(6): 384–399.

Tuckman, B.W. and Jenson, K. (1977) Stages of small-group development revisited. *Group and Organization Studies*, 2(4): 419–427.

Tudor, K. (1999) *Group Counselling*. London: Sage.

Tudor, K. (ed.) (2007) *The Adult Is Parent to the Child: Transactional Analysis with Children and Young People*. Lyme Regis: Russell House Publishing Ltd.

Tudor, K. (2008a) To be or not to be in personal therapy, that is the question (part I). *ITA News*, 35. Burwell: ITA.

Tudor, K. (2008b) To be or not to be in personal therapy, that is the question (part 2). *ITA News*, 36. Burwell: ITA.

Tudor, K. (2011) *The Turning Tide: Pluralism and Partnership in Psychotherapy in Aotearoa New Zealand*. Maungaraki: First Edition Ltd.

UKAHPP (2012) *Guidance and Advice on Therapy and Counselling*. Online. Available at: www.ahpp.org/page.php?pageid=30&sectionid=1 (accessed 9 April 2012).

UKATA (2008) *UKATA Statement of Ethics*. Online. Available at: www.ita.org.uk/pages/policy-documents/ita-statement-ethics (accessed 2 July 2013)

UKCP (1992) *Entry Requirements and Curriculum Contents*. Humanistic and Integrative Psychotherapy Section Training Standards Committee. London: UKCP.

UKCP (1993) *Training Requirements*. Training Standards Committee. London: UKCP.

UKCP (2007) *Training Standards of Humanistic and Integrative Psychotherapy Section of UKCP*. London: UKCP.

UKCP (2008a) *Submission Response No. 2 to the HPC Call for Ideas*. London: UKCP.

UKCP (2008b) *UKCP Standards of Education and Training Guidelines for Sections for the Development of Training Standards in Child Psychotherapy: Full Training*. Online. Available at: www.psychotherapy.org.uk/hres/pwcc%20section%20training%20standards%20_%204%20year%20courses%20_%20may%202008.pdf (accessed 28 May 2013).

UKCP (2008c) *UKCP Standards of Education and Training Guidelines for Sections for the Development of Training Standards in Child Psychotherapy: Post Qualifying Courses*. Online. Available at: www.psychotherapy.org.uk/hres/pwcc%20section%20training%20standards%20_%20post%20qualifying%20_%20may%202008.pdf (accessed 28 May 2013).

UKCP (2008d) *UKCP Standards of Education and Training Guidelines for Section and Institutional Members for the Development of Codes of Practice and Professional Conduct for Working with Children*. Online. Available at: www.psychotherapy.org.uk/hres/pwcc%20ethics%20july%202008%20doc.pdf (accessed 28 May 2013).

UKCP (2009) *Ethical Principles and Code of Professional Conduct*. UKCP London.

UKCP (2011) *Training Standards of Humanistic and Integrative Psychotherapy Section of UKCP. May 2006 Training Standards (revised May 2007 and amended January 2011)*. London: UKCP.

UKCP (2012) *UKCP Standards of Education and Training (2012) The Minimum Core Criteria Psychotherapy with Adults*. London: UKCP.

UKCP (2013a) *About Psychotherapy*. Online. Available at: www.psychotherapy.org.uk/public_frequently_asked_questions.html (accessed 3 January 2013).

UKCP (2013b) *Colleges*. Online. Available at: www.psychotherapy.org.uk/colleges (accessed 21 March 2013).

UKCP CCP (2009) *Constructivist Section Training Guidelines and Requirements for Members*. London: UKCP.

UKCP CFCST (2009) *Modality Criteria and Requirements, Section and Institutional Member Organisation, Standards of Education and Training, Family, Couple, Sexual and Systemic Section*. London: UKCP.

UKCP CH-P (2008) *Hypno-Psychotherapy Section Modality Specific Standards of Education and Training*. London: UKCP.

UKCP CPJAC (2012) *Formal Documents of Training Standards and Membership Committee of the CPJA*. London: UKCP.

UKCP PCIPC (2008) *Psychotherapeutic Counselling and Intersubjective Psychotherapy College Standards of Education and Training for Psychotherapeutic Counselling*. London: UKCP.

Urwin, C. and Sternberg, J. (eds) (2012) *Infant Observation and Research: Emotional Processes in Everyday Lives*. Hove: Routledge.

Vallance, K. (2004) Exploring counsellor perceptions of the impact of counselling supervision on clients. *British Journal of Guidance and Counselling*, 32: 559–574.

Van Emden, J. and Becker, L. (2010) *Presentation Skills for Students*. Basingstoke: Palgrave Macmillan.

Von Haenisch, C. (2011) How did compulsory personal therapy during counselling training influence personal and professional development? *Counselling and Psychotherapy Research: Linking Research with Practice*, 11(2): 148–155.

Vygotsky, L.S. (1978) *Mind in Society*. Cambridge, MA: Harvard University Press.

Walsh, R., Perrucci, A. and Severns, J. (1999) What's in a good moment: a hermeneutic study of psychotherapy values across levels of psychotherapy training. *Psychotherapy Research*, 9(3): 304–326.

Wampold, B.E., Minami, T., Baskin, T.W. and Callen, T.S. (2002) A meta-(re)analysis of the effects of cognitive therapy versus 'other therapies' for depression. *Journal of Affective Disorders*, 68(2–3): 159–165.

Warren, G. (2010) *Set Up a Therapy Business: A Step-by-Step Guide*. Bristol: Ethical Business Publishing.

Watts, M. (2006) Therapeutic training after Freud: to what extent is personal therapeutic experience and external validation essential in therapeutic training? *European Journal of Psychotherapy and Counselling*, 8(4): 415.

Wertsch, J.V. (1985) *Cultural, Communication, and Cognition: Vygotskian Perspectives*. Cambridge: Cambridge University Press.

Wheeler, S. and Richards, K. (2007) The impact of clinical supervision on counsellors and therapists, their practice and their clients: a systematic review of the literature. *Counselling and Psychotherapy Research: Linking Research with Practice*, 7(1): 54–65.

Widdowson, M. (2011) Depression: a literature review on diagnosis, subtypes, patterns of recovery, and psychotherapeutic models. *Transactional Analysis Journal*, 41(4): 351–364.

Widdowson, M. (2012) TA treatment of depression – a hermeneutic single-case efficacy design study – 'Peter'. *International Journal of Transactional Analysis Research*, 3(1): 3–13.

Wilkinson, M. (2010) *Changing Minds in Therapy: Emotion, Attachment, Trauma, and Neurobiology*. New York: W.W. Norton & Co.

Wing, J.K., Curtis, R.H., Park, S.B.G., Hadden, S. and Burns, A. (1998) Health of the Nation Outcome Scales (HoNOS): research and development. *British Journal of Psychiatry*, 172: 11–18.

Index